"With a focus on processes of power underpinning 'difference' across such axes as class, race and gender, this text provides a sustained critique of essentialist thinking. Its innovative reworking of the concepts of intersectionality, stratification, and political economy is likely to set new agendas on addressing questions of inequality. Incisive theoretical and political analysis at its best."

— Avtar Brah, Professor Emerita of Sociology, Birkbeck College,
University of London

"Floya Anthias offers a nuanced and astute account of the changing forms of social inequality in the contemporary global environment. She challenges simplistic accounts of belonging and identity and seeks to show that we need to move beyond dominant paradigms and perspectives."

— John Solomos, Professor of Sociology,
University of Warwick, UK

"This book is a masterpiece: with a translocational lens, Anthias focuses on insights from studies on intersectionality, bordering and belonging, migration, nationalism, racism, violence, intimacy and social class and demonstrates how they are entangled in complicated ways. Yet, she is not satisfied with depicting dilemmas but instead provides heuristic tools and theoretical frames for their adequate analysis."

— Helma Lutz, Goethe University Frankfurt, Germany, co-author of
Gender and Migration: Transnational and
Intersectional Prospects

"*Translocational Belongings*, introduced by incisive personal memories of growing up in an activist migrant family, captures the human condition of the migrant, offering a distinctive account of border crossings, in the real world and in sociological theory. Scrutinising intersecting hierarchies of race, gender, class, ascribed cultural differences and social inequalities, the author grounds new horizons for solidarity politics beyond fixed belonging."

— Aleksandra Ålund, Professor Emerita,
Linköping University, Sweden

TRANSLOCATIONAL BELONGINGS

This book explores the multiform and shifting location of borders and boundaries in social life, related to difference and belonging. It contributes to understanding categories of difference as a building block for forms of belonging and inequality in the world today and as underpinning modern capitalist societies and their forms of governance. Reflecting on the ways in which we might theorise the connections between different social divisions and identities, a translocational lens for addressing modalities of power is developed, stressing relationality, the spatio-temporal and the processual in social relations. The book is organised around contemporary dilemmas of difference and inequality, relating to fixities and fluidities in social life and to current developments in the areas of racialisation, migration, gender, sexuality and class relations, and in theorising the articulations of gender, class and ethnic hierarchies. Rejecting the view that gender, ethnicity, race, class or the more specific categories of migrants or refugees pertain to social groups with certain fixed characteristics, they are treated as interconnected and interdependent *places* within a landscape of inequality making. This innovative and groundbreaking book constitutes a significant contribution to scholarship on intersectionality.

Floya Anthias is Professor Emerita of Sociology and Social Justice at Roehampton University, London, UK. Amongst other works, she is the author of *Ethnicity, Class, Gender and Migration*, the co-author of *Racialised Boundaries* and the co-editor of *Woman, Nation, State*; *Into the Margins: Migration and Exclusion in Southern Europe*; *Gender and Migration in Southern Europe: Women on the Move*; *Paradoxes of Integration: Female Migrants in Europe*; *Rethinking Anti-racisms: From Theory to Practice*; *Contesting Integration, Engendering Migration* and *Work and the Challenges of Belonging*.

Routledge Research in Race and Ethnicity

Crisis and Coloniality at Europe's Margins
Creating Exotic Iceland
Kristín Loftsdóttir

Anti-Muslim Racism on Trial
Muslims, the Swedish Judiciary and the Possibility of Justice
Marta Kilankiewicz

Life Trajectories Into and Out of Contemporary Neo-Nazism
Becoming and Unbecoming the Hateful Other
Christer Mattsson and Thomas Johansson

Ethnic Subjectivity in Intergenerational Memory Narratives
Politics of the Untold
Mónika Fodor

Cool Britannia and Multi-Ethnic Britain
Uncorking the Champagne Supernova
Jason Arday

Translocational Belongings
Intersectional Dilemmas and Social Inequalities
Floya Anthias

For a full list of titles in this series, please visit: www.routledge.com/sociology/series/RRRE

TRANSLOCATIONAL BELONGINGS

Intersectional Dilemmas
and Social Inequalities

Floya Anthias

LONDON AND NEW YORK

First published 2021
by Routledge
2 Park Square, Milton Park, Abingdon, Oxon OX14 4RN

and by Routledge
52 Vanderbilt Avenue, New York, NY 10017

Routledge is an imprint of the Taylor & Francis Group, an informa business

© 2021 Floya Anthias

The right of Floya Anthias to be identified as author of this work has been asserted by her in accordance with sections 77 and 78 of the Copyright, Designs and Patents Act 1988.

All rights reserved. No part of this book may be reprinted or reproduced or utilised in any form or by any electronic, mechanical, or other means, now known or hereafter invented, including photocopying and recording, or in any information storage or retrieval system, without permission in writing from the publishers.

Trademark notice: Product or corporate names may be trademarks or registered trademarks, and are used only for identification and explanation without intent to infringe.

British Library Cataloguing-in-Publication Data
A catalogue record for this book is available from the British Library

Library of Congress Cataloging-in-Publication Data
Names: Anthias, Floya, 1945– author.
Title: Translocational belongings : intersectional dilemmas and social inequalities / Floya Anthias.
Description: 1 Edition. | New York : Routledge, 2020. | Series: Routledge research in race and ethnicity | Includes bibliographical references and index.
Identifiers: LCCN 2020005249 (print) | LCCN 2020005250 (ebook) | ISBN 9781138304291 (paperback) | ISBN 9781138304284 (hardback) | ISBN 9780203730256 (ebook)
Subjects: LCSH: Social stratification. | Equality. | Women—Crimes against. | Sex role. | Emigration and immigration. | Ethnic relations.
Classification: LCC HM821 .A548 2020 (print) | LCC HM821 (ebook) | DDC 305—dc23
LC record available at https://lccn.loc.gov/2020005249
LC ebook record available at https://lccn.loc.gov/2020005250

ISBN: 978-1-138-30428-4 (hbk)
ISBN: 978-1-138-30429-1 (pbk)
ISBN: 978-0-203-73025-6 (ebk)

Typeset in Bembo
by Apex CoVantage, LLC

CONTENTS

	Prolegomena: a personal borderscape	1
1	Introduction. Marking places: dilemmas of difference and inequality	9
2	Branding places: dilemmas of ordering	30
3	Assembling places: dilemmas of articulation	61
4	Hierarchising places: dilemmas of class and stratification	91
5	Transgressing places: dilemmas of gender, intimacy and violence	116
6	Territorialising places: dilemmas of b/ordering the nation	141
7	Epilogos. Transforming places: towards a politics of translocation	176

References   *190*
Index   *211*

PROLEGOMENA

A personal borderscape

Give me my voice my free voice
To let myself loose in all the universe
Spirit of my age, a cell of art
Nerve and steel and fire and tempest
A whirlwind and breeze and kiss
And a ruthless bite

. . . .

And a drunken sunflower
That chases the sun
From dawn to dusk

(From the 'Human Epic',
Tefcros Anthias)

The tramp's whistlings

The title above pays homage to my father, Tefcros Anthias, whose first book of poetry of that name, published in Athens in 1928, brought him to the attention of the Greek literary scene, was reprinted seven times, and is still recited by old and young in Greece and Cyprus. Written with an existentialist sensitivity, and compared to the work of Baudelaire and Walt Whitman, it lyrically sings the adventures and struggles of (his) life as a tramp, homeless on the streets of metropolitan Athens in his early youth. I like to think of this book, too, as a set of whistlings, written with the spirit of the engaged vagabond, refusing the safe place of accepted and received wisdoms. I like to think of translocational belongings as reflecting the condition of the wanderer, of the non-fixities, of the fluidities and of the flows characterising the human condition in our turbulent times today.

Writing this book has been a process over some time as it brings together many of my ideas around boundaries and inequalities, and builds upon them.

2 Prolegomena

Whilst writing is a solitary exercise the ingredients that furnish this exercise are anything but solitary, constituted through our encounters with others. Firstly, much of this writing has been to the accompaniment of the voices, laughter, cries and demands of my grandchildren, mainly joyous but always a cause (and excuse) for distraction. My work has been enriched in myriads of ways: through my family, my trips, symposia, friends, colleagues and my travels between the country of my birth, Cyprus, and my long-established home in London. It has benefitted from dialogues and conversations within research projects, with my students and through the many conferences and workshops and other fora that I have been invited to talk at. I would like to warmly thank all those people who chose to invite me to present my work and who have encouraged me in the development of my ideas, and they are too numerous to mention. But I warmly thank you all. Particular thanks are due to all those people who have provided at various times support and inspiration, some of whom, sadly are no longer with us (but happily most are very much so): these include Stuart Hall, Mike Kelly, Nira Yuval-Davis, John Gabriel, Ali Rattansi, Maria Hadjipavlou, Marina Pierides, Avtar Brah, Ann Phoenix, Steve Fenton, Nikos Trimikliniotis, Mirjana Morokvasic, Mojca Pajnik, Maria Kontos, Aleksandra Alund and John Solomos: they are some of the many. I am also lucky to have a home in two places of the mind and of the heart. To my family of Cypriot friends, I thank you for everything you have taught me about the traumas of living in a divided island, traumas that do not override its deep beauty and the warmth and hospitality of all its people. I long for us to climb together the Pentadaktylos mountains, unhindered by Green Lines, passports or barricades, converting the Dead Zone to a living breathing land we can all share. My father, Tefcros Anthias, inspired in me the love for freedom and justice and the hatred of inequality and exclusions of all types with his own passionate struggles to build a better world, showing me the power of the word in the heritage he left behind for his beloved small (and universal) island. He also, by example and in his creative work in poetry and prose, and in his 'provocative' journalism, showed me that it is okay to be a maverick or αλίτης, a whistling tramp, and not to search for a fixed belonging. My mother, Anastasia Pagoni Anthias, taught me about the power of love, commitment and care with her piercing intelligence, sense of justice and modesty (which I cannot live up to), and she never burdened me with the 'imposter' syndrome which haunts so many of our sex. I would like to dedicate this book to her and to all our mothers, the unsung heroines of all our lives, and to my father and all those whose life work has been to fight for justice and equality.

My family, Ron Ayres, Alexander Ayres and Natasha Ayres, have always been a source of inspiration and support. Thanks to Alex for his last-minute technical help. Most importantly, they have provided a safe, warm, fun and stable 'home' for me to travel from, intellectually and emotionally. My four beautiful grandchildren are a source of immeasurable joy and laughter – Irissa, Phoebe, Isla and Elliot. What would I be without my brother Tefcros, whose modesty and brilliance have always been shining examples, and my sister Andry, whose energy, intelligence and creativity I value more than she can know? I miss my 'other' brother, Kokos, who sadly passed away not so long ago; my mother became his mother when her sister died in childbirth. He came to us again after many years of hiding (but that is another story) for me to rediscover afresh the bonds of shared and forgotten memories (as well as his intellect, warmth and flair). My lifelong partner, Ron Ayres, has been a wonderful source of love, joy and support, a veritable lifeline, providing me with 'a safe haven' from which my wings have never been clipped. He has listened, intelligently, to many of my ideas, and contributed through his questioning to any refinement they have, accompanied me on long walks through parks, woods and along beaches and coast-lines, and held my hand in many cinemas and theatres.

Personal borderscapes

In a book such as this, it is not out of place to insert the role of the personal. I came to the study of social divisions and inequalities out of a keen theoretical and political interest, no doubt filtered through my personal journey. I migrated to Britain as a small child with my parents from the small conflict-ridden island of Cyprus in the Eastern Mediterranean. My mother, Anastasia Pagoni Anthias, having herself been merely educated in a village in Cyprus up to elementary school level (her father thought she should not 'have' to work) passionately wanted her daughters to fulfil their potential. My father was a Communist, an activist, teacher, poet, writer and journalist whose ideals were passionately expressed in his political action, and who dedicated all his life (whilst working mainly as a journalist for the official newspapers of the Cypriot Communist Party (Akel) in Cyprus and in London) to his political work. In Central and North London, we lived on various council estates and I went to several primary and secondary modern schools in the East End of London, finally, post 16, to go to a grammar school and then to the London School of Economics. My experiences as an outsider in British society were amplified by my school experiences in London, where my failure to be part of the local working-class culture was compounded by my 'foreignness' (being a 'greasy Greek'), and my designation (through my love of reading and books) as 'the teacher's pet'. I felt an outsider as a migrant whose mother couldn't speak English, invisible and wanting to pass, but my mother's presence at the school gate and my own name gave me away. I was an outsider also in terms of class position, in an ambivalent way, since I was probably poorer than some of the other children, but my father was middle class by education and cultural interests, although himself born of a poor peasant family (an unwritten book about my father haunts me more and more). I felt most at home when I met children from Cypriot backgrounds at the mother tongue classes and Greek School in Camden Town. We also met at the many functions, political and cultural, at the Royal Hotel in Bloomsbury where we danced, sang

4 Prolegomena

and played. I should say, however, that this did not generate in me a strong belief in ethnic difference but quite the opposite – a strong scepticism about ethnicity as a master narrative, clearly present in all my writings.

In my own personal trajectory, the experiences of migration and associated border-crossings are some of the most important. But borders are not just those we physically cross. The first memory I have is standing in a hallway at the age of what must have been three years old with my brother, in a cool flag-stoned house in old Nicosia, the capital city of the small island of Cyprus, at the time still under British colonial rule. We were watching my father set off on his bike to catch a ship to England. I was crying, or rather chanting, in a two-person choir with my younger brother, 'we want our papa, we want our papa'. Tears of anguish were streaming down our faces. He was departing for London, as the first step in our family migration to that land of promise and opportunity. For him not economic migration but a search for new horizons and joining the 'international proletarian struggle'.

And another memory, now I was somewhat older but back in Cyprus (after a sojourn of a few years in London), tears streaming down my face as the British 'commandos', as we called them, entered our house, one December night, at break of dawn, and took my father into Dhekelia detention camp, because he was an active member of the Communist Party and for his anti-colonial writings. Already in 1931, over 25 years earlier, he had been exiled to a Turkish Cypriot village (Androlykou) for participating in the anti-British riots which culminated in the burning of the Governor's house. In Androlykou, he infringed all the rules by teaching the villagers how to write Greek, and about communism, and he spent 18 months as a political prisoner for these infringements.

Let me return to the moment of first realising about borders: my father leaving for another country (the projection of staying for just a few years in London became a lifetime, as is the case for many migrants). Then came the boats and trains: a seven day journey from Cyprus via Venice and then on to Paris by train and then boat across the Channel and train into grimy foggy London and in the eager arms of my papa. So many borders were crossed that day. The border of leaving home and then, again, the chant 'I want my yiayia and thia' (grandmother and aunt on my mother's side) who lived with us the few months after my father left and before we went to join him. Memories of sweet-scented pink roses (the wild damask roses whose petals we collected in our aprons to make rose-water) in our garden, or should I say Mirofora's garden, whose house we rented and shared in Strovolos, a suburb of Nicosia, of sun, of home (a dream waiting to be found).

The border between home and school, a vivid memory of deepest exclusion and denigration. Going to my first class in the local primary school in Archway, and all the other children being asked a question I could not understand (as I did not speak English) before they were given a small pot of flowers. And I could not understand why I didn't have one also, why I couldn't belong to the club of flower pots. I was crying when my mother came to pick me up, but no

Prolegomena 5

explanation came. Being called a 'greasy Greek' when I *could* understand the words: at lunch-time 'Go on eat your cabbage, you greasy Greek', came the chant from the children, and then I felt the smack on the hand by the teacher.

Let me take you to another border. Some years on, now back in Nicosia, and to those commandos, and at another school. Being the little *englezouda* (little English girl), as I spoke better English than Greek this time round. The bodies of young men soaked in blood in the streets: *whose bodies were they, theirs or ours?* Running home one day and being told by a small child that my father had been killed by EOKA (the right-wing national liberation group in Cyprus) and then seeing my mother who comforted me. It was not true; the little girl was just being malicious because my father was an active Communist (EOKA was anti-Communist as well as anti-British). Going to stay in my mother's village for a few days and the little friends of my cousin chanting 'your dad is a bad Communist, Communist ya ya', and finding out for the first time that 'Communists don't believe in God'.

So far, the story has been about the border of homeland and the migration experience: loss and displacement. The border of fear, of losing your family, of not understanding, of not being accepted. The border of being a colonial subject threatened and imprisoned for your desire for freedom from the colonial yoke, and the loss of the father behind the barbed wires of the Dhekelia camp, visiting him, seeing his tender face behind those bars. The border of political belief, of castigation for taking a different stand to the nationalist one in those years of passion and deepest conformity to the Enosis ideal. The border of communism and how it separates you out from your neighbours but also as an inclusivist community of fellow believers. The simultaneous otherness and belonging.

And then the other border, the one that is strongly imprinted on all societies of ethnic conflict: the border with and against your 'other' who is around the corner, but who cannot be in your homes. In my case in Nicosia, it was literally around the corner. We lived in the old quarter of Nicosia, and in a side street, a rarely visited (by Greek Cypriots) dead-end, were a cluster of run-down little houses, (for me at the time they seemed full of exciting, new things), and this is where some Turkish Cypriot families lived (or Turks as we called them). Being told by neighbours not to go there. But why oh, why, it was fun, they were good at playing ball and skipping: but 'no' they are not like us, they have different habits, best to stick to your own. I never told my mother, was too fearful of what she would say and stopped going around the corner, past that imaginary but all too real border. No need for a flag, for barbed wire, for soldiers, the mere existence of that 'other' was enough. For our neighbours, this was also the 'other' of 'the Turkish policeman' being used by the British to conduct their dirty business, employing them against the Greek Cypriots during the anti-colonialist struggle.

I loved those stories of Nasrandin Hodjas, the mischievous Muslim we all, Greek and Turkish Cypriots, loved to hear: all those years of hybridity, of common phrases, of common bonds with the earth, of conversions to avoid taxation,

6 Prolegomena

of sharing the table of sweated labour, sweetened Turkish coffee (whoops or should I say Cypriot?), of *mahalepi* sold in the streets, of *loukoumia* and *loukoumades* (sweets), of the shepherds' song. What has happened to this history?

Hence here the border of the rejection of the 'other' where I was not that name but the 'self', coexisting with the communist other and the little *englezouda* other that I was.

And then there was the border of the written word, of the book, of being a bookworm in my secondary modern school, being 'too clever by "alf"'. As a small child I used phrases like 'n'aff nice' 'n'aff bad' but never knew what this meant. I remember asking my father who said he thought it must mean 'not half' but I couldn't quite come to terms with this, for 'n'aff' seemed a word in its' own right. Hence also the border of familial expectations, of class aspirations. My mother taking me to a school and, embarrassingly, telling the head teacher of this secondary modern school, on our return from Cyprus, that she wanted me to go to university. And I saw the smirk on his face, as though to say, oh yes, from here, you should be so lucky, we'll see. So many borders to talk about and I have only just started . . .

My mother called me 'the spirit of antilogy' and those who know me well and know my work might be able to recognise this in my impatience with received wisdoms. Why I became a sociologist? Could it be because it allowed me to ask these awkward questions as a professional pastime? Being a feminist: I can't remember when I realised this, but I have felt the injustices in being a woman, of my mother, my aunt, my grandmother all my life.

Who were the dead men (or rather boys) in that blood-stained earth on my journey home from school? *Are they theirs or ours?* What does it mean theirs or ours? Are they 'Greek' (the fighters), are they the Communists, hunted and killed by these young fanatics, are they the young British soldiers posted to Cyprus, being asked to kill as a duty, are they Turkish Cypriots, killed by Greek Cypriots or Greek Cypriots killed by Turkish Cypriots? All this blood, these killings. Please no more ours and theirs, no more borders of violence, let the borders be those of trees, of seas, of bodies, of voices: BANISH THOSE OTHER BORDERS.

Now the Green Line of Nicosia stares us in the face, a black gash in the heart of the earth, in the heart of the city. Not the borders of the Venetian city walls. They are part of another story of my childhood when we were not allowed outside these walls by those British commandos as part of a family curfew. Within those walls and at their feet we spent many a time picking the wild marguerites and fragrant little narcissi. The borders now in the city are those of Ledra Palace, a grand old hotel that symbolises this only divided city in Europe, the border guarded by soldiers from all over the world, through the United Nations. Those you encounter at the barricaded entry point on the border are Cypriot-Greek and Cypriot-Turkish officials.

The first time I crossed since 1974, in 2004 when the Pergamos border was opened, my heart was racing at this border, a mixture of excitement, fear, anticipation. Going to find my father's grave in Kontea, where he was buried in 1968,

Prolegomena **7**

before the Turkish invasion of 1974 and the division of the island. Into Northern Nicosia, this hidden, forbidden, militarised half-city, in a time-warp apart from the khaki uniforms, the military symbols, the guns. Hiring a car to travel on the old road to Famagusta: destination Kontea. Small poor village, birthplace of my father, where my grandmother in old age sold tomatoes and trinkets from a cart (sometimes a donkey) she wheeled around, where my grandfather borrowed from moneylenders to tide him over (the same happened to my mother's father). Family bankruptcy and poverty led my father to wander the villages reciting his poems from the age of nine, accompanied by his father on an accordion, to support his family. Small poor village, from where he was sponsored by a kindly and progressive priest (ironically to then become opposed to organised religion in all its forms), to the Lykion (High School) in Larnaca, and to the Ierodidaskalion, the church-run teacher's college. He emerged (although this might appear unlikely) a bohemian radical, questioning his religious education with a passionate hatred of poverty and the social systems that sustained it (my mother's is another story of escape, but this is not the time to tell it).

Although Kontea is no longer of that name and all signs of the Greek language have been wiped out, erased, the landscape remains the same flat, golden pasture dotted with olive trees and orchards – and way out on the horizon, from the 'other' side now rise the five peaks of the Pentadaktylos mountain range. They also, like the barbed wire, but more majestically and for all Cypriots nostalgically, separate the two territories: contemplative, moved beyond expression, full of anticipation. Kontea, unknown and mythologised village (I visited it only a handful of times before the invasion of 1974). Kontea, how would I find you?

The house that my grandparents lived in has now become a pen full of sheep, the stone arch crumbled. No one with memory of the place, no one to ask, what happened to Elpida's old coffee house, where is Haralambos's house, who lives in it now? They fled in 1974 with only the clothes they were wearing. Where is the graveyard? Who would know, who would care? The church, golden stone, like an ancient ruin, crumbled, whitewashed inside (although since beautifully restored with money from Europe) and standing alongside, its twin, the white Tekke, or Mosque. Some of the people in this village are Anatolians, some are Turkish Cypriots: but I was too anxious and moved by this experience to linger, didn't find the graveyard (since then I have sojourned many times and my father's grave has been partially restored, again with European money). Oh, the border of the political, the border of language and memory, the border of displacement for those who left and those who came. And then the quick trip to the site of old Salamis, guarded by a man and two dogs. But I couldn't get out of the car to see the ruined old kingdom, my heart was in my mouth.

Two lands now, but one people, a common history remembered differently, divisions and solidarities and the new presence of settlers both old (from 1974) and newer ones, as well as migrants and refugees, leaving their own homes to escape poverty, searching for a better life. But one question: where are the

8 Prolegomena

flowers in their tin pots so omnipresent in the Cypriot tradition, both Greek and Turkish, where are the small and large leaved basil plants, where are the vines heavy with fruit? Many people don't feel a stake here, as though their suitcases are already packed to be sent on their way once again.

These memories resonate today in the writing of this book and unfold their traces over me, with sweetness, sorrow and hope.

1

INTRODUCTION. MARKING PLACES

Dilemmas of difference and inequality

Introduction: the book

Walls and borders are everywhere around us. They are not only represented in the wall that Trump wants to build with Mexico, or the borders that desperate migrants and refugees seek to cross on their perilous journeys. They are also the borders between 'us' and 'them', between rich and poor, between men and women, between citizens and non-citizens, between the dominant and the dominated, between the 'normal' and the 'deviant'. The borders are not only physical or territorial but also social, political, economic and symbolic.

The multiform and shifting locations of borders and boundaries in social life, related to difference and belonging, along with the associated hierarchy-making practices around them, underpin the concerns of this book. In this book, I address categories of difference as 'places' in the order of things, how to conceptualise them and how to connect them in social relations. The aim is to contribute to understanding borders and boundaries of difference as a building block for forms of belonging, inequality and oppression in the world today and as underpinning modern capitalist societies and their forms of governance. I therefore treat them as aspects of political economy, and part of the cultural/material nexus in social life (see Chapter 4 particularly). They are then central to relations of production at the concrete level of analysis and to forms of violence and oppression. The book is organised around contemporary dilemmas of difference and inequality. We have seen both a disassembling and re-assembling of borders and boundaries. These point to the unprecedented importance of boundary and bordering practices, and how bodies are marked and sorted, in a world that is purportedly discarding traditional understandings and normative values and practices around fixities and moving towards greater fluidity and multiplicity. There has been a simultaneous dismantling of categories of difference, on the one hand,

10 Introduction

and the growing entrenchment of these within state and other discourses and practices, on the other, denoting a central contradiction in modern neo-liberal democracies.

A translocational lens for addressing modalities of power is developed in this book, stressing relationality, the spatio-temporal and the processual in social relations, building on what has come to be called an intersectional heuristic.[1] As such, space did not permit an extensive range of concrete examples, historical excavations or developments empirically (a potential project for another book). It is therefore an unfinished work, and I treat it as a synthesising of, and development of, my analytical contributions so far to this field. The book brings together many of my ideas over the last few years and builds on my earlier work on the links between boundaries and hierarchies in social life as inequality-making processes that underpin modern capitalist social relations. Hopefully, also, others will take up the challenge, as many young scholars have done in applying the notion of translocational positionality,[2] and in the burgeoning work on racialised and gendered capitalism and the new bordering processes that are emerging worldwide.

Many of the dilemmas I engage with relate to the categories of gender, ethnicity/race and class but this does not exhaust the issues at stake. In engaging with these categorisations, I do not want to minimise the importance of other categorisations and lived experiences, such as age, disability, migration, citizenship, which also constitute ways in which people are ordered and hierarchised. There are *inevitably* multiform ways in which boundaries and hierarchies manifest themselves (as noted by Butler (1990, p. 143) in the use of the 'embarrassing "etc"'), but we should not put them in the bin of the 'etc'. Such categorisations and many others are important in doing some of the work of ordering and hierarchising, as situationally emergent constructions and practices. The categorisations involved are heterogeneous and variable in their effects at different points. Nor should we collapse them together. Some of these are more entrenched and virulent than others at different times, and people are haunted by them differentially (e.g. see Lewis and Hemmings 2019). The processes relating to the workings of categories are intersectional and translocational, articulating in concrete social relations, on the one hand, and operating across place, scale and time, on the other. Whilst relatively new work on borders has thrown into relief the importance of attending to power relations and governmentality in the area particularly of migration, such work has failed to engage with gendered border practices – and to a lesser degree with classed ones because of their political economy orientation (e.g. see Mezzadra and Neilson 2013; de Genova et al. 2018; van Houtum and van Naerssen 2002). In this book I develop an approach which attempts to correct this limitation, treating borders and boundaries as translocationally constituted.

Our concepts are not innocent of social structures and are always politically inflected – they too are part of the discursive apparatus for the making of power. They are also potentially able to interrupt and destabilise. I see theorising, like

Pat Hill Collins (1990), to be a form of political practice, and that which can be transformatory as well as legitimising of the status quo. Recognising the importance of the tools that we use is also to recognise the operations of power that place us, diminish us or lift us, the conditions of existence of such powers, both within category formation and the concrete relations they are embedded in. Reframing our concepts is an important political exercise which intervenes and potentially disrupts the borders and boundaries of fixed identities and essentialised conceptions of our interests, of who 'we' are and who 'they' are. To interrogate the concepts that we use in this understanding is itself a form of intellectual political revolutionary practice which can inform and is informed by political activism.

Chapter 1 is an introduction to the book and sets out a framing for thinking about categories, fixities and fluidities through engaging with salient contemporary issues. A main argument is that there is a particularity to the current set of contradictions that modern societies face which lies in processes of dismantling fixities, on the one hand, but also tendencies towards their entrenchment and reproduction, on the other. It is argued that this is part of the mechanism for dealing with crises at different levels, denoting a central bifurcation in modern neo-liberal democracies. The chapter points to the mutual co-existence and indeed co-dependency between the twin poles of de-ordering and re-ordering. Such processes are expressed particularly around the boundaries of categorisations and the concrete social relations involved, around race, ethnicity and nation, migration, rights, sexuality, gender and class and at their intersections. It argues for an approach that considers categories around difference as modes of power which also inform people's sense of belonging as well as relating to processes of differential inclusion, oppression, and resource allocation. It provides an account of the notion of translocational belonging, with its focus on spatialised temporalities, beginning the process of presenting a translocational intersectional lens which is developed more fully later in the book.

Chapter 2 focuses on the work that categories do in relation to borders and hierarchies, enabling systems of differential inclusion and resource allocation. It argues that categorisations, and associated forms of belonging, involve the marking and making of *places* of difference, mapping out the borders and boundaries of entitlements, resource allocation, inclusion and exclusion, and inequality. The chapter considers the under-theorising of categories of difference in the sociological canon and briefly examines some of the limitations found in the work of notable social thinkers, amongst them Bourdieu and Foucault. It also discusses the limitations, heuristically, of the diversity problematic. The chapter then explores some of the commonalities of the major social categories of gender, ethnos and class in terms of the work that they do in the social order of things and as concrete social relations of hierarchisation and unequal resource allocation.

Chapter 3 considers the strengths and potential of an intersectional lens but also some of the quandaries raised in the project of theorising the effectivities of

12 Introduction

categories of difference through the postulate of their intersection and mutual constitution. It explicates some of the quandaries and dilemmas faced by those who engage with intersectionality and proposes a provisional way of addressing these. In doing this, it engages with the dilemma raised by using, on the one hand, categories of gender, race, class and sexuality (as well as others) as points of reference (and therefore, at some level as separate), and on the other hand, the idea of their mutual constitution, which points to these categories as always already intertwined, and therefore inseparable. The chapter develops a dialogical and multi-level framework (see also Anthias 2013a) for thinking through their translocational nature alongside the specification of societal arenas as conceptual and methodological tools.

Chapter 4 aims to develop a more integrated and intersectional approach to social stratification, arguing for an approach which differentiates between class and social stratification beyond the classical way of focusing on stratification as relating to an interplay between class and status. It also argues that class and other major categories, like gender, ethnicity and race, are inflected by both the economic and the symbolic which constitute *the economic/symbolic or material/cultural nexus* in social life. Symbolic struggles for representation are treated as intricately woven with resource struggles. The chapter argues against the separation of the economic and the symbolic/cultural arenas in ways that privilege the former in relation to class and the latter in relation to gender and ethnicity/race. It develops a way of thinking about class places within an intersectional stratification analysis which treats class as a necessary but insufficient condition for the understanding of inequalities, and it argues that gender and ethnicity/race are already inscribed in class places.

Chapter 5 looks at dilemmas relating to sex and gendered forms of boundary making. It argues that a central contradiction found in gender categories lies in the mutuality and violence/subordination twin and that this constitutes a particularly biologistic discursive apparatus that feeds into naturalising social relations of subordination within modern societies. Gender lends itself particularly as a stigma or branding that translates into the naturalisation of social effectivities. Positing biological proclivities or psychic traits and predispositions functions to legitimise the different roles that gendered subjects play in the fields of the economic, the political and the representational. Gender categories facilitate exploitation and differential exclusion in ways that invisibilise the forces at play. The forms of domination found in the gender category and its relations appear as forms of symbolic and physical violence. This includes intimate partner violence, familial gender violence and the physical violence inflicted on the bodies of rape victims. Gender categories reinforce the naturalisation of power; they also reinforce dominant national imaginaries and class relations of exploitation. The chapter discusses, within an intersectionally inflected framing, gendered and transnational violence, women's migrant labour and care work as well as looking at some of the dilemmas faced within feminisms in the transgendering debates that have currently grown in importance.

Chapter 6 turns to dilemmas of borders, boundaries and othering in relation to nation, migration and race, as interrelated aspects of territorialising resource allocations and subordinations within an imperative of closure and differential/subordinated inclusion. Nation, 'race' and migration mark important spaces where struggles about where and how borders are placed for control and management of populations and resources are played out. This chapter looks at a range of bordering processes relating to collective categories and their contestations, and ways in which belonging is politicised and policed in various ways, hierarchising resources of different types. Borders around collectivities and national boundaries throw into play some of the violent and dislocating aspects of the categories of the collective 'other'. The chapter delineates a family of concepts relating to collectivity, and then engages with the saliency of the 'migrant' category in relation to the so-called 'migration and refugee crisis' or the 'turbulence of migration'. The chapter also examines racisms and nativisms, and the projects of racialisations, as both modes of exclusion and modes of exploitation. It also looks at the trope of diversity in the management of migration and difference and the related governmentalities through integration discourse and practice.

Chapter 7, the concluding chapter, deals with dilemmas of theory and politics, considering further some of the problems of theorising, and engaging with a politics of translocation as a way of thinking with translocational belonging in resistance and solidarity politics. It locates, firstly, the main dimensions of the argument of the book and its theoretical thrust. It then looks at the political potential of an intersectionally inflected approach. Intersectionality has produced critiques and backlashes concerning its potential 'whitening', neo-liberal agenda, policy framing, its individualisation of difference, and claims and counterclaims about its origins. There is therefore the issue of the form of politics which it fosters, whether it be identity politics or solidarity politics which are discussed and which the chapter does not see as always incompatible. The chapter provides some provisional reflections on how we might pursue a 'politics of translocation' which has direct relevance to the issue of the politics of intersectionality.

A contradictory moment: fixities and fluidities in unsettling times

To say we live in unsettling times may seem like a tautology given the history of the world. Life has been unsettling for many people all over the world throughout time. Poverty, inequality, hatred, collective violence, war and allegiances of religion, race and ethnicity, gender, sexuality and class (in different forms relating to economic and political inequalities) have characterised human societies in different ways and within different cultural, political and economic systems since time immemorial. Exploitation, subordination, exclusion and expulsions have been rife through history. It is a figment to think of these as modern or recent phenomena. Wallerstein's ideas about the world being 'out of joint' (2014) could be used to refer to most of human history, as indeed the writings of Marx spell

14 Introduction

out through his social critique of forms of economic and social organisation, developed within his theory of historical materialism (Marx 1859). Agamben's characterisation of refugees as 'bare life' (Agamben 1998) could be marshalled also to explain many manifestations through history, where people become reduced to 'nature' to 'zoe' (as opposed to bios), without political rights and deprived of that which, in some views, constitute the human as beyond the animal. Whilst such a view is compelling and important, it's also central to re-insert the role of the agentic and agonistic in human life, as that which resists, contests and is engaged in struggle around the 'givenness' of the social order, the doxa that often underpin such forms of violence.

From the beginning of this book I do not want to make claims to any strong exceptionalism for modern times in this regard, nor risk a Eurocentric and Westocentric approach that ignores the upheavals, movements and violence produced by the footprints, wounds and foul debris (Stoler 2013) of imperial forms of domination (amongst others), sometimes referred to as postcoloniality or as limited decolonisation. These still have a *dynamic* presence of course today (not just as vestiges of the past scattered along our way). Nor should we ignore internal conflicts over resources, the control over peoples' minds, and the disciplining of their bodies. The issue of the specificities of the current moment is complex and I cannot address it in any serious way. I would like to remark, however, that what we have is a greater technological apparatus for the exercise of power and domination, and greater capacity of people to exercise their autonomy, for example, with the 'autonomy of migration' (De Genova 2017), enabling them to escape conditions which are unliveable (as well as greater means to police these movements by the state).

There is a global division in what Hall (1992) famously called 'the West and the rest', in the very capacity to sustain life in different parts of the world today. More than half the world lives in poverty and disease. The United Nations estimates that there are 783 million people who live below the international poverty line of US$1.90 a day, more than 11% of the world's population.[3] Large numbers of people have faced displacement through wars and conflicts as well as poverty, escaping in various ways to seek safer spaces, sometimes to face death or further violations and dehumanisations (70.8 million people, of which 25.9 million are refugees, according to UNCHR (2018a) – for more information see UNCHR (2018b). Many of the world's refugees sit their time out in encampments, waiting to be 'ordered' and 'sorted' (see Chapter 6). Some find themselves facing life or death situations, risking their lives on boats, interned in refugee camps, for example in the unfortunately named Calais 'jungle' (now closed) and in the disgusting and inhuman febrile environments that refugees face in Libya and elsewhere (and the mass exodus of people from Venezuela). These conditions are overlaid by gendered violence, with many women being raped in the camps (Donnelly and Muthiah 2019), and with the effects of racialisation and class dividing people. Some form enterprises, dance and sing and find new forms of sociality and comradeship. Some find ways of evading border controls and enter

Introduction **15**

through the porous borders of the Mediterranean or the Balkans, working in vulnerable and low paid jobs, illegal migrants who states may turn a blind eye to in the exercise of exploitation. They are not mere victims of structures or mere objects of biopolitics, they are never reduced to 'bare life', even if they sit in no man's land, in the buffer zones of life itself. Others can cross state borders more easily through their ability to acquire visas or nationality, with many countries conferring citizenship to those who can pay (see Chapter 6).

Pensioners, single mothers, those living on benefits, the long-term unemployed, the sick, the disabled, migrants and refugees are terms we use to describe the boundaries we place between different categories of people (although these are not mutually exclusive), categories embodied in state practices and regulations, and unequal economic and social positions around income, housing, employment opportunities, education, skills and social rights as well as forms of social honour and rank. In the process we reduce people to these labels and we fix them. We also avoid looking at the construction of the places of liminality and subordination and how people are marked by them, interned within them, and how these markings intersect for individuals in translocational ways within socio-spatial temporalities.

Category dismantling and retrenchment

We live in a highly contradictory moment. All societies through time manifest processes which are multiple and contradictory, but there is a particularity to the current set of contradictions. This lies in processes of dismantling fixities, on the one hand, but also tendencies towards their entrenchment and reproduction, on the other. This is part of the mechanism for dealing with crises at different levels, denoting a central bifurcation in modern neo-liberal democracies. This contrasts with the views of Agamben (2005) who talks about the normalisation of 'states of exception' where political ideals of democracy have been superseded by permanent crisis management. Social regulation cannot be reduced to the level of the monolithic ordering process or the totalitarian state to use Hannah Arendt's (1951) term. I point to the mutual co-existence and indeed co-dependency between the twin poles of de-ordering and re-ordering instead. Such processes are expressed particularly around the boundaries of categorisations and the concrete social relations involved, around race, ethnicity and nation, migration, rights, sexuality, gender and class and at their intersections. Some of them are manifested in the making of new spaces of vulnerability, inequality and degradation, found in the present refugee crisis and in the growing forms of precarity. Yet others are manifested in new political spaces of right-wing populisms and the growth of alt-right parties such as New Dawn in Greece, Elam in Cyprus, the Front National in France and many others worldwide.

At the same time, there are new spaces of solidarity, resilience and even empowerment. Despite the violence and moral depravities of modern-day capitalist neo-liberalism with the mammoth god of profit, and the struggles to deal

16 Introduction

with the failings of capitalist governance and governmentality, there are large pockets throughout the world of active citizens and non-citizens. There are mobilisations against war and inequality, around ecology and climate change, support for refugees and migrants, struggles against violations of rights, and around social justice, found in grass roots organising and the re-energisation of anti-racism through the Black Lives Matter movement (despite its retention of identity politics). They are making a difference, for example, in the multiple resistances of migrants (or the 'migrant commons' – see Trimikliniotis et al. 2015), within the refugee camps and in humanitarian practices (despite their contradictions – see de Genova 2017; Chouliaraki and Georgiou 2017). They thereby struggle to avoid and evade the complex, and at times, contradictory ordering of the state, demonstrating in the streets, organising in political mobilisations of different kinds. Bifurcations and contradictions also open up potential spaces of hope and transformation and new forms of mobilisation.

Whilst there has been some dismantling of binary categories, particularly around gender, sexuality, nation and race, this has not been accompanied by the equivalent dismantling of inequalities and violence on their basis. There might be more acknowledgement of the difference within difference, but greater inequalities characterise our current period.[4] Whilst the issue of 'inequality' is currently being focused on politically and academically, it often acts as a rhetorical device, a buzzword, for example in the call 'to tackle inequality' proclaimed by right-wing populist parties in the UK and Europe (e.g. in the platforms of Nigel Farage and his followers and in the empty promises of the erstwhile British Prime Minister Theresa May amongst others in the UK). At one and the same time the earth is facing imminent disaster through climate change and pollution. This has given rise to new forms of participatory citizenship as well as attempts to order it, co-opt it or neutralise it. But the human spirit lives on and will refuse to be relegated to abject nature, as long as it can.

Whilst this book argues against the ways in which notions of fixities of position, location and belonging operate in social relations, and argues, analytically, for a move away from fixing and essentialising categories and concepts, it's important to remember that fixities are characteristic of social life. Many of these fixities operate as 'doxa' (Heller 1975; Bourdieu 1979), that is, as taken for granted assumptions about the nature of the world. Many of the fixities around us today are not new although they may manifest themselves in different and variable forms. Fixities of gender, religion, race and class have survived many years beyond their analytical dismantling by philosophers and social scientists. They have survived political interventions and economic arrangements and rearrangements although arguably many of these have been weak at best and disingenuous at worst. These are often zombie-like, without substance, empty signifiers and indeed veils for the operations of power. The differentially bright or blurred walls and borders loom strong and high, even though the occasional crack or gap might create noise and consternation for a time. However, the point is not just to understand them but to change them as Marx famously pronounced.

Arguably this understanding, although never enough in itself, has political resonances that can help us better to dismantle these walls.

The fundamentalisms of culture in one form or another, such as religious or sexual values and practices, classed ways of being, ideological obfuscation or the camera obscura principles of hegemonic sociabilities and their manifestations under capitalism should not be underestimated. These underpin many forms of subordination and inferiorisation, facilitating exploitation. They are far from recent phenomena, but they are not merely iterations as they are manifested in different guises, giving rise to new forms.

The rise of feminism, anti-racism, the LGBTQ movement, the move away from traditional ideas about sex and marriage (an ambivalent secularism in the Christian world) and the increasing formal and informal acceptance of homosexuality, transgendering and gender equality/feminism are important. But they have not meant the decline of gender categories in terms of their political use, or the decline in homophobic and transphobic attacks, but indeed their harnessing in new ways often through co-optation of the struggles and their effects. Hence, some have referred to these processes in terms of femonationalism (Farris 2012a) and homonationalism (Puar 2007) demonstrating how ideas about equality around gender or sexuality themselves are used strategically for political projects that are far from equality projects and become part of a neo-liberal agenda.

Many of the fixities, and the political imaginations and practices around them, are manifested at times as hysterical or kneejerk reactions to the unfixing that is taking place and the disassembling of the foundations for a Westphalian social order with its 'everything in its place'. These include right-wing populisms, the growth and amplification of racisms of different kinds including anti-Muslim, anti-Roma and anti-Jewish racism, anti-migration policies and discourses, new bordering practices, the Trump and Brexit phenomena – which some might see as business as usual (Benson 2019). At the bottom-up level, they also hold the emotional traces of nostalgias for a container model of the state built on supposedly culturally if not ethnically homogeneous citizens (where any 'diversity' is a gloss on essential conformity), and evocations of empire and greatness. These nationalist tropes have strengthened in these times of austerity with growing inequalities and divisions around jobs, housing, income and wealth. Greater inequality has also led to responses which are doxic, where inequality becomes so normalised that it recedes into a hazy smoke and becomes part of 'the way of the world'. Some might see these developments as political manifestations of 'resentment' (Barbalet 1992) fuelled by people missing out their turn in 'the queue' of social advancement through a perceived jumping of that queue by newcomers or 'outsiders'. This is salient, for example, in the discourses around Brexit in the UK where new forms of 'nativism' have emerged (Benson 2019), claiming greater rights to belonging.

However, such reactions are not only on the ground, arising out of people's social locations and their own at times fundamentalist beliefs and values, and ways of managing their sense of loss and disaffection, expressed in what some

18 Introduction

have called vernacular racism (Amin 2010). They are produced, reproduced and controlled by powerful social agents in the governance and governmentality of the modern state, arguably particularly important today through digital media platforms (Skeggs 2019; Georgiou 2018). They are instantiated in the practices of individual functionaries or agents (police officers, housing clerks, social workers, migration officers) who perform their roles in at times arbitrary and contradictory ways. Individual decisions are made by the police, border guards or social workers or personnel in job centres, pointing to the importance of bureaucratic functionaries who can never be just office holders following rules (c.f. Weber in Gerth and Mills 1946). Such practices cannot be allocated only to the debris of coloniality or the post-racial turn (Lentin 2016). They are constantly reproduced and transformed through the operations of power at different levels – structurally and discursively – and through positionalities in all their contradictory and translocational ways.

Althusser's positing of ideological state apparatuses (1971/2001) is more and more apt with the greater move towards a brave new world. There is surveillance from cameras, Google and other search engines and data collection for marketing purposes or for the services of the police. For example, in the UK, a new requirement was recently mooted by the police that rape victims be asked to permit access to the data on their phones, at the risk of not having their rape allegations investigated otherwise. Such instances confront us daily in our everyday life, monitoring and indeed often filming and photographing us wherever we go, whatever we do. Our biometric data are collected and stored at airports and other spaces. A babble and cacophony of discourses and narratives spread their voices constantly through digitalities which are colonised by a range of social actors, both states and global capital, testifying to our consent and indeed addiction to social media forms, such as Facebook and Instagram. There are also more and more legal duties on citizens to act as vigilantes for the state, in their role as teachers, doctors, nurses, landlords and citizens (see Chapter 6).

Foucault's (1975) narration of the panopticon, a word taken from the Greek, 'the all-seeing eye or observation point', has become more and more resonant as a principle of social life itself rather than a particular instance of it. Nonetheless these invisible hands/eyes are not just the inevitable workings of the social in modernity, a diffuse power in the very act of acting, an action upon an action, as Foucault has defined it (1982). They are manipulated and essentially configured, and reconfigured, if not in their totality, by the powerful, but fractured and clunky, machinery of the modern state apparatus, and by powerful (and on the ground less powerful) social actors with particular economic and political interests and values or through legal requirements of their roles. Nancy Fraser's (1989) turn to Weber to correct some of the excesses and limitations of the Foucauldian notion of power is instructive here. Power cannot be so easily disassembled from violence and domination, a disassembling marring the work of the early texts of Foucault (Brenner 1994; Cronin 1996). These forms of domination have become more and more transparent, and their visibilities raise possibilities for contestation too.

Introduction **19**

However, at the same time we have seen shifts towards fluidities, largely as a result of action on the ground undertaken through various political mobilisations, of ideas and of practice, around sexuality, gender, race, migration and democratisation which I see as partially made possible through complex and contradictory locations. Such fluidities, however, are not just testaments to solidarity struggles but also play off each other. Promoting gender rights, in the name of gender equality, may be made at the expense of racialisation, where supporting Muslim women can involve the demonisation of Muslim communities. Rights to cultural difference, in the name of race equality, may be made at the expense of gender equality, where supporting cultural difference involves turning a blind eye to the plight of women who face subordination and gender-based violence (see Anthias and Yuval-Davis 1992; Farris 2012b).

At times fluidities may be generated by the economic needs of concrete economic systems, pulling women in and out of the labour force or bringing migrants in to fill the jobs that indigenous workers are not available for, or as cheap or compliant labour. Such shifts hold the potential to make more transparent the workings of power relations. This can supplement the classical Marxist imaginary where these operate primarily through class mobilisations. Indeed, *contradictory locations* are found in relation to working-class struggle with its roots in male dominated labour markets. In a patriarchal society this throws up disparities in the relationships that men have with women and racialised minorities (where they are dominant), and relationships they have with their employers (where they are subordinate). In the case of middle-class women, who were important in western feminism, we can see an opposite effect, where class and race/whiteness ordain dominance over others, and yet gendered forms of domination haul this back, preventing full social engagement.

The importance of *relationality* of position and *intersectionality* are central here and the idea of contradictory locations flagged by the notion of *translocational positionality* (which I first presented in Anthias (2002)) is its apogee. I am not arguing that *contradictory* location (or contradictory inclusion) is the sole or even necessary element at work here; rather that it is part of the process for social transformation of fixities that we have witnessed. Putting people back into the homology of difference is one way such antagonisms can also be fought – returning women to the home after wars or re-affirming the gendered nature of unpaid or low paid labour of care, through the care work done by migrant women. Whilst fluidities and border-breaking point to some of the successes of mobilisations and contestations, they also enable the projects of capital, providing pools of cheap labour at different times. Developments in technology and the move of the organisation of production to poorer countries means that there has been a growth of the service sector and the lower middle classes, as well as precarious labour. However, there is still the requirement for the labour of reproduction, much of it now part of the official labour market (cleaning services, nannies and nurseries, domestic workers). These build on old notions of gender and race which are thereby reinforced, as the categories of people who fill these labour market reproductive roles are

20 Introduction

women and migrants. The persistence of these fixities constitutes some of the essential failures of Enlightenment thought, on the one hand, but also the successes of the projects of androcentricity, coloniality and empire, on the other.

Some of the fluidities are manifested in the steady undermining of the binary nature of social categories, gender fluidity through the transgender movement, opened up, arguably by the lessons learnt with struggles around multiculture and hybridity, as well as against homophobia and heteronormativity. This includes the slow but steady recognition about the need to dismantle gendered positions in the labour market and in the home, through struggles by feminists, some of whom have not been so keen to embrace the transgender movement, however (as we shall see in Chapter 5), as well as through the commodification of labour power more generally. This is one central reason why joined up struggles within solidarity politics are so important (see Chapter 7).

In addition, within contemporary developments in sociology there has been a move away from monolithic categories. In the area of the study of ethnicity and migration, for example, there has been an interest in what have been called transethnic, transnational and hybrid identities which often place people in contradictory locations rather than in-between positions (for a critique of the idea of cultural in-betweenness see Anthias (1998b)). In terms of class theory there have been several writers, who some time ago now, focused on hybrid and contradictory class positions, for example, Wright (1985), Carchedi (1977) and Poulantzas (1980), particularly regarding supervisory roles and in Poulantzas's case on the contradictory location of the petit bourgeoisie. Such class contradictions manifest themselves particularly in the gig economy of self-reliant, self-employed but super-exploited workers – between autonomy and enslavement, unable to collaborate and supremely individualised (although some are beginning to show the capacity for action). Such class relations require new ways of thinking about class, not only through a complexification of class positions away from the binary class schemas of old or the proliferation of class positions based on occupational groupings or capitals (c.f. Goldthorpe 1987; Savage et al. 2013). It's necessary to understand forms of class distinction even within occupational categories. For example, in the recent work of Sam Friedman (2019) on elite jobs we find 'class ceilings', although he doesn't look at gendered class ceilings where there are differential rewards and pay structures for men and women doing the same jobs (e.g. as TV presenters). This is in addition to the recognition of how categories of gender, race and class, when looked at together in all their simultaneity and entanglement, produce diverse effects (a point now being taken up by some class theorists e.g. see Segal and Savage 2019).

Whilst fixities around gender have been challenged for a long time by various forms of feminist struggle, and more recently by the LGBTQ movement which includes struggles around transgendering, throwing into relief sexual citizenship (Richardson 2017), there are counterforces at play. Various new forms of heteronormativity and sex-based violence and reaction have crept in to taint even the most apparently radical practices. For example, whilst rape is a criminal offence, only a minority of women press charges and even fewer rapists are sentenced.[5] Within the feminist movement, itself, we have seen some feminists opposing the use of women's toilets by transgender women on the grounds of the misaligned bodies such women inhabit, and their intrusion into safe women's spaces, with the resurgence of the trope of the 'real biological woman'. New forms of identity politics have been emerging out of the persistence of state and other violence towards Black people; in America one of the most important being Black Lives Matter with the response from the All Lives Matter rallying call, deliberately distorting the slogan of Black Lives Matter which was essentially 'Black Lives Matter *too*'. This shows the complexity of the mechanisms at work and some of their contradictions on the ground.

The migration crisis and governing diversity

The focus on difference and belonging today is particularly married to the twin poles of the so-called 'migration crisis' (which also encompasses discourses on refugees) and the 'governing of diversity'. Borders are policed, both through specific technologies at the border and through integration and surveillance (in the UK e.g. through the notorious Prevent programme – see Chapter 6) of those who are already within them. These have become central planks for the control and management of populations within the contradictory parameters of capitalist globality and resurgent nationalism. These involve the twin processes of dismantling borders for capital, whilst simultaneously rearranging them and re-erecting them for people, proliferating bordering processes. Increasing numbers of poverty stricken and persecuted people are fleeing their countries to find safety nets in Europe and the West, many of these wars and violations themselves facilitated by the very countries that migrants and refugees flee to, risking their lives and those of their children to find a safe space. Arguably, migration today epitomises and embodies the centrality of bordering and inequality regimes and their associated technologies, throwing into play the related projects of modern-day capitalism, nationalism and societal forms of governance, all of which marshal various means of determining 'belonging', non-belonging or differential belonging. This exercise is not just about technologies which create algorithms of membership, but it also entails technologies for resource allocation. Crossing borders is a way into memberships and entitlements although one can be a member without some of the entitlements of citizenship and indeed one can hold formal citizenship without full entitlements to safety and security.

This is also tied to constructing spaces of contradiction, liminality and ambiguity. Within these spaces sit subjects at the extreme ends of humanity, those incarcerated serving their time at the edges of society, the homeless, refugees, those in so-called safe places or refuges, such as women suffering domestic violence and many others. Some are constructed as the 'permanent temporary', in black holes or dead-ends, such as Palestinians in Gaza, or Cypriot refugees in Cyprus. Some inhabit border-zones waiting over many years to cross or to be

22 Introduction

fixed in place. Others are workers on zero-hour contracts in the gig economy, and the temporarily unemployed whose unemployment has become more, or less, permanent.

These are spaces where people are being subjected to a process of fixing, waiting to be sorted and ordered, which I would call the '*fixed unfixed*', incarcerated in the waiting room of life. Such spaces embody the principle of total denigration and loss of political voice. They have sometimes been referred to as 'gray spaces' (Yiftachel 2009), outside the normal rule of law, and their subjects as 'bare life' (Agamben 1998). Mbembe calls this necropolitics (2003) showing how social and political power is used to dictate whether people live or die. On the other hand, for Rancière (2004, 2010) the process is one of dissensus, where people are divided into those who can and those who can't speak which is foundational to the current order of things.

These terms have resonances with in-betweenness and indetermination, or with extreme dehumanisation. However, the spaces of contradiction and ambivalence – in the waiting rooms between the fluid and the fixed – can also play multiple functions. Some of these spaces are occupied by 'surplus populations' to be sorted and allocated a role within the contradictory intersections of the forces of capitalist modernity and national border making and marking. Others are permanently marked as surplus and dispensable, thrown on the scrap heap of human life. Not only do such processes divide and stratify people but they also facilitate multiple and intersecting violence and violations, including extermination, expulsion, genocides, inferiorisation, exploitation, subordination and stigma.

Nationalism and its twin, nativism, are key discursive and ideological drivers of the practices around border controls of various types, which distinguish between desirable and undesirable others. Desirable others shift and change with different economic and related political projects. The desirability of capital inflows provides a rationale for investment visas where rich people are able to buy permanent residence and citizenship (in the UK an investment of over £2 million buys a Tier 1 investment visa.[6] Work visas or permits are differentially available indicating the desirability of different categories of workers – in the US there are 185 types of visa (Grossman, Golden and Thurnell 2009). Issues of Brexit in the UK throw a lens on the complex nature of the processes as the divisions over Brexit reveal some of the contradictory effects of capitalist difference making and the boundary making involved. The divisions over Brexit have crosscut, in British political life, divisions of class and politics more broadly, and arguably throw the spotlight on the crisis of neo-liberal democracy. They demonstrate how migration is emblematic of the concern for 'control' within the extreme right populist moment in western societies, simultaneously throwing into relief *and* shifting attention away from the crisis in western capitalist societies' management of the economy and government. This raises the question of who the working class are, and the whiteness assumed in the term, even, or particularly by, the socialist movement (Valluvan 2016, 2019; Virdee 2014).

Unfixing borders through transnational and global movements of different populations, for work or to escape poverty, war and disease, has characterised the western world (and 'the rest' where internal migration has been particularly important). However, new borders and border-making practices have emerged to manage and to curtail some, but not all, migrants. The differentiated nature of seepage into borders again is not new but is now taking place through controls over borders which distinguish persons not just through ethnicity or national provenance alone, or even for labour market shortages (i.e. they are not just dependent on an ethnic or racialised imagination or crude economic interests), but through ideas of desirable versus undesirable populations and individuals, using complex algorithms for control and ordering.

Such individuals or groupings of individuals are not only signposted as potential terrorists but also in terms of a range of other attributions or human property conferments, given to individuals as members purportedly of hostile or undesirable groups (cultural or social contaminators, unable to integrate, and people whose ways of life do not conform to the hegemonic ideal), and also in terms of their economic ability to pay for entitlements to enter and stay. The classed as well as ethnic, religious and gender aspects are clear. In the case of gender, not only do women enter on the basis of different skills or aptitudes but to fill different needs, particularly of social reproduction, as domestic maids, carers, cleaners and nannies. Skin colour or explicitly racist notions are still important, but the tropes used are multivalent and heterogeneous, and coalesce around the notion of *compliance* with the mainstream social fabric as a basis for desirability, and the capacity to pay. The importance given to the curtailment of an impending and threatening dissensus (Rancière 2004) cannot be overstressed. As I argue in Chapter 6, some of the processes bear the marks of racialisation in its broadest sense denoting *danger, deviance, deficit* and at times harnessing ideas about *disgust,* currently using religious faith and culture as pivots for distinguishing such persons or groups, with 'skin colour', body covering or religion being the most prominent alert for such persons; in the first two, flagging the role of visible difference.

The related ideas of danger, deviance, deficiency and disgust (the four Ds as I have called them, Anthias (2014); see Chapter 6) have always underpinned the boundaries of race, ethnicity and national provenance in justifying exclusion or differential inclusion (Anthias 1998b; Mezzadra and Neilson 2011), but *compliance* (rather than sameness or community) alongside 'our national interest' have now a central and separate role that differentiates within various categories of the racialised and the objects of racialisation. In this way, crosscutting markers operate in both more basic and more sophisticated ways, with, for example, ideas of good versus bad 'differences' and 'others', integrated versus non-assimilable ones or good and bad Muslims. This requires meeting quite complex algorithms of differential and subordinated inclusion in the bordering regimes of various states or regions. Many of these 'otherings', including hatred and everyday racism towards Black people, Jews and Muslims, and hostility to refugees and Roma

24 Introduction

populations appear to be reactive in the sense that they manifest themselves as forms of protection against the loss of resources, including power hierarchies (i.e. are both *exclusionary* and *usurpationary* to take Parkin's (1979) use of Weber's binary and treat it as hybrid). These are fuelled most strongly during times of austerity and economic decline, an argument that Max Weber insightfully made about class but failed to make for ethnicity, seeing the latter as more dominant in times of economic stability (Weber 1946).

Civil society has been designated an increasingly important role in the policing of borders and boundaries; this includes legal duties given to teachers, academics, health professionals, employers, landlords and so on, who are being required to police borders. One recent example, from the UK, is that teachers and health professionals might have a public or legal duty to report those under their care that they suspect might commit acts of violence (if it is agreed). This would then sit alongside the legal duty they already have to report undocumented or illegal migrants.[7] In terms of borders, certain roles are becoming effectively functionaries of the state (whilst the state personnel itself has diminished) and could themselves be regarded as forms of the 'state apparatus' (to use Poulantzas's (1974) term), in preventing or rather safeguarding seepage into borders, by denouncing those who are working illegally or who claim authenticity 'falsely'. Individuals, both as citizens and as workers, are required to be handmaidens of the state, increasingly reinforcing the power of Althusser's designation of schools and other institutions as ideological state apparatuses, whilst at the same time converting all citizens to becoming part of the state's surveillance mechanisms, as objects and subjects (see Yuval-Davis et al. 2019). Such practices affect all members of society as all members can potentially be subject to such surveillance and border controls, particularly if they are visibly different, black, Muslim and young.

Belonging

Belonging, in the title of this book, is a border-making organisational principle in social life, but complexly inflected and articulated. As a political and heuristic tool it has become particularly important through recent foci on bordering mechanisms with the so-called migration crisis and the concern over the plight of refugees. Research around boundary and border forging, maintenance and contestation has partially supplanted identity-based research with the growth of mobilities, securitisation and bordering practices of all types, both formal and everyday. I treat belonging and non-belonging (or differential belonging) in this sense, as a process and an outcome of boundary and border making and the marks these leave on human experience, location, and modes of identification.

In addition, borders and boundaries imposed by modern states more explicitly use notions of belonging. Instances of the unmaking of belonging (e.g. in the Windrush scandal in Britain) and constructions of non-belonging are rife, particularly in this latest phase of concern with migration and its impact. There are newer impediments to entry and settlement. These relate to compliance and conformity with hegemonic cultural norms and practices, as well as to the differentiation of migrants by skill and in accordance with the economic requirements of the labour market.

Belonging and non-belonging relate to access, participation, safety and incorporation (Anthias 2006). The related notion of identity flags much more issues around the self or the construction of common selves. Although it is broader than the notion of inclusion, belonging, like inclusion (and exclusion) can be, and indeed is, differentiated (Anthias 1998b), and can exist on subordinated terms (Anthias 2001b). This is clear in many forms of work that minorities and migrants do, and in their lack of full citizenship. As such, as I have argued before (Anthias 2009), belonging includes under its ambit a range of facets, both formal and informal – citizenship, nationality, ethnicity, locality and family forms as well as those related to gender and class and other salient border-making categorisations and practices. The arenas of the social and the political infiltrate all social life, including our feelings, values and orientations.

As belonging raises questions about boundaries of 'difference', collectivities and social bonds, it also points to when and how differences count, their normative and political evaluation, and how they are struggled over. Struggles about membership, entitlements and belonging become ever more politicised where there is competition over resources. It is important to treat belonging also as a technology of power as the criteria both at the more formal and informal level are part of how people are categorised and disciplined and part of the ways in which resources of different types are allocated. These also pit people against each other by making some commonalities disappear into thin air, whilst reinforcing others.

Belongings can be fixed or fluid under different conditions and for different groups. However, it is important not to essentialise them as whether they are more, or less, fixed, or more, or less, fluid, they are enactments in social space that articulate power relations, and the discourses around them; actors and groups use these as resources and as meaning-making tropes. They involve life or death situations also, witnessed in the savageries and death tolls left by refusals to grant belonging, including the case of Shamima Begum's baby[8] and those seeking refuge from wars or insecurities of life that have drowned in our seas. The differential valuation given to differentiated human bodies makes them subject to the violent and dehumanising effects of processes of identity making and breaking, and the inclusionary and exclusionary practices of belonging.

The notion of belonging enables us to ask questions about the technologies of belonging: how categorisations mark belonging, embodied in legal and formal ways as well as in everyday life and as central to delivering differentiated inclusions. It can enable us to ask questions about belonging to 'what' rather than, as with identity, who an individual 'is' or who and what they 'identify with' (which are in fact two different questions). It replicates, in Mezzadra and Neilson's (2013) terms, 'border as method', where we might substitute the term belonging for border. Belonging is essentially a bordering mechanism, and bordering

26 Introduction

is a way of determining where to mark belonging. Belonging entails not only attributions and claims, but also asks us to consider the actual spaces and places to which people are accepted as members or feel that they are members. Compared to the notion of identity, it enables broader questions about social inclusion as well as the forms of violence and subordination entailed in processes of boundary or border making. The place-making elements of belonging are stressed, for example, by Antonsich (2010), as well as in my work on social locations (Anthias 2002, 2008).

Belonging ties in much better than identity to the focus of this book, and the simultaneous concern with walls, borders and boundaries on the one hand, and resource allocations and struggles, as well as agentic and agonistic positionalities (captured with the notion of translocational positionality, e.g. see Anthias 2002, 2013a). This is because of its relationality to place both physical and symbolic and because it denotes spatial and temporal contexts. Moreover, the struggles around belonging in terms of who belongs, to what extent and in what ways, and the criteria used become much more embedded in struggles of national and territorial resources rather than being posed, if not actually constituted, by struggles over representation and culture (which have been tied to identity politics). For example, struggles around membership, nationality and citizenship much more clearly entail struggles of belonging than struggles about 'identity'. To seek citizenship does not entail identifying but a desire to be included. Belonging in such a formulation is a broad notion related to differential inclusions (and exclusions/expulsions/precarities) found in all the kinds of membership denoted: formal, informal and in terms of values, attachments, claims and attributions of different kinds, of which the clearly political in terms of political mobilisation or in terms of political control is only one specific form of the political. In other words, belonging, although overlaid by affective and claims-making elements is always political in different ways.

A translocational lens – translocational intersectionality

In this book, I propose a 'translocational' lens as a way of addressing some of the quandaries about how different forms of hierarchy interconnect. In a term like translocational it is necessary to home in on the use of the term 'location'. Places are both physical and social, as argued very convincingly by Doreen Massey (2013), but location here is a broader term than place. It also transcends the idea of the local as found, for example, in discussions of the translocal (Brickell and Datta 2011) particularly used in relation to cities and urban geographies. Translocal is a term that came to prominence as an accompaniment to transnational, pointing to the way in which localities are bound together through movements and flows at the very intimate levels of neighbourhoods, on the one hand, or larger units but beneath the level of the transnational and national, on the other hand. Translocal references particularly space in the physical sense or in the sense of symbols, values or positionalities tied to that physical space.

Social location, on the other hand, in my use of the term, refers to social spaces defined by boundaries on the one hand and hierarchies on the other hand. It references how *places as locales are intertwined with social locations as boundaries and hierarchies of difference*. The notion of 'translocation' flags place, time and scale in the understanding of the ways different modes of division are entangled in each other. It brings together the spatial, the temporal and the scalar as place in a *hierarchical social ordering*. The latter includes the role of social attributions, representations and resource allocations relating to a range of categories such as gender, ethnicity, class, race, as well as lived experiences of various kinds. It also recognises the situated nature of claims and attributions and their production in complex and shifting locales (and the contradictory processes in play). We not only need to think of them in relation to each other in time but also *over time*. Here the processual level is key. Difference and inequality are conceptualised as a set of *processes* with an emphasis on *historicity*, and not possessive characteristics of individuals.

One central argument here is that we should aim to move beyond treating categories as prima facie, as this would start our understanding away from their production as signifiers and embodiments of power (which I treat constructions of difference to be). It means abandoning a methodologically nationalist frame-work but does not mean abandoning looking at the ordering and contestations over national borders and nationalist ideologies. It also means abandoning an ethnic lens (Anthias 1998a), but again does not mean that ethnic struggles are not important facets of struggles both within nation state borders and between them.

It is useful to say a little more about the use of the prefix 'trans'. This centres movement/flow, change, contradiction and historicity, moving away from a still shot approach. It overcomes the static and binary nature of the 'inter' (referenced in the neologism 'intersectionality'), depicting both fluidity and change. It is useful to think of it in relation to the idea of 'situated' or 'situational', acknowl-edged in intersectional work also (e.g. Collins 1990). Whilst such a notion is important, nonetheless it holds the danger of providing still shots or pictures (see Chapter 7). Since positions carry over their traces from other moments, places and scales, the notion of 'situational' may not fully capture the simultaneity of persistence and change. Such historical traces are part of re-imaginings and new forms present themselves in specific contexts. Using 'trans' in this con-text enables the concern with process which requires a diachronic lens, thereby avoiding fixed categories (since they are always in and of themselves transversal – see Guattari 2015). The contextual or situational is accompanied therefore by the '*trans*-locational', acknowledging historicity and the diachronic. Here, fixity and fluidity are simultaneous processes relating to the agonistic nature of social life (i.e. with the meaning of the Greek *agonas*, as struggle rather than 'action').

'Trans' also functions to override and overdetermine (signalling *beyond* as well as *interrelation*). It denotes the potentially porous nature of boundaries (they are never fully effective), and it treats them as open to being dismantled. It references, therefore, another 'trans', the transformatory, motored by the oppositional and

28 Introduction

contradictory, giving hope in a world where there is a push towards retrenchment of the past and the gestation of new fixities. It therefore counters those forms of theory that point to the intractability of power. It opens the lens to the transgressive and the dialogical. The notion of translocational therefore seeks to capture the complexity, multidimensionality and symbiotic, albeit often contradictory, simultaneity of these processes as well as the importance of place, time and meaning.

One of the criticisms, discussed in Chapter 3 of the intersectionality framework is that it lacks a theoretical anchor which means that whilst positing the mutual constitution of categories, it is unable to account for how they operate analytically at more than the descriptive level. A related criticism is that it has tended to ignore issues of class and the ways in which capitalism and its social relations provide a framing for the different intersectional processes at work. Although I do not make the distinction between a *heuristic* and a *theory* (see Chapter 3), nor claim that intersectionality always needs the same theoretical anchor, in my approach to intersectionality as a heuristic frame, an anchoring is provided by the centrality of the production and reproduction of the resources that are necessary for life itself. There is an *impetus* towards their uneven distribution, despite equality talk in various guises over time, which lie at the heart of modern capitalisms today. At one and the same time contestations appear with the impetus towards the redistribution of resources. Moving away from the idea of given 'groups' or 'categories' (such as amongst others, gender, race, ethnicity and class), which then intersect (which some intersectionality approaches imply), also highlights the importance of both *material and symbolic resources* and conflicts over them, and the production of complex and at times *contradictory social locations*, positionalities and processes with an emphasis on spatiality and temporality. It denotes the translocational nature of borderings, belongings, performativities and social inequalities.

Having introduced the concerns of the book, I will now look more closely at the issue of the work that categories do within modern capitalist societies.

Notes

1 See Anthias (1982) for early formulations of the intersections between gender, ethnicity and class.
2 See Anthias (2002, 2009, 2013b) for a discussion of the concept of translocational positionality.
3 Un.org, retrieved October 13, 2019.
4 Greater inequalities are found between and within countries over the last few years. In the UK it has been estimated that more than a fifth of the population live on incomes below the poverty line after housing costs are deducted. One in three children live in poverty. The average household wealth for Britain's richest decile is 315 times that of the poorest. This is based on the Institute of Public Policy Research Commission on Social Justice report for 2019. See ippr.org for more details.
5 See Chapter 5 for more details.
6 www.gov.uk–tier–1 – investor.

7 A consultation was launched by the Home Office in Britain in April 2019 to look into the creation of a multi-agency 'public health duty' to require that schools, social services and hospitals raise concerns about children at risk of becoming involved in knife crime.
8 Shamima Begum is a British-born woman who left the UK in 2015 when she was only 15 to go to Iraq and Syria to join the Islamic State (ISIL). She asked to return to the UK in 2019, but this was refused by the Home Office in 2019 and she was deprived of UK citizenship and told she could never return. All three of her children died in the camps, the last baby dying whilst she was pleading to return to the UK to save his life.

2

BRANDING PLACES

Dilemmas of ordering

Introduction: constructing places in the order of things

Categorisations, and associated forms of belonging, involve the marking and making of *places* of difference, mapping out the borders and boundaries of entitlements, resource allocation, inclusion and exclusion, and inequality. They are constituted through social regulations and other taxonomic devices within an imperative of differential resource allocation, enacted in spatio-temporal terms. They become manifested in the hailing process of collective imaginings and embodied practices, naturalising and invisibilising their operation as modes of power. Categorising people is a major facet of sociabilities and the management of resources, entailing central technologies of power. The common-sense assumptions of actors (the taken for granted order of things or doxa), and juridical categories of the state are part of this process. Boundaries and hierarchies are complex and intersectional as they play out in social relations and they are central and connected parameters of social life.

Whilst boundaries mark out places of difference and belonging, they have various degrees of porosity, as they play out in spatio-temporal ways, in relation to one another and within wider social relations of power. In their *fixing* of identities, they are never fully adequate to the task as there is an excess found in the agentic and the contestational, and they are imbricated in modes of struggle (based on claims of identity, for example) which pose at times problems for both governmentality and a politics of solidarity. These are tied to resource struggles of different kinds, found in the organisation of production and reproduction (such as labour markets, the economy, sexuality and the family), and those relating to territoriality and collectivity. Categories not only place people and order them in ways which are hierarchy making, therefore, but they also become generative of forms of resistance. They are sources of agency and collective struggle, either in terms of their contestation and through disidentification, or through their refashioning (as with reclaiming the category Black or queer), denoting the importance of the agonistic and indeed contradictory in social life.

The social relations around categorisation are not only central to the formation of solidary bonds and other intersubjectivities that underpin struggles around the marshalling of resources for life itself, but they are complex and changing. As categories articulate with domination *and* struggle, they are permeated with changing forms of valuation; constructing hierarchies of value, merit and desert. As they are involved in contestations over resources of different kinds, they thereby facilitate the conflict and antagonism that lie at the heart of capitalist society, as well as binary cleavages, both exclusionary (involving closure) and usurpationary (involving claims and contestations) that contribute to the fractured nature of human sociality, on the one hand, and to social change, on the other.

The attributions and identifications relating to boundary and hierarchy-making categories are neither given nor arbitrary constructions, essential or accidental by-products of sociality. Categorical formations set out *places to be filled by collectivised subjects* who are deemed to possess the appropriate attributes or identifications, as properties are conferred on them. But the places themselves are already constructed out of the targeting of bodies, in temporal and spatial locations. They constitute then ways of placing populations, encountered and acted upon through a range of ways, through the colonial encounter, through the appropriation and exploitation of labour, through the imperative of the national border, through technologies of social reproduction and the reproduction of labour itself (found, for example, in the family form). Both the places, and the bodies that inhabit them, are permeated by forms of *valuation* which provide fuel for the allocation of resources and act as legitimisers of their unequal access and distribution. The valuation of the *places* and the valuation of the *bodies* are dialogically constituted, historicised, and subject to the various and at times discordant technologies of power within capitalist modernity.

Once individuals – and their bodies, properties, psyches and actions – are placed into categories (although they are not mutually exclusive) in temporal spatialities, they endow individuals with attributions and possessive properties which are then seen to have necessary social effects, thereby *naturalising* them. This *branding* of individuals is an important exercise in marking out the spaces of their social engagement and their differentiated inclusion and exclusion (Anthias 1998a) and is implicated in a group-making process. This involves both positing collectivised subjects (such as Blacks, women, Jews, migrants, the working class) and how people take up positions, as forms of subjectification and positionality. The social organisation and dynamics involved is not only embedded within institutional arrangements or organisations (Tilly 1998), but it is also an accomplishment by actors in their everyday lives (West and Fenstermaker 1995). Ideas of performativity are found especially in the work of Goffman (1956) and Judith Butler (1990). Pat Hill Collins (1990) is probably the foremost thinker that locates intersecting divisions in the discursive field of power, on the one hand, and as forms of domination, on the other, in the tradition of critical race studies and feminist standpoint theory.

Rejecting the view that gender, ethnicity, race and class, or the more specific categories of migrants or refugees, pertain to social groups with certain fixed characteristics, I treat these as interconnected and interdependent *places* within a landscape of inequality making. Indeed, we can rephrase the concern with categories with a concern with '*categories in place*' and with '*hierarchical social locations*'. I suggest we look at them with the analytical gaze of deciphering how power is imbricated in them. To gaze on categories *in place* is to think of them *as relational* (to one another) and *in relation* to place making (in the sense of hierarchical place) but also as historicised. The categories and social locations of difference themselves are *both* analytically distinct *and* constitutive in relation to each other and broader social processes, requiring analysis at different levels of abstraction (see Chapter 3).

Theorising and under-theorising

Analysing categories, practices and relations of difference, their effectivities and their inter-relations, must lie at the heart of the sociological enterprise. Such an exercise is also central, though by no means sufficient, politically, to contestation of the naturalisation of these categories. Although social categorisations of the population, which are naturalised and essentialised, are a prominent feature of societies in general (taking different forms), traditional sociological theory has tended to give less emphasis to some rather than others. For example, gender, ethnicity, nationalism and 'race', have been given less prominence in the overall sociological canon than class. There has been a tendency, traditionally, to treat these non-class 'modes of being' as Dietze et al. (2018) call them, and the related population groupings and processes, as natural or primordial (or alternatively as different historical manifestations of an essence), and therefore as given features of social life which then social life affects in terms of their specificities. This emphasis is the product of a number of factors, such as the heritage left from Enlightenment thought and 19th century classical or historical sociology rooted in androcentric and Eurocentric forms of social theorising. The relative underemphasis on gender and 'race' categories, processes and divisions may be located in 19th century sociology's construction of the social actor as essentially male and 'white', with social transformation or conflict being located within social class processes in industrial society. The construction of the individual as ahistorical, ungendered and unracialised is a prominent feature of many theoretical approaches to the individual and society, whilst taking for granted that the relations of patriarchal subordination and colonialist forms of exploitation and violence were not a central object of study and indeed that they were powered by the 'natural' which was something sociology did not need to engage with.

Sociology grew out of a concern with social order (rather than the problem of social ordering), a problematic tied especially to the growth of industrial capitalism with its production of the landless, disenfranchised and potentially volatile and revolting proletariat. Although not singular in nature, drawing on different philosophical and political traditions, it emerged during the period of the Enlightenment, and under capitalist social relations in Europe, as a self-conscious discipline whose object of reference was 'the social'. The 'problem of order' (as opposed to the problem of 'ordering') has often been conceptualised as a question of discussing the prerequisites for sociality to be possible, and yet this was rather the problem of maintaining order in relation to the '"dangerous" classes'. Some looked to the order that lay in the division of labour, which harnesses individual needs and interests in a sphere of co-dependency with others (e.g. in the work of Emile Durkheim). Indeed, Durkheim's ideas of organic and mechanical solidarity (1893) are somewhat Janus faced. On the one hand, the division of labour within industrial society which is based on organic solidarity is regarded as constituting a better mode of sociality than that found in less complex societies where there is mechanical solidarity, based on people having similar and often multiple roles in the division of labour. On the other hand, such a theorisation functions, potentially, as a justification of different (and unequal) positionings of individuals and groups within industrial societies.

Whilst it is not my intention to review the field, to have a discussion of social categorisation without a nod to the work of important theorists whose work has engaged with the technologies of power would be amiss. Given that there is limited space in a book of this kind I can only draw out some of the implications of their work to the understanding of the working of categories. Social thinkers such as Foucault, Bourdieu, Agamben, Butler, Tilly (to name some of the most important), have opened the way towards a non-economistic but nonetheless highly critical examination of modern power relations. In different ways they have engaged with the work of Marx and concomitantly there has been an engagement with their work in conjunction with Marx (e.g. see Raaper and Olssen 2017). Michel Foucault's work has been identified with post-modern theory and post-structuralism and he has produced important work on sexuality (1972), but very little on gender, ethnicity or race (see later for a short discussion of his limited contribution to 'race'). Pierre Bourdieu's work has been identified with more culturalist approaches, whilst his attempt to rethink structure and agency has at times been described as 'canonical structuralism' (Margolis 1999, p. 75). Field and habitus are primary and influential concepts in his work, and he develops an approach to social class focused on capitals (Bourdieu 1986). His work, unlike Foucault, has addressed gender more explicitly through ideas of the gendered habitus and symbolic violence where masculine domination is located (Bourdieu 1990). Judith Butler's work is focused mainly around sexuality and gender (1990, 1993) and her work has also engaged, but to a lesser extent, with race (Butler 2006, 2010). Charles Tilly (1998) has been explicitly concerned with the social organisation of difference in general, and forms of what he calls

34 Branding places

'durable inequality'. In his book of that name, he develops an approach which locates the ways categories function within organisations. In the work of Giorgio Agamben who uses a biopolitical frame, drawing on Foucault, we find an almost complete absence of the concern with the categories of class, ethnicity and gender. Agamben (1998, 2005) has produced an approach that treats refugees, like Arendt (1951), as the epitome of the modern and as representative of 'states of exception' where the rule of law no longer applies, but his work does not engage with migration or race and ethnic *categories*, and gender is singularly absent. All these theorists, apart from Agamben, have seen extensive discussions of their work in relation to feminisms. Agamben and Bourdieu have been used in the study of migration (e.g. Anthias 2007; Erel 2010; Ryan, Erel and D'Angelo 2016; Dines et al. 2015), Butler, Bourdieu and Foucault have been particularly influential in work on gender and sexuality (e.g. Adkins and Skeggs 2005; Lovell 2000).

Given the prominence of Bourdieu in social theory today and particularly in relation to work on classification and inequality, I want to say a little more about some of the contributions and difficulties in his work with reference to the project of this book. For Bourdieu power operates at the subjective and intersubjective level through the habitus, the dispositions and cognitive apparatus relating to the social position of actors, in the social field, which construct the taken for granted nature of the social world. The habitus is related to the possession and distribution of different forms of capital, economic, cultural and social, all of which gain their effectivity through symbolic capital (Bourdieu 1986). Symbolic violence is produced by the *habitus* as it elicits misrecognition, and the workings of power are experienced as free choices of the individual. This individualises the process of misrecognition, however, rather than treating it as structurally formed, in as much as it is essentialised within the individual, and agonistic only at that level. Shared habitus amongst actors is a product of occupying the same positions (e.g. occupations correlated with similar possessions of forms of capital) rather than forged through collective action (e.g. control) operated on workers, or common actions by workers (resistance).

Symbolic violence includes dispositions to acting which involve forms of classification, subordination, hierarchy and domination (Bourdieu 1980). These are related to social fields such as language, education, religion, family structures and state power (Bourdieu 1985). Masculine domination[1] is a prototypical example of symbolic violence. However, Bourdieu does not address issues of sexuality or gender as constituting forms of power in themselves, nor does he engage with feminist struggles. This is surprising given the period in which he was writing, with the growth of the feminist movements in France.

In Bourdieu's work there is a significant lacuna with regards to race, particularly strange also since his writings on Algeria (1977a) deal with colonialism and the revolutionary potential of the colonial working class, acknowledging that colonialism gives rise to demands for rights and that these embody the counterpoint to symbolic domination. It is also surprising given the differential treatment of the large number of people of Arab descent within France itself and the writings of Franz Fanon (1967) and others about their conditions. His few reflections on ethnicity and race appear unsatisfactory, and Jenkins (2002, p. 92) also claims that Bourdieu does not consider ethnicity except in his early research in North Africa, and that this constitutes an important gap in his work.

In reading Bourdieu it is unclear how change can occur given the overriding importance of dispositions (the habitus) and the lack of a clear mechanism for their change. Individuals may be involved in classification struggles as they play the rules of the game within fields, in an individualistic jostling for power where they seek higher forms of various capitals. But this doesn't happen in unison and there is no obvious mechanism that produces any collective struggles over classifications. The notion of misrecognition, so central to his analysis of symbolic power, has the danger of trapping people in unequal relations, therefore, and Bourdieu fails to consider ways in which misrecognition can metamorphose. This has been a lynchpin in many critiques (Burkitt 2002; McCall 1992; McNay 1999). It's important to note, however, that Bourdieu argues that his theory of practice is not a theory of total determination. For example, in *Pascalian Meditations* (2000) he states that subjects have a degree of freedom, particularly at points of crises, but this aspect of his work remains underdeveloped.

Bourdieu's notion of the social field as 'a series of institutions, rules, rituals, conventions, categories, designations, appointments and titles which constitute an objective hierarchy, and which produce and authorise certain discourses and activities' is deterministic (Webb et al. 2002, pp. 21–22). The field structures and predisposes, imprinting itself on the habitus. However, there is some space in the notion of habitus for transformation as it is 'creative, inventive, but within the limits of its structures' (Bourdieu and Wacquant 1992, p. 19) and 'it is made and not simply determined' (Bourdieu 1977b, p. 78). Bourdieu and Wacquant assert that change comes from a 'symbolic revolution that questions the very foundations of the production and reproduction of symbolic capital' (Bourdieu and Wacquant 1992, p. 17). There are a number of ways in which change is possible (Bourdieu and Wacquant 1992). Individuals can change their own position (but not the field itself) through acquisition of different forms of capital over time by adhering to the rules of the game and increasing their capital (Bourdieu 1977b). This occurs at the individual level and there is very little indication of how collective agency emerges (Burkitt 2002, also see Nentwich et al. 2014). Despite Bourdieu acknowledging that there has been some progress in women's trajectory, for example through their insertion into the labour market and within education, it is not apparent, in his work on masculine domination (2001) how more collective forms of symbolic struggle emerge. Hence the 'canonical structuralism' noted earlier by Margolis. This explains to some extent why Butler (1997) is quite dismissive of this aspect of Bourdieu's work.

The second possibility for transformation lies in changing doxa (taken for granted understandings) and the logic of practice (Bourdieu 1980, 1985). This entails a situation where the habitus no longer works practically within another context or field, and allodoxia or confusion occurs (reminiscent of the work of

36 Branding places

Alfred Schutz (1944) on the 'Stranger'). This links also to Bourdieu's notion of the habitus *clivé* (Bourdieu 2000; Friedman 2016) which creates hysteresis, entailing a lag between that which is appropriate in one situation and another situation. However, there is little discussion *of the ways* that the habitus is transformed through allodoxia, given that there is little indication of how one habitus acts on another. They are differentiated in time rather than in terms of the co-existence (already) of concurrent contradictory elements within the predispositions themselves.

Overall, the notion of the habitus appears to replicate the idea of socialisation in its emphasis on proclivities and inclinations (but here tied to class locations), which take over individuals, determining their dispositions, and leaves very little room for agency. Feminists have taken exception to the idea of women's complicity with male domination (e.g. see Skeggs 2004). One could argue that domination may be resisted in a myriad of small ways (in Foucault's terms through acts on other acts), but any reliance on acts is missing in Bourdieu. In addition, one could argue that those who suffer domination (e.g. masculine domination) may be aware of this without necessarily being able to act to redress it because they lack structural power. Moreover, since he makes a distinction between categories of analysis (the domain of the intellectual/sociologist) and categories of practice, he falls into an elitist conception of knowledge where only the former can expose the 'rules of the game' that are doxa in the logic of practice.

Whilst the notion of habitus is more historicised than Marx's ideas about the ideological imprint of capitalism on individuals (Burawoy 2018) as it develops over the lifetime of the individual, it is not located within a structural system where predispositions become the effects of class *relations*. Rather, they become the effects of *inhabiting* a particular class category/habitus and this position can end up as tautological. Moreover, his concern with symbolic power/misrecognition can be linked to Lukacs's idea of reification (1967), Marx's idea of false consciousness (1859), Gramsci's ideas on hegemony (1971) or Freud's notion of the unconscious (1912/2005), but there is little engagement with these concepts in his work.

Having briefly discussed Bourdieu it is also useful to make some comments, however short, on the work of Foucault despite not being able to do full justice here to the significance of his theoretical contribution overall. As a counterpoint to Bourdieu, we find in the work of Foucault the important insight about how categories, which are discursive, emerge as knowledge and power, enabling the governmentality of the modern subject. However, whilst Foucault's work has been built on the importance of the knowledge-discourse nexus as power, and biopolitics works on controlling populations and their bodies, there is little in his work on the social organisation of difference and he is more concerned with 'the population' rather than the construction of different categories of 'the population'. There is also very little concern with capitalist relations of production and how they tie into the biopolitical framing and to governmentality. Foucault does not concern himself with the categorial constructions of gender, race and class, amongst others, or consider their role in the discursive production of power as

Branding places **37**

such. However, there is space in his approach to treating them in terms of the ordering of populations, working on the 'abnormal' in biopolitical terms. There are the beginnings in his work around race in his 1975–76 lecture series titled *Society Must be Defended* (Foucault 2004), where he refers to state racism.[2] Foucault stresses that 'races' in the 17th century did not refer to physiognomic or biologistic notions but to cultural units. And it was only in the 18th century that the idea of 'race' emerged as a biological category. Referring to Nazism he states:

> The new racism specific to the twentieth century, this neoracism as the internal means of defense of a society against its abnormal individuals, is the child of psychiatry, and Nazism did no more than graft this new racism onto the ethnic racism that was endemic in the nineteenth century. I think, then, that these new forms of racism, which took hold in Europe at the end of the nineteenth century and the beginning of the twentieth century, should be linked historically to psychiatry.
>
> *(2003, p. 317)*

He treats racism as a subset of society's defence against the abnormal which ties in with the birth of the psychiatric subject. According to Foucault, racism against the abnormal interacts with what he regards as a more traditional, 'ethnic racism'. However, it is not limited to ethnic groups, since the Nazis attack Jews, homosexuals and Roma as well as those Aryans who are regarded as a genetic threat to the 'race'. His use of the word 'race' here relates to the conception of ethnic and cultural units as races. This latter is explicit in his argument that historically there were race wars which emanated from resistance to sovereign rule and became manifested in struggles over hegemony in terms of nations. As Taylor argues (2011, p. 750), 'the claim that racism, in the modern age, is "racism against the abnormal"', seems, oddly, to dispense with race'. Instead racism becomes a broader notion which functions to classify people into the acceptable and the degenerate or deviant. Such a notion of racism is unable to consider the functionalities of specific racialisations of populations which are not dependent on notions of deviance but instead on notions of securitisation or cultural contamination. To be able to locate the border-making role of racialised discourse is central to understanding the different manifestations of racist discourse and practice, including notions of diversity and integration (see Chapter 6), as well as discourses of nativism that are not dependent on ideas of degeneration.

In terms of power he makes a sharp distinction between domination and violence treating the latter potentially as outside the scope of governmentality. Foucault's view of power is expressed in the following way:

> multiplicity of force relations immanent in the sphere in which they operate . . . as the process which, through ceaseless struggles and confrontations, transforms, strengthens or reverses them . . . as strategies in which

38 Branding places

> they take effect . . . embodied in the state apparatus, in the formulation of
> the law, in the various hegemonies.
>
> *(1985, p. 92)*

But what is absent here is a category whose interest it serves – a dominant group, and as Charles Taylor says strategic patterns can only relate to the purposes of identifiable social agents (Taylor 1984). In addition, Foucault does not engage with how categories relate to the formation of solidary groups who contest and challenge, nor how change becomes possible.

Butler (1990), on the other hand, flags the transgressivity (or gender trouble) emergent in gender performativities which challenge gender binaries and thereby open the way to change, immanent in the act of performance (Lovell 2000). For Butler change comes from performative and transgressive actions by actors subverting the normative, challenging dominant norms, and these can 'displace the very gender norms that enable the repetition itself' (Butler 1990, p. 148). However, the context determines how effective this is as there needs to be public acknowledgement. In relation to Bourdieu, her view is that he 'fails to take account of the way in which social positions are themselves constructed through a more tacit operation of performativity' (Butler 1998, p. 122). A question that Butler, however, is also unable to answer is the mode by which transgressivity emerges and how its performance alone can effect change.

With regard to race, Butler's more recent work tries to apply her notion of performativity to race (Butler 2010). Race becomes fixed to bodies and performed and understood through what she calls racial frames, giving rise to differentiating bodies into those with entitlements to rights and those without them. Looking at the fight against terrorism in the US, she argues that those who are non-White are constructed as a threat. Although this is a characteristic of the racialised agendas of states, such a view is one that is central to many approaches to racism and found in a range of literature (e.g. in Hall and colleagues' work on policing the crisis – Morley et al. 1978). Moreover, this approach is unable to deal with differential racialisations which are not based on body-coding, such as nativisms. There are a number of writers on race that have used Butler's work on performativity. For example, Nayak (2006) in the UK uses Butler to argue against an essentialising view of identity, but again many other writers have been arguing such a position (see Anthias 1982, 2002; Brubaker and Cooper 2000; Jenkins 1997).

Charles Tilly (1998) more than any other theorist has a worked-out approach to the ways in which categories operate in organisations to produce 'durable inequality'. This inequality is the product of strategies of exploitation and of exclusion (in the form of opportunity hoarding by dominant members). For example, uniforms, titles and so on, are ways of marking *internal* categories (such as occupational or organisational roles) within organisations. The provision of gendered gym classes and the sex typing of jobs shows how broader *external* categories impact on inequality within organisations, as they map onto internal categories. The argument is that when there is a matching of interior with exterior categorical boundaries there is a reinforcement of inequalities (1998, p. 78). Such a reinforcement leads to a potential for exposing inequality, and to possible strategies to contest exploitation and exclusion which are dealt with by organisational provisions for emulation and adaptation. It is impossible to do justice to Tilly's pioneering work in unpicking the operation of categories in organisations, but for the purposes of this book, it remains a partial analysis. This is because it does not relate explicitly to the ways different categorical formations impact on each other and thereby become transformed in the process. Nor does it consider how the arenas of intersubjectivity or experience impact on actors' framings within organisational scenarios, or on collective solidarity formation. Particularly, a consideration of any contradictory projects at play within organisations is missing in Tilly's account. These might pull in different directions at different periods in relation to the attainment of specific organisational goals.

Despite some difficulties, all these approaches in different ways have made strong contributions to the analysis of categories and their centrality to the modern neo-liberal state. However, the modern neo-liberal state involves a contradictory management with the evolution at one and the same time of more egalitarian or democratic procedures within civil society, such as consultations by local government about the 'needs' of ethnic communities or tenants' associations, alongside a honing back of the preconditions for their effective deployment, on the other. This involves the central role of the other half of the binary of the control-contestation nexus, that of contestational politics. Concessions and adaptations are continually made in modern societies to deal with economic and political crises and they are also a response to struggles and contestations. Discursive (or in the case of Tilly, organisational) power is never quite enough and there is an excess found in the question of agency, on the one hand, and collective struggle on the other. The latter is fired by an impetus towards resource usurpation and re-allocation, on the one hand, and de-branding or destigmatisation on the other (and not just emulation and adaptation which are the twin mechanisms for Tilly of countering opposition). These struggles for material resource gains and de/classification/de-branding are dialogically interrelated, each feeding off the other. They are often built on the very same identity categories (through identity politics, for example) whose classifications they seek to resist.

Broadly speaking (with the exception of Tilly who has a more organisational focus), these tendencies in the analysis of categories of difference focus on the discursive and/or the cultural, indicating arguably the colonisation of the social by the cultural. We can find this cultural turn, for example, in the significant take up of the work of Michelle Lamont, relying in large part on a Bourdieusian framing (see her discussion of Bourdieu in Lamont (2012)). Beyond both the important biopolitics and cultural/capitals turns, we find the resurrection of a concern with the political economy of categories of difference. The ways in which categories are implicated in the pursuit of different economic, political and national projects has been a central concern in theorising social divisions.

40 Branding places

This is found, for example, in arguments about the connections between race, colonialism and class in the work of Cox (1970), Robinson (2000), Miles (1989) and Gilroy (1993, 1987); gender and class in the domestic labour debate (see e.g. Molyneaux 1979); the 'reserve army of labour' debate (e.g. Beechey 1977; Anthias 1980); and earlier approaches to gender, race and class (e.g. amongst others in the work of Anthias (1982); Anthias and Yuval-Davis (1983)). The importance of race exclusions and the creation of racialised subjects in plantation slavery and in the interstices of the emergence of modern capitalism are developed in some important more recent work (such as Virdee 2014; Shilliam 2018).

Regarding gender categorisations and processes, newer connections have been made between gender and class, found in the political economy of women, drawing on earlier debates within Marxist feminism but developing these in new directions. This is found in the work of Nancy Fraser (1989) who also draws on Weber, and in social reproduction feminism (Bhattacharya 2017). This includes work by Sarah Ferguson (2016) and Silvia Federici (2012) amongst others. This complements some of the insights on discussions about gender and nation prioritised in the work of Anthias and Yuval-Davis (1989). Homonationalism (Puar 2007) and femonationalism (Farris 2012a) have been added to our vocabulary to signify how equality, on the basis of gay rights or women's rights, can be harnessed to produce further othering and inequality of marginalised groups, for example, on the basis of nationality, race or religion, (noted also in Anthias and Yuval-Davis 1992).

The heuristic of 'diversity'

The terms we use to analyse social categories and to understand them is crucially important as it frames them theoretically and politically, and this is the case with those approaches that focus on difference/diversity and research it. Diversity belongs to a family of concepts whose heart is 'difference' but not as an ever-present reconstitution in social life at both symbolic and social/material levels, but as a given, and as a sorting exercise. Diversity can refer to a range of boundaries in social life – often treated as cultural. This can include and has included concerns with lifestyles and with cultural practices by different groupings, acting as a code for ethnicity and 'race'. The term is also used to refer to disability, faith and gender although rarely to class. Diversity is a promiscuous notion that can be attached to any construction of difference and entails a boundary-making exercise. It also has strong political and normative dimensions, from positive to negative (see Chapter 6). Diversity talk not only has difficulties because it is so fuzzy, but it also holds dangers. Talking about 'the diverse' slips into the dangerous terrain of marking the 'other' or range of 'others', in juxtaposition to the non-diverse or homogeneous 'self'. Both the terms difference and diversity, act as a code for 'otherness' and, borrowing from Stuart Hall, are linked to modalities of power (Hall 1996a). Therefore, difference and the related notion of diversity are not givens nor self-evident objects of reference.

In the Global North we hear that diversity is everywhere and indeed that we are living in a super-diverse world (Vertovec 2007; Berg and Sigona 2013). But merely referencing multiplicity and pointing to its various manifestations is rarely adequate. With greater asymmetries of cultural production and diffusion, many people are disempowered, constituting members of highly disadvantaged groups, many of whom are women, the young and migrants/minorities. There are both structural and discursive processes worldwide, which construct, solidify and embalm 'difference', including the concepts used in research. Migration controls, racialisation, securitisation discourses and discourses of diversity are important in this process (see Chapter 6). But more importantly, rather than pointing to discourses of diversity, we can point to the poverty of the discourse *on* diversity. A focus on diversity constitutes an inadequate *theoretical* means for analysing and understanding social relations of categorisation and differentiation. This supplements the critique that 'diversity' (which points to different differences) has proved to be inadequate for enabling the social correction of inequalities of different kinds between and within socially defined categories or social groups (e.g. see Ahmed, 2004, 2009, 2016; Anthias 2013a; Ahonen 2014).

'Diversity' in and of itself does not provide tools for understanding and cannot be a heuristic term. I argue that we need better tools for addressing the shifting landscapes of difference and identity, and their interconnections and ruptures, in the highly mobile and complex global mobilities system today.

The problem often arises of constructing sameness and difference against and across the location of difference, finding commonalities between 'groups' and differences within 'groups'. One way of looking at this is that the individuals appear in those spaces as ready-made, as befitting and homologous only to those spaces. However, it is better to treat the places as inhabited by individuals in particular socio-spatial and temporal contexts, not because they are already prior to the places, but that they are hailed or interpellated into them through particular gazes, positionalities, institutional framings, and meaning-making practices. This is not to disembody individuals, far from it, but to recognise that there a translocational process at work where different places, at one and the same time, can be inhabited by the same individuals, and subject to their multiple effectivities and historicities where they are *marked* and *processed*. Difference is itself always politically inflected and never a neutral way of classifying. It can be constructed as part of a strategy of governance, containment, domination or contestation, or in very contradictory ways as found in discourses of integration and diversity (Anthias 2013b – see Chapter 6). Hegemonic groups within the state often make claims that 'others' are different, naturalising their own difference, hailing the 'others'. For example, ethnic groups are often defined as those which are subordinate and white majorities and dominant white minorities are divested of ethnicity. Whiteness itself becomes invisible as a modus operandi of power. Another example is how the British abroad are referred to as expats rather than migrants, as the latter has overtones of 'othering'. They are treated as not having an ethnicity, being defined merely in relation to their country of origin. In such

42 Branding places

a formulation, difference or diversity is something that the 'other' possesses and very rarely applies to the dominant self who stands beyond such depictions.

We can see, therefore, that 'difference' is not something that we actually have; it is a range of positions in social space that we are attributed or allocated, that we claim, that we embody, that we narrate and that we live. 'Difference' points to certain aspects of our world, constructing them as such, making them socially meaningful. What type is being signalled, where are the boundaries placed between the same and the different, how is this evaluated and who is marking the difference and why – all are questions to be raised. How is such marking received by those who are marked as the different and what strategies do they employ in return either to negotiate or to struggle/resist such markings and most importantly the social practices that accompany them? Gloria Anzaldua (1999) the writer of *Borderlands*, tells us that such struggles exist not only between us but also within us:

> The struggle is inner: Chicano, Indio, American Indian, mojito, mexicano, immigrant Latino, Anglo in power, working class Anglo, Black, Asian – our psyches resemble the bordertowns and are populated by the same people.
>
> *(p. 109)*

It is evident that 'diversity' is never an innocent description of the plenitude and multifarious nature of social life or the multiplicity of actors and their delineation. Therefore, I prefer the term 'diversity-making', that is, a concern with the processes whereby categories of difference are made, organised, managed and practised across time, space and scale. To focus on *diversity-making*, we need to move beyond the use of the term diversity.

We should pay close attention, not just to the language used (whether it be the language of multiculturalism, integration or diversity) but to what the political arguments attached to it are. Pointing to diversity (rather than commonalities) may also be a way of pursuing a politics of exclusion found in arguments that there is too much diversity, particularly of the 'wrong' kind, and that it undermines social consensus and national values (e.g. in Trump's concern to build a wall against 'invaders'). On the other hand, when Stuart Hall (2000) argued that the multicultural question (which links to the idea of diversity) is the most important question facing the world today, he was doing it from a position that saw multiculturality and equality as prime principles of political engagement and justice, as do many writers who use the term diversity (e.g. Berg and Sigona 2013). But despite this, defining the multicultural question as centred around the problem of how people with very different cultural traditions, ways of life and different understandings can live together (see, in contradistinction, the discussion of conviviality in Chapter 6), unintentionally inflects difference with problems. Struggles over resources (rights, respect/representation and redistribution), often underpin conflict, and these struggles may manifest themselves in terms of cultural differences. As Bourdieu (1990) has rightly reminded us, resources or capital take forms which are cultural, symbolic and social as well as economic. Therefore, I prefer to turn Hall's multicultural question on its head (Anthias 2006), and ask 'under what conditions is difference regarded as a problem and how do we change those conditions'?

As a term, like other terms, the ability of 'diversity' to work as a heuristic device depends on how it is used. This also means that it has the potential to alert scholars and researchers to the importance of attending to the multifarious and complex heterogeneity of social relations at different societal levels.[3] Because it usually signals the diversity of persons (organised into groupings of human subjects based on a purported commonality – either as attribution or claim), it fails to challenge and indeed reinforces everyday assumptions of fixity that characterise categorisation in everyday life. Diversity as a description of variation and heterogeneity cannot denote the mechanisms by which difference is allocated socially, how it is organised and what its social practices entail. It lacks a modus operandi. Merely signposting social differences of various kinds (and therefore analytically and politically privileging them) yields little but a reification or reproduction of frameworks of meaning current in the social order and is both tautological and analytically unproductive.

More recently there has been a take up of the term 'super-diversity' (Vertovec 2007) to refer to the diversification of diversity (sic). This aims to move beyond ethnicity and explore other factors also, such as the proliferation of legal statuses, migrant trajectories and so on. The term super-diversity points to a migration that is more various and larger in scale, characterised by greater ethnic differences but also differences in legal status, trajectories of migration, motivations, and processes of settlement. The object of reference, however, as with many uses of 'diversity', remains the 'other' (migrants and their descendants) distinguishable by language, competences, statuses and trajectories. So, from that point of view, ethnic difference remains key to the term but complexified by differences within. Although it has been a fertile basis for academic research and debate, such a 'summary' term, as Vertovec (2019) himself has noted, needs to be accompanied with more analytical tools for analysing the processes involved. Given the descriptive nature of 'super-diversity' which it shares with diversity, it does not provide tools to understand the processes which have produced the outcomes it identifies. The exponential growth of the popularity and take up of the term has in fact encouraged research into the features that migrant categories have, rather than the broader societal relations within which migrants are placed. One particular issue relates to when to apply the notion of 'super-diversity': it is not clear when diversity becomes super-diversity, that is, the point at which diversity, which now, in this understanding, has become normal, changes into super-diversity, which characterises a new phase in migration. In any case, in terms of the latter, we need to be historically accurate in understanding the great movements of people in the past, including settler societies like the US and Canada. When looking at these societies today, we may return to the question 'what or who are the diverse/super-diverse', how do we identify them, what are their characteristics?

44 Branding places

A central shortcoming of super-diversity is that it does not easily engage as a term with the amplification of inequality worldwide (see also Ndhlovu 2016), or the differential effects of austerity or the growth of different forms of power, including the growth of powerful global actors in different market sectors of international capital. Nor does it flag the centrality of racisms and related forms of subordination, exclusion and violence. In order to move away from the problematic of diversity, it's important to look at inequality-making categories beyond the saliency of difference. They are never a priori but always emergent and generated by socio-political projects that are tied to complex and socio-spatial boundary-making processes. They become part of complex social arrangements and social relations in organisational, intersubjective, experiential and representational domains or arenas of power (see Chapter 3). These places of containment and regulation are filled with particular marked body types (male/female, black/white, European/non-European, able-bodied/disabled, heteronormative/queer), already formed through their journeys to, and habitation of, places in a historically intersectional process. For example, the migrant is not a fixed category, but a place inhabited variably and differentially (see argument in Chapter 6): the migrant in some cases can pay for citizenship, or the migrant from some countries with a different valuation of the bodies gets different treatment, from the blackened or gendered body, or the Islamised body of the Syrian refugee. Therefore, categories of 'difference' are more than categories and indeed more than about difference, as noted earlier in this book. The markings of the bodies come to be seen as indelible, represented in biological, primordial or genetic ways which fix them, serving to also legitimise the inequality processes attached to them and the violations and violence at play. They engage the body in different ways, which is thereby read as a self-evident text, and subject to stigma, inferiorisation, differential valuation and differential resource allocation and hierarchisation.

The problematic of 'groups'

Much has been made over the last few years of the problem of 'groupism' (e.g. see Brubaker 2004). It is clearly important to make the distinction between category and group and to avoid a notion of group which entails what Brubaker calls groupism, whereby groups are seen as given (see also my critique of the idea of diaspora groups (Anthias (1998a)) and which under-stresses the group-making process. However, it is premature to throw out the existence of 'groups' as objects of analysis and as forms of social organisation, although we have to be careful in this exercise. Categories sort people into groups at the imaginary and organisational level as well as at the juridical and legal level. Such sorting and ordering often has profound effects on people's lives, their social place, their social identities and their actions. It's impossible to dispense with the idea of groups as they are socially salient. For example, being defined as a member of a minoritised or racialised group will affect how one sees oneself, feelings of safety, ideas of belonging and otherness, as well as affecting life chances. This may also have an important role in determining social participation, fuelling claims for social representation and recognition, with such claims acting as vehicles for a range of political, cultural and economic struggles.

What is problematic is not so much pointing to groups as elements of the social landscape, but rather that the socially constructed nature of the categories often becomes reduced to people belonging to groups that are endowed with a given and inalienable quality. This ignores the crosscutting differences within them, and they are treated as homogeneous categories of people with particular characteristics. For example, groups relating to women or ethnic groups are often presumed to have particular needs and predispositions, and assumptions are made about how they should be inserted into the labour market and in society; these are often underpinned by ideas of 'nature'.

It's important to recognise that groups exist at a number of levels, which include the imaginary, practical, juridical and institutional levels. They are made by procedural rules and categories, by the auditing and regulatory systems of the modern state but are also made by actors in their forms of mobilising, and their socialities. They are often the connective tissue of social bonds. Claiming or being attributed to them has real effects. But no categories of the population can be called 'groups' in any inalienable sense: they are claimed or attributed as such or produced through practices of affiliation or identification and contestation. Groups exist as *outcomes* of group-making processes, particularly exclusionary *and* solidary processes of border making. Categories are involved in a range of group-making and group-breaking processes and outcomes but in complex ways within different *societal arenas* (organisational, representational, intersubjective and experiential), and in terms of different technologies of power and different *historicities* relating to the diachronic (processes) and the synchronic (outcomes). At this level, there is the consideration of the combinatory of the categories and divisions (and therefore their intersections) as they are played out in spatial, scalar and temporal contexts. Such groupings are always in the process *of becoming* in the sense that the claims and attributions shift in time and place depending on what is being 'marked'.

As an example of the need to distinguish between category and group, we can take the issue of ethnic categories. Whilst claims about culture and origin often act as the border guards of group membership (and related resource allocation), ethnic group formation does not derive its dynamics either exclusively or necessarily from the ethnic category. Rather, ethnic group formation may be a product of a complex process that involves broader types of social relations, including processes of gender and class (but how and the extent of this is a question of looking at ethnic formations at concrete levels of analysis (see Anthias and Yuval-Davis 1989, 1992; Ferguson 2016; Mulholland et al. 2018). For example, groups can become ethnicised as part of a political project of inclusion, where funds become publicly available for ethnic groups (as in the case of multicultural funding in 1990s Britain), or exclusion. The Roma, Jews, Asians, Blacks have

46 Branding places

at different times claimed to be ethnic groups, whilst at other times they have defined themselves or been defined as religious or national groups.

Therefore, whilst groups do not exist in any a priori fashion, this does not mean that they should not be the object of investigation, as 'groups' are made and unmade in social practice. It is important to stress that they are produced agonistically and not just enacted through the hailing process of various hegemonic and less hegemonic representations. Here I place much more emphasis on both struggle and contradiction than Foucault, despite his idea that agonistic power is 'a set of actions upon other actions' (Foucault 1982, pp. 220–221 – see discussion in Deveaux 1994). I also place much less emphasis on the analytical separation of the economic from the cultural or super-structural than found in the work of Marx and some of his followers. Here I see categorial formations as both modes of control (Foucault) but also as forms of struggle (in the sense of 'agonas-resistance'), which, arguably, both Foucault and Bourdieu underemphasised. They not only constitute ways in which inequalities become embedded, reinforced and reproduced, but also ways we struggle against inequalities (e.g. through mobilising group identities, which constitute central forms of identity politics). This does not mean that political mobilisation, based on categorial identities, is inevitable or indeed always desirable. Foucault was himself averse to the tropes of identity (1985), although Spivak's 'strategic essentialism' (1985) has been resonant with many feminists.

Which categories? Differential saliency

Although social categorisation is a universal process, as it is an essential part of the classifying principles found in human societies (Durkheim and Mauss 1967; Levi-Strauss 1949), what categories exist and how they operate is not.[4] In the current period, all sorts of categories of difference impact on, and relate to, structured forms of inequality, such as migration status, legal status, citizenship, age, health, religion, styles of life and so on. Indeed, one could end up with categories which are as numerous as all the identifiable range of socially salient differences in human populations. This could lead to an endless proliferation of descriptive categories, as well as a homology of difference, treating categories as equivalent. This takes us on a descriptive journey without the tools to sort out the dynamics involved. Hood-Williams and Cealey Harrison (1998) use the metaphor of the 57 varieties of Heinz – a market brand most famous for its baked beans! This entails an infinite regress, ending up, potentially, with an individualising of difference.

Forms of identification and belonging, attached to categorisations, are differential and situational as is the formation of collective or solidary bonds, as well as contestations and struggles. Stigma, avoidance, violence and differential humanisation/dehumanisation are important aspects of this as are differentiated forms of closure, inclusion and exclusion, found particularly in national, race and ethnic categories. In capitalism and class relations they are characterised by exploitation which takes place in the context of relational and subordinated inclusion (although this also entails closure in terms of the denial of access to the resources of the exploiting group). Relations of exclusion can take the form of avoidance and ghettoization, found in the case of the caste system and certain forms of racism (such as apartheid). Avoidance is also found in class stigmatisation and non-sociabilities between classes, and in the case of women in some cultures at certain times of the month and in certain contexts. During the menstrual cycle, for example, women cannot enter sacred spaces, and at other times sit separately, as in the Greek Orthodox tradition and in Islam. The separation of jobs into male and female work (in combination with ethnic and race categories), although illegal in many countries today, is still a de facto reality, with many jobs primarily male or female, attesting to the continuation of the gender and ethnic ordering of employment relations and beyond to other forms of 'work' and sociality, including networks, friendships and cultural consumption. These are deeply entangled and intersect with race and class, in particular (see Anthias 2001a, 2001b). The logic of extermination has been applied where the threat of the 'other' is seen as too great and/or complete dehumanisation of the group has taken place (as in genocides against Armenians and Kurdish populations, and in Rwanda and the Holocaust). The logic of expulsion (Sassen 2014) is also central to the workings of nationalist projects, as in the case of the Greeks in Smyrna or the Turks in Crete and, in more recent times, expulsions of settled populations such as Palestinians in Israel, Greek Cypriots from the Turkish-held territory in Cyprus and expulsions of those who suddenly find they no longer meet criteria of inclusion as happened to the Windrush generation in the UK.

Some forms of categorisation do more work for the sorting and management of populations than others in different contexts. For example, the category of the refugee has emerged as a particularly central node in the modern state (see Arendt 1951; Agamben 2005). Such a category relates to the saliency of the national boundary in determining political and social rights and is counterposed to that of the citizen-subject. In the case of refugees, the national boundary and the citizenship boundary have led at different times to various forms of exclusion, violence and dehumanisation. Agamben (2005) argues that the figure of the refugee is exemplary of the normalisation of the states of exception of the modern nation state in the global order. However, such an exemplary figure already builds on the categorisations of those who are outside the boundary of inclusion on ethnic terms since in the modern state it is this primarily that gives incontestable rights of nationality and citizenship, based on claims to be the originary owners of the land and the territory. All others *earn* rights through other claims to membership. Only a 'native' who has been extraordinarily denied the rights of authenticity, through treason or other forms of criminality towards the nation state would be subject to such a positioning outside the borders. Refugees inhabit a twilight zone between inclusion and exclusion if they have not been deported or expelled and sit in the waiting rooms of ordering, temporally suspended in limbo land. The category of refugee is a label that permeates the lives of the displaced. In some cases, it is reproduced generationally through state and political discourses (e.g. around the resolution of the so-called Cyprus problem). It can provide a mode of identification and a group-making process under

48 Branding places

certain conditions. For instance, the children and even grandchildren of refugees on both sides of the national divide in post 1974 Cyprus are hailed by the state as refugees as well as being named as such within their own communities and neighbourhoods. They have internalised a 'refugee' identity with the interpellation 'I don't forget (*Den xehno*)'.

Such processes exemplify how power relations operate within the nation state form which intersects with those of capitalism. They indicate that capitalism cannot be seen purely in terms of its logic via a purist Marxist analysis (see more on this point in Chapter 4). Such practices also cannot be regarded as feudal remnants alone. They are manifestations of how the nation has become a container model for competition over resources, but not only over territory and land but also over rights to citizenship, culture, recognition and quality of life as well as freedom from dehumanisation and disenfranchisement. This occurs not only through discursive power in the acts and agonism of a myriad 'small' acts (as found in the work of Foucault) but through embodied practices and collectivised struggles and the management of antagonism and contestation using differential reward structures, pitting populations against one another. For example, as noted in Chapter 1, rights of women may be claimed or forged at the expense of demonising whole cultures (e.g. with the body covering of Muslim women being used to embody 'danger'). Rights of cultures can be promoted at the expense of silencing, and sanctioning violations against women. Some cultural rights under multiculturalism (see Sa'ar 2005) were promoted irrespective of the ways they subordinated women. These serve political and economic projects of inequality, found at different times within capitalist societies and the neo-liberal state, inasmuch as they are plastic rather than immutable, like the slime so popular with children today.

However, at the level of the placement of individuals within hierarchical social relations, it is never purely a question of a hierarchy of individuals within a category, such as gender, class or race, for example, because their bodies are marked in a range of ways. If the inscriptions can be read as 'grids' (as I argued in Anthias 1998a) their salience will not only vary in different times, places and contexts, but individuals are interpellated by them in different ways. There are complex forms of hierarchy across a range of different dimensions, and individuals may be placed differently hierarchically in these constellations of signs, figurations and babbles. The interplay of the different grids always needs to be considered in any analysis of social outcomes or effects, producing a tangled and at times *reinforcing* or *contradictory* web of inequality and privilege/subordination, captured through a translocational and intersectional lens.

Gender, ethnicity, race, sexuality, class

This book has chosen to focus on categories with particular reference to gender, ethnicity/race and class (which includes also a concern with a range of related ones such as migrants and refugees). However, as pointed out earlier, this does not exhaust or relegate others. Clearly, we can broaden or narrow our conception depending on the object of our analysis and on the salience for social relations at different times and places (e.g. with the category migrant and refugee being particularly salient in the technologies of ordering today). Not all are salient all of the time, nor are they all equally salient in terms of political or economic projects at different times. Some categories or divisions group individuals in legal terms or otherness relating to nation state boundaries, such as the categories of migrants and refugees; these constitute particularly socio-legal categories. Such categorisations of people are particularly prone to change over an individual's lifetime (assuming they are not in a permanent state of limbo), for example from being categorised as a refugee or a migrant or legal or illegal, and in different socio-spatial contexts (where you might be a migrant in one place but not in another – Crawley and Skleparis 2018).

The categories of gender, race, ethnicity, sexuality and class, amongst others, have been considered, at times, to have diminished in salience or seen as too 'traditional'. Some prominent developments have critiqued intersectionality's fixation with them, and instead prefer to talk about 'the diversification of diversity' or super-diversity, discussed earlier (e.g. Meissner and Vertovec 2015). I do not want to enter the debate again here, as I have engaged with this position earlier, but I want to note that I believe that this is quite a mistaken position. Indeed, I would go to the opposite extreme and say that they have not been given enough centrality in social analysis, in terms of the work they do enabling inequalities and hierarchies, and how they operate within both juridico-legal frameworks and socio-economic relations which involve differentiated exclusions and inclusions. Moreover, they are also central to the symbolic value which fuels both those modes of operation, and indeed beyond the symbolic, operate as moral domains regarding worth and desert. They are also at the heart of the salience of other contemporary and not so contemporary social categories such as migrants and refugees in an intersectional way, for example in the making of the domestic carer category or in the differential placing of men and women within the liminal space or grey zone of the refugee camps.

A *definitional* approach to the contested terrains of gender, ethnicity, race, sexuality and class is unhelpful, if only because this would go against the grain of the fluidities of categories that I have been arguing for. Instead, I think it's useful to treat the central categories of difference as grids (see Anthias 1998b) for analysis, that is, in heuristic terms. To look through each of the grids (and they cannot be neatly packaged in the abstract) yields a different set of *issues and problems* at different times and places. It is these that must be attended to rather than definitions. They may shape each other, emerge simultaneously, assemble and re-assemble, be reflective of each other or operate at the concrete level in ways that make it difficult to separate them: indeed, we can refer to all of these as *intersecting*, with a permissive notion of the term. The form that connections take cannot be known in any a priori way. That is why we need a *plastic* notion of 'mutual constitution' rather than attempting to decipher it as a specific type of connection (see Chapter 3 for an engagement with 'mutual constitution').

50 Branding places

In my view, even though, in social relations, the categorial formations involve constellations which are performed and experienced simultaneously, and form assemblages of power, the categories cannot be collapsed together. We need to *separate* them as a first step in any analysis of their interconnections, as these categories are *social facts* (in the Durkheimian sense, see Durkheim 1895/1970). They are social constructions which are embodied in structures, procedures and people's actions. Of course, individuals themselves in concrete locations cannot live them in this way, as separate. However, people can differentiate the locus of the practices in quite clear ways, at times, for example where there are direct forms of sexual or race abuse (found in the testimonies of victims of sexual or racially based violence). We can also see how class location is affected by gender and race when we look at the distribution of jobs or pay levels – subjects too are often well aware of the procedures whereby this happens, and the obfuscations involved (ideas such as being mothers or less ambitious, the role of old boys' networks or being told that they cannot want the responsibility of a senior position). In peoples' lived experience, forms of violence may be imbricated in such ways that rape of the women or men of the enemy in war, or rape or trafficking of a domestic maid, whilst at the intersection of gender, race, nation and class amongst others, may be experienced primarily as a violation of the person related to the sexed and gendered body, even though such forms of violence require an intersectional understanding (see Anthias 2014 and Chapter 5).

Commonalities?

There is very little work on the issue of the similarities amongst salient categories of difference (but see Tilly (1998), McWhorter (2004) and more recently Brubaker and Fernandez (2019)), possibly because of the need for historical specificity and a situational approach (found in Tilly's organisational focus). There is also a fear of homologising and flattening the work of the categories and not paying attention to historical variability. Whilst all these are important, it's still useful, in my view, to try and find some common grounds in the specifications of difference that operate in modern societies as pivots for inequality. We can see these common grounds in terms of tendencies which are part of the exercise of what some have called biocoloniality (Narayan 2019). Some categories of difference and their historical specificities are grounded in the colonial enterprise, others within the formation of capitalist relations of production, others particularly have unfolded from within the dynamic of nation state formation, and others as modes for intimacy, control of sexuality and relations of biological and social reproduction. Some writers have argued that particular forms have emerged out of coloniality as a historical economic and political enterprise (e.g. race: Cox 1970; Robinson 2000; Virdee 2014). Others have focused particularly on sexuality (Butler 1990; Foucault 1972) as a form of biopolitics related to control of populations, others have looked at nation and ethnicity in relation to their links with capitalism. The Marxist tradition has treated class division as the motor of capitalism and the primary division in relations of economic and other inequalities. Modern class categories, by definition, are specific to particular social systems, both in their generality and their specificity. Other systems of economic and social hierarchy are found in caste and systems of slavery – sometimes in conjunction with ethnic and race attributions and cultural difference. Despite pertaining to different projects these are all intricately linked to differential forms of resource allocation and social valuation.

The question of what these categorisations share or how they differ has been an under-explored issue. Despite the risks involved, exploring their commonalities can help us investigate their operation, not as generalisations but as ideal types for comparison (see Weber 1946), even if only in terms of the kinds of questions we might want to ask. The commonalities which inform their social operation and their role as inequality regimes, modes of governmentality, as forms of discursive power and the ways they construct belonging and exclusion, are useful although hazardous questions.

Categories of gender, sexuality, ethnicity and race (and those of disability or age which this book does not engage with), unlike class, for example, are particularly prone, in different ways, to fix the difference in more essentialist and binary ways, often across different socio-spatial contexts, because of the more biologically or originary principles found in them, depending on physical typology, nomenclature or territorial or cultural origins and traits. This does not mean that they are produced in these ways but rather that they are socially and discursively constructed as such. Whilst not necessarily stable they are treated *as though* they are stable. However, the valuation and social outcomes relating to such categorisations will vary for individuals depending on the social contexts, and the meanings attached to the categorisations as well as how they intersect with other categories (e.g. being middle class and Black or being a white woman).

In terms of the common principles found in their discursive production as *boundaries* and in their *hierarchical* outcomes, it's useful to draw out some facets as a point for comparison, that is, as a heuristic exercise. In my view, we can look for tendencies towards binarisation, naturalisation and homogenisation in the ways they are constructed. We can look at unequal social outcomes, on the other hand, relating to hierarchisation, inferiorisation (including stigma) and resource allocation. Here I develop some of the ideas found in my earlier work (see Anthias (1998a) particularly).

1. Binarisation

Binary oppositions are common in western social and political thought and these involve asymmetrical relations within the binary and are therefore never free of evaluative connotation. Hertz (1978) talks about the left and the right, where one side of the binary is regarded as dominant and superior over the other. For example, gender and race/ethnic categories are relational, constructing asymmetrical attributions of difference and identity involving, commonly, binaries and

52 Branding places

dichotomies. Derrida (1982) argues that difference (as 'differance') establishes a space between objects giving rise to hierarchy and binary categories. Although there are also tendencies towards greater multiplicity and fluidity (both in relation to gender and ethnicity/race, as argued in Chapter 1) the binary in terms of dominant 'self' (the authentic or ideal) and subordinate 'other' (differentially included or excluded) still operates in complex ways. For example, there may be multiple others whose commonality comes from a united 'otherness', but there is only one ideal 'us' against multiple or diverse intruding minorities. Such a binarisation is blinded to commonalities across the boundary. It cannot consider that the individuals that are placed in each category may occupy a different position in the other categories, for example white women are subordinate using the gender grid but dominant using the race grid (see Hertz 1978).

2. Naturalisation

Gender, ethnic and race categories are underpinned by a naturalisation of the difference (with the idea of people being born into them). Age, ability (as in class) or disability and sexuality are treated as 'natural'. These categorisations play a central role in essentialising social relations, aiding in the perception of existing arrangements as a product of biology or cultural absolutisms. In gender, necessary social effects are posited to sexual difference and biological reproduction. There are assumptions concerning the natural boundaries of collectivities or the naturalness of culture. Stronger forms of biological essentialism are found in racial categories. Natural differences in capacities and needs based on gender or on ethnicity/race come to be regarded as explanations for particular kinds of economic or familial and other roles, inclinations and achievements (ironically reproduced in the work of Bourdieu with his rather deterministic account of the classed and gendered habitus). These act as legitimisers of inequalities in class position (see also Anthias and Yuval-Davis 1983). The subordinate position of women may be legitimated differently, across and between classes and ethnicities and cultures, as social categories are not universally formulated but contingent to cultures and localities as well as political projects.

Both gender and 'race' are social categories which are seen, generally, to be filled by people who share some fixed, unchanging essence. In the case of gender this is related to gender being inscribed onto bodily 'sexual difference' (or a natural proclivity to being trans) and in the case of 'race' to 'human stock difference' (colour, physiognomy) or 'cultural difference' (sic). This is underpinned by a central and powerful fallacy. In the case, for example, of the race category the attribution of racial stock has been totally discredited as are any necessary links between physiognomic, colour or ethnic difference and capacities and needs which are in any case socially constructed (Miles 1989, 1993; Guillaumin 1995). In addition, even more scientifically presented arguments about the differences between the brains of men and women have been recently challenged (Rippon 2019).

Branding places **53**

In terms of the concept of ethnicity, there are naturalising assumptions concerning the boundaries of ethnic groups, particularly through the importance often given to the historical origin or common descent of the group, or in terms of the taken for granted character or naturalness of cultural difference in constructing solidary bonds. Although the borders of the ethnic group may not be as fixed and rigid as those of 'race' categories, nonetheless there are markers as well as policies of border-making in most states, regarding who has the right and who hasn't the right to belong to the group, that specify parentage, descent, origin or even destiny. Whereas, with nationhood, it is possible to accede through gaining political rights of citizenship or acquiring cultural or linguistic skills, the acquisition of the latter does not automatically entitle an individual to ethnic belongingness, although in some cases marriage or religious conversion may.

Ideas about class also naturalise in a society underpinned by the idea (but not the practice) of opportunity and mobility. Those who fail to take advantage are then deemed to be deserving of their lot, despite the wealth of research and writing that points to the mechanisms whereby such inequalities are produced and reproduced.

3. Homogenisation and collective attributions

Gender, 'race' and ethnic and race categories, amongst others, construct their subjects in unitary terms. The gender category homogenises women; that is in its very nature. It uses the attribution of sexual difference and certain postulates about its necessary social effects to treat all women as a unity. The unity of *experience* on the other hand is one hailed by many feminists in constructing the idea of sisterhood which underpins much feminist identity politics (for early critiques, see amongst others, Anthias and Yuval-Davis (1983); Spelman (1988)). Even here, in the feminist project there has been a homogenisation of women with the concerns of white (and often middle-class) feminists determining the constructions of a patriarchal model of social relations which is treated as universal. Again, it is mainly with the rise of intersectionality that this has been corrected, and then only partially (see Anthias and Yuval-Davis (1983), The Combahee River Collective (1977/1982), and the writings of bel hooks (1981), Pat Hill Collins (1990) and other black feminists). The categories of 'race' and ethnicity also homogenise, and difference, contradiction and multiplicity may be unrecognised or absent within such conferments. Collective attributions are often endemic to categories of the population overall, as to categorise, such collective attributions need to be in place – as in the categories of age, health, disability, sexuality and so on. This also leads to blind spots and oversimplification in social analysis.

Such attributions have a profound effect on people. Homogenising collective attributions may become internalised and paralysing, as well as mobilising forces. The poignant title of Fanon's important book, *Black Skin, White Masks* (1967), indicates the power of racist attributions in producing negative self-concepts and in endowing positive value to whiteness. The plethora of images that purvey

54 Branding places

idealised versions of the objectified female body is another case of the negative effects of sexualised gender idealisations. The effects such values and norms have on the self-esteem, quality of life or behaviour of individuals is debated frequently, not only in feminist circles, but also in the mainstream media.

Collective attributions are also situated and may be discordant with the ways that people understand their values and practices. An ethnic or racial category may be constructed and construct itself in different ways: as stronger, more logical, less emotional, as great warriors or lovers, as honourable and so on and on the other hand may be seen as disciplinarian, insular, unassimilable and isolationist. There may be stress on the importance of conformity to religious, gender or other cultural practices which may be regarded by others as fundamentalist and violating women's rights. Often the behaviour of women is crucial, where the collective attribution of being a good ethnic subject may depend on the sexual control of women and their behaviour (Anthias and Yuval-Davis 1989): Mediterranean rural societies, Muslim cultures, and a range of others place special emphasis on the performance of differentiated gender roles.

4. Hierarchisation

Whilst the issue of the analytical need to *differentiate* amongst the categories whilst acknowledging some of their common principles and how they intersect in translocational ways is an issue which will be taken up in Chapter 3, it's useful to say a few things here. In the case of central social categorisations that have tended to fix categories of people, the biological or essentially based difference is often seen as having necessary social outcomes. Bodies are hailed, disciplined, and subjected to a range of operations of power through political practices in their broadest sense which encompass the family, the state and the nation. The argument here is that the social relations manifested by the categories cannot be explained by them, nor can they be explained purely with reference to technologies of power around them. Such technologies also touch the intersectional level, operating on different women or men through articulating with race and class (amongst others). Hence intersectional categories mimic those of single axis categories. In other words, intersectional categories (such as black working-class women) are also salient categories in the auditing system of states, as well as within a social justice framework (the latter is a position upheld by Crenshaw (1989)), but of course the outcome will depend on any contesting social forces that intersectional categories can produce.

5. Unequal resource allocation

Resource allocation has often been conceived in terms of economic resources which have generally been theorised in terms of class. The empirical evidence that 'race' attributions and gender attributions are correlated with economic position in general terms has meant that many of the explanations concerning the dynamics of 'race' and gender have reduced them to some form of economic category. Much of the debate on 'race' and class (Anthias 1990) takes as a starting point the economic position of Black people and explains this with reference to economic processes and their link to racism (Castles and Kosack 1973; Castells 1975). As Miles (1989) however points out, there are a range of exclusionary practices in society that are not merely coterminous with racism but are 'a component part of a wider structure of class disadvantage'. In other words, the position of any racialised category cannot be explained solely through the workings of racism: if this were the case then we would expect to see them all having the same class position. This is despite the fact that there is a wealth of empirical evidence that shows that women and ethnic minorities suffer durable disadvantages in the labour market (see Miles 1989; Castles, Booth and Wallace 1984; Modood et al. 1997; Anthias 1993; Breach and Li 2017; Li and Heath 2018). Unequal resource allocation also involves political, cultural and representational resources.

6. Inferiorisation and stigma

One of the assumptions that underlie binary social categories is that one side of the binary divide is seen as the norm, and as expressive of the ideal. For example, the yardstick for gender becomes male capacities or achievements, male needs or interests. These assumptions are often reproduced in struggles against the disadvantage conferred on the 'wrong' side of the binary divide. This is found in feminist struggles that argue for equality of capacities and needs, taking as given that those expressed in the masculine are the yardstick. It is also found in arguments for gay marriage which are fired by an equality agenda, but which also play, arguably, into existing normative framings of gender and sexuality (for further discussion see Chapter 5). This leads to forms of theory and practice that are concerned with redressing disadvantage relative to the 'normal/right' side. It may lead theoretically to treating the 'normal/right' side as the explanatory field for the 'other/wrong' side. This is expressed in those arguments within feminism, for example, that treat men as the cause of women's oppression or those arguments by antiracists that treat Whites or racist individuals as the problem that needs to be countered, rather than locating the sources of racism within broader social relations. At the same time, normality and pathology become ascribed to individuals in two ways: firstly the 'other' becomes pathologised and secondly individuals who do not perform the ascribed roles in a satisfactory way also become pathologised. In the first way pathology is seen as endemic to particular categories (Blacks, ethnic outsiders, women). In the second way, pathology is derived from failing to perform adequately the appropriate roles imputed to a particular category.

The work of categories and their intersections

Modern capitalist formations involve complex and heterogeneous practices of power and contestation, which cannot be reduced to a single causal principle,

56 Branding places

such as 'structure' or 'social action', with its greater emphasis on agency.[5] This does not mean that we should abandon an attempt to analyse and understand beyond merely the recognition of complexity and fluidity, however. Such an exercise requires an anchoring – a theoretical framing. Indeed, one of the central critiques of both post-modernism and intersectionality, which were born of the post-Marxist turn, is that they both lack a theoretical anchor, that is, a mode for analysing and understanding the processes involved (see Chapter 3 where I argue that different theoretical anchors can be attached to the project of intersectionality). This can end up as merely charting a fragmented and complex social system. However, to describe involves selecting 'what' to describe and 'how' to describe it. Often hidden conceptual and indeed ideological and political conceptions underpin what appears to be description. Recent work on policies, aimed at minorities, has shown that these often entail hidden and essentialised conceptions which reinforce existing modes of exclusion and inequality (e.g. see Anthias (2013b), Titley and Lentin (2008), Lentin (2019) for examples of how diversity and integration policies can function to alienate and demonise categories of the population).

In my approach, a theoretical anchor is provided by the centrality of the production and reproduction of the resources that are necessary for life itself, and the *impetus* towards their uneven distribution, a central prerequisite of capitalist relations, if not their total modus operandi. Indeed, equality talk, which is part of this process today, takes for granted *the necessary inequality of income and wealth* (often used to determine class position), whilst being stronger on mechanisms for trying to equalise gender, race and ethnic position (however unsuccessfully and indeed, one could argue, cynically pursued). However, the impetus to unequal resources is not only related to the economic, nor does the notion of resources extend only to the kinds of capitals that Bourdieu was concerned with (such as social and cultural capital), where he saw them as valuable if they could be transferable to the economic (Bourdieu 1986). Once we think of resources in terms of a broader notion of the conditions of existence of the liveable self (Butler 2006) or in terms of human capabilities (Sen 2004; Nussbaum 2011), which includes of course legality, political rights and citizenship or using another terminology in terms of quality of life, we can think of issues of safety, sociality, recognition, citizenship as important resources. Depriving some populations of these is a mode by which categorisations often work, in Agamben's term, converting some categories, such as refugees, to 'bare life' (1998), and others to beasts of burden (such as in plantation slavery in the Americas) or disposable surplus populations, as expendable and expellable (migrants on borderlands or the long-term unemployed). Whilst I take issue with the idea of 'bare life' given the agonistic nature of life itself, such a project at times can succeed (as in total institutions, e.g. where agency gives way to total compliance and subjugation). This does not displace the central role of the distribution of economic resources, but these other facets make possible the access to them on the one hand, and, on the other hand, make economic resources meaningful for life itself beyond subsistence.

Understanding the workings of modern capitalisms, and their regulatory mechanisms, requires also a recognition of colonial and imperial pasts and their traces or debris (Stoler 2013), as noted in Chapter 1. However, the emergence and transformations of categories of difference cannot be reduced to the workings of colonialism either, despite their heavy and blood-stained footmarks. Uneven and hierarchical resource distribution, which characterises modern capitalism, is facilitated by the workings of shifting and persisting categories of difference, their construction and ordering, and these fill particular roles at different times. This is related to their tendencies to fixities (and at times fluidities and fixed/unfixities), manifested in the ways they harness binary and naturalised categories of people, and construct homogeneous and collectivised categories, with shifting boundaries. Sometimes, in the process, they become de-individualised, de-personalised or can be treated as disposable (or surplus) and ultimately dispensable, replicable or replaceable.

This process is not only one that is done *to* people but a process that people *do*, that engages people actively in the very heart of their everyday lives and struggles (see Chapter 3). This approach therefore distances itself from the Bourdieusian dependence on habitus (dispositions or taken for granted ways of thinking and being) as fully determining the 'doings' of people. As the placement of people in the different relations of power related to categories articulate they generate complexities and contradictions that potentially yield a way of resolving some of the difficulties in the notion of habitus that were identified earlier, particularly its totalising and determinist inflections. Actors occupy a range of positions in social space through their habitation of a variety of categories as part of a wider system of classification and social relations of difference and inequality. Therefore, dispositions or proclivities (stressed by Bourdieu) arising out of fields generate struggles that are played out in their interstices and intersections. Such intersections give rise to contradictions at times. The differential placement of the same individuals in each one of them potentially alerts individuals to the operations of power, which can work in various ways. One of these is through the multiplication effects of subordinations, where, as in Crenshaw's metaphor of the basement (1989, p. 149), at the bottom lie those who are multiply disadvantaged. Another is through the contradictory placement of those who occupy dominant positions in one or more categories, and subordinate positions in one or more (moving between floors thereby seeing what lies above and below).

Cross-categorial disparities of position can potentially disrupt the homologisation of categorial positions that is often normalised in cases where they reinforce each other. Such contradictory locations are more and more likely in multicultural societies where there is an ethic and practice of legislating for equality of treatment on some fronts and not others, or where some of these policies are more effective than others. This might relate to equality provisions for women or minorities or widening educational participation for the working class. The greater the number and force of disparities and contradictions, the more potential arises for unlocking the gaze out of the basement, and through the window,

58 Branding places

making visible the existence of power inequalities, where they matter. This is not to say that there are any necessary effects involved and this may vary considerably. Inhabiting both dominant and subordinate positions simultaneously may yield a range of effects (and this may be a fruitful point for investigation), through experiential and identificationary dissonance, where coming up against procedural and institutional mechanisms on either side of the subordination-domination twin can pave the way to greater understandings of their social construction and relationality.

Some work is already available on class contradictions, particularly in the study of education and social mobility and in the role of the petit bourgeoisie (Poulantzas 1974; Wright 1982; for a review see Abercrombie and Urry 1983). Some of the possibilities link to insights from the sociology of knowledge (Marx and Engels 1932; Mannheim 1929) and from an adapted form of situated knowledge, where this situatedness is never complete or fixed and is always ambivalent. Such an approach re-inserts positionality and agency as well as contradiction into the recent take up of approaches such as the important work of Agamben (1998, 2005). This work has embraced a biopolitics framework that is in danger of treating people as mere objects of power, rather than also as negotiators and resisters of power (echoing Foucault in the less than agonistic agonism that he claims).

Here, we can question, and complexify, the determinist nature of habitus found in the work of Bourdieu, as well as begin to point to the limits of governmentality in Foucault's work which largely relies on the acquiescence that it rests on, rather than violence or domination. Both thinkers in different ways fail to engage with the ways in which acquiescence should not be taken at face value. For example, Genovese (1971) shows how black domestic slaves used their agency to find ways of subverting the power of the slaveholder whilst maintaining acquiescence, and they were amongst the first to revolt against slavery. Similarly, with regard to patriarchy, Kandiyoti (1989) has talked about the 'patriarchal bargain', a mode of reciprocity that women deploy that belies the totalising power of gender predispositions. Such forms of complexifying erase therefore the pre-given registers that both Foucault and Bourdieu use in different ways.

Concluding remarks: building blocks for inequality

Categories of difference are important in a range of ways as a building block for both forms of inequality and belonging/unbelonging in the world today, and they underpin modern capitalist societies and their forms of governance. The categorial formations act as pegs for inequality (Anthias 1998b), having changing configurations and centrality in social relations and people's lives. Their apparent plasticity (and people's own investments in them) belies their role as a modus operandi of power. They are inequality-making processes as well as constitutive of subject positionalities. They are 'inequality regimes' (as Acker (2006) so aptly puts it), on the one hand, and modes for the control and management of populations (as a form of biopolitics, Foucault 1982, 1997), on the other. Ideas of belonging or who can be included, how they can be included, when they can be included and to what they can be included are always undergirded by questions about the resources which are being claimed, allocated, contested and struggled over. As such, these category-making and group-making practices can be regarded as central to the projects of capitalist social formations since they act, in a range of ways, to facilitate inequality, subordination and exploitation. They can be fixed or become more fluid as modern capitalism and its governance seeks to manage the crises endemic within its inequality project.

Firstly, at the *organisational* level, they are central to economic or political projects of various types. For example, exploitation, regulation, auditing or social correction, or in Foucault's (1982, 1997) words governmentality and biopolitics. Persons are hailed, defined, organised into groups, legislated on and so on. They delineate legitimate and illegitimate positions and subjects of entitlement: entitlement to inclusion within the border, or exclusion and expulsion. The processes are intricately woven because some categories may exist inside some borders but outside other borders, such as being illegal migrants but workers occupying the liminal zone of a modern–day migrant reserve army of labour. This involves differential and subordinate inclusion at one level but exclusion on the other (inclusion or exclusion are not oppositional because of forms of subordinate inclusion (Anthias 2001b – see also Mezzadra and Neilson 2013). They are also tools for allocating *roles in the production system* and in related reproductive mechanisms of capitalism, such as the family and the boundaries of differential exclusion and inclusion in the nation. They figure in the institutional and structural arrangements in society.

Secondly, at the *experiential* and *intersubjective* levels, categories and practices of differentiation are implicated in modes of identity and belonging, relating to enactments and performativities (Butler 1990), linked to mobilisations and contestations of different kinds. They are central elements in the ways we relate to others, that is, in social encounters and their patterns and rules (e.g. see Goffman 1956). They have a central place in our experiences and understandings of ourselves and others, structuring as well as being structured by them. They confer value and allocate specific traits, stigmas and roles; they are important facets of our subjectivities and emotional well-being. They are also ways in which we mobilise, either for seeking inclusion or for rights and representations or by actively de–normalising and refusing the project of inclusion and integration within existing rules of the game. De Genova (2010) points to the queer negation of the concern with inclusivity: 'we are queer, we are here, get over it'. Mobilisations of illegals may make the same interdiction: 'we will not disappear, we cannot be expelled, we will return'. Palestinians who rebuild their houses again and again when they have been demolished endlessly by the Israeli army are taking a stand, refusing the normative arrangements of the status quo, asserting their autonomy and agency as forms of resistance. This differs from claims made in the name of identity politics, found in desires to legalise gay partnerships or for marriage which Richardson (2017) has termed sexual citizenship.

60 Branding places

Thirdly, at the *representational* level, major categories and practices of differentiation constitute central social doxa (Bourdieu 1980) being naturalised and taken for granted, despite their changing configurations; this allows us to treat them as *generative* of particular social relations. They appear as dominant social and psychic imaginaries, texts and discourses about the world. Capitalism itself has relied, in part, on some of the ways such categories naturalise inequalities and differential treatment of people, thereby facilitating exploitation and its corollary, governmentality, within capitalist social relations. Unequal and subordinating treatment has been legitimised variously through ideas about merit, desert, preference, eligibility (e.g. being a native, being physically strong), biological traits and cultural dispositions and needs.

I now turn specifically to the project of intersectionality which lies in assembling the social relations of inequality further, and consider some of the quandaries this raises, continuing the conversation about theorising categories as boundaries and hierarchies of 'belonging' through a translocational lens.

Notes

1 According to Burawoy (2018) Bourdieu's notion of masculine domination is a pale imitation (unacknowledged) of Simone de Beauvoir's ideas in *The Second Sex* (ref).
2 Foucault predicts 'a racism that society will direct against itself, against its own elements and its own products . . . the internal racism of permanent purification, and it will become the basic dimensions of social normalisation' (ref).
3 See Nieswand (2017) for an argument supporting the use of diversity as an analytical frame.
4 However, see the contested argument by Levi-Strauss (1949) on the primary role of sexual difference in the development of human culture.
5 Structure and agency is a lynchpin and rather obfuscating binary within the sociological canon, and underplays the importance of 'process', binarising the individual and the social.

3

ASSEMBLING PLACES
Dilemmas of articulation

Introduction: the relationality of categories

One of the most prominent approaches that addresses the relationality of social categories of difference and hierarchy is what has come to be called 'intersectionality'. This term has now escaped the confines of both Black feminist politics, where its origins lie, and academia, to be referred to almost everywhere, including the popular media. For example, Black Lives Matter and the Me Too movement in America have represented their politics as intersectional. There is even an internet site where people are invited to test their intersectionality.[1] Of course, the term has been open to much use and some have argued, abuse, on its 'travels' (see Tomlinson 2013; Crenshaw 2016 and for a very different position see Lutz 2014).

As I have noted before (Anthias 2013a), the idea of the existence of inter-relations in the domain of the social is not new and constitutes the very foundation of classical sociological theory. Relationality is a central premise of work ranging from Marxism and critical theory to earlier feminist and race analyses. Marx, for example, was concerned with the dynamic and dialectical ways in which configurations at different societal levels produce forms of political engagement and social transformation. In his work we find a concern with the intersection between economy and society (Marx 1859/1977) and in the work of Durkheim we find ideas about complexity and systems, as well as forms of materiality and representation which are relational. Durkheim's premise about the *sui generis* nature of society (Durkheim 1895/1970), and of social facts points towards one of the central underlying principles of contemporary intersectional frames, that is, the irreducibility of social relations to others on the one hand, and the need to look at the social as a complex system of interrelated parts. Weber too, whilst working within a methodologically individualist approach, is concerned with

62 Assembling places

inter-relationships in the prominence he gives to the intersubjectively constituted nature of social life, and in the concern with the intersections of economic class, status groups and political parties (Weber 1947/1964). This is also apparent in his discussion of the links between economic conditions and the actions of ethnic groups (Gerth and Mills 1991). Whilst not attending to gender, as such, the idea of gender as status group is compatible with his formulation. The notion of status group is articulated in a range of work, such as social stratification analysis (e.g. Goldthorpe 1996; Crompton 1998; Crompton and Mann 1986; Scott 1994) and work that is concerned with issues of redistribution and recognition (e.g. Fraser 1997, 2000).

The analysis of the links between different forms of identity and hierarchy is not new either, and there has been a long-standing interest, both theoretical and political, in exploring the connections in social relations between different forms of subordination and exploitation. This includes the work of Lenski (1966) on social stratification, Lerner (1973) on black women in America, and feminists working within a political economy approach relating gender to class (e.g. Gardiner 1975; Beechey 1977), as well as race theorists exploring the connections between race and class (e.g. Myrdal 1944; Sivanandan 1976; Miles 1989). In other words, recognising the interconnections between social divisions existed without this being named as 'intersectionality'. Of course, its entry into our political and theoretical vocabulary does mark a significant development if only because it acts to further destabilise fixed and essentialising understandings of the operation of social categories of difference and identity, and it provides a further challenge to traditional stratification theories.

If relationality has been central to much social theory what is new about intersectionality? Clearly the focus is new in as much as the approach is embedded in a concern with the intersections between central categories of difference, particularly those of gender and race (and somewhat less class) and their power relations as they articulate or co-constitute each other. Clearly intersectionality has had a distinctive trajectory but its history can be narrated in many different ways that mark out different authoritative voices (Collins 2019). A central difficulty is according intersectionality a specific set of analytical tools and methods which would then constitute it as more than an analytical sensitivity or a heuristic device (see Anthias 1998a) which focuses on categorial inter-relations and social power. This is being increasingly acknowledged today by primary intersectional thinkers, such as Kimberle Crenshaw who has more recently called intersectionality a prism and a provisional concept (2011), and it is referred to as a heuristic in a recent book co-written by Collins and Bilge (2016). However, others have regarded intersectionality as a theoretical paradigm (Hancock 2007) and Collins (2019) recently has argued that it can be a metaphor, a heuristic or a paradigm, without herself taking a position on this. However, others have argued that treating it as a heuristic constitutes a 'downgrading' of a theoretical contribution by black feminists (e.g. Lewis 2009). This contrasts with the view that treating it as a heuristic device lends itself to treating it as a tool for understanding broader

Assembling places **63**

social relations, including the intersections between advantage and disadvantage (Anthias 2008, 2009).

Pat Hill Collins, one of the most theoretically sophisticated and nuanced writers working in the field, has sought in her latest book (Collins 2019) to produce an archaeological excavation of intersectionality through engaging with critical social theory and with relational thinking. She cites its core constructs as relationality, power, social inequality, social context, complexity and social justice. She regards its guiding premises as the interdependence of race, class and gender as systems of power in the production of complex social inequalities which shape individual and group experience, as well as maintaining that intersectional analyses are needed for solving social problems. This depiction is useful in pointing to its programmatic, but it doesn't interrogate the dominant conception of mutual constitution (which will be discussed later in this chapter), nor how this involves an explicit rejection of additive forms of interconnection. Instead she lists addition, articulation and co-formation as three possible ways, all potentially fruitful, for understanding the relationalities involved. This is an important reminder that the interconnections cannot be stipulated a priori and that we shouldn't reject outright different ways in which social processes collide and assemble within a social landscape of power. A useful aide memoire is that

> Intersectionality is situated at the crossroads of multiple interpretative communities that are characterised by discursive histories, concerns, and epistemic standards.
>
> *(Collins 2019, p. 128)*

The location of intersectionality at the crossroads of critical race theory, feminism and inequality theorisations (as well as identity theorisations) makes it potentially broad-sweeping as well as analytically promiscuous. For Collins, however, intersectionality is above all else a dialogical knowledge project that puts a range of different theories in conversation with one another, and proceeds by abduction, that is, through 'collaboration, iteration and reflection' (p. 149). I would argue that this is indeed the hallmark of all good theory and one argument here, which I would endorse, is that intersectionality above all else points to the modes by which we should conduct our analyses and investigations, on the one hand, and on the other, points to a particular subject matter which is the complexity of hierarchies and inequalities, and their understanding and overcoming.

In this chapter, I consider some of the quandaries and dilemmas faced by those who engage with intersectionality and propose a provisional way of addressing these through a translocational multi-level lens that considers social categories and their interconnection at different levels of abstraction. In doing this, I particularly engage with the dilemma raised by using, on the one hand, categories of gender, race, class and sexuality (as well as others) as points of reference (and therefore, at some level as separate), and on the other hand, the idea of their mutual constitution, which points to these categories as always already

64 Assembling places

intertwined, and therefore inseparable. I try to formulate this in ways which do not present paradoxical positions, and I develop a dialogical and multi-level framework (see also Anthias 2013a) for thinking through processes of power and their translocational nature (see Chapter 1 and later in this chapter for an elaboration of the notion of translocational). The substitution of 'social locations' for 'sections' or identity categories, and 'trans' for 'inter' (stressing *processes* in the making of hierarchies), already paves the way for this exercise.

Intersectionality, which is an umbrella term for a range of approaches, is aligned with a primary insight: that you cannot *explain* the workings of a category of difference (and its effects), such as gender, or power relations relating to heteropatriarchy, purely self-referentially, that is, with reference to gender processes, as it is co-produced and entwined with other categories of difference and related power dynamics, such as race/racism and class (amongst others). Such a framing has tried to correct the tendency to assume an equivalence between a population category (e.g. a socially defined grouping such as women, men, ethnic group, class and so on) and the ways in which the group-making processes and inequalities occur. This makes a distinction between the object of analysis (e.g. gender relations which can be thought of as the *explanandum* in this example) and the *explanans* (mode of explanation) which relates to how they are produced and their outcomes.

However, intersectional frames aim to go beyond this and to address the complexity and multidimensionality of the social relations of advantage and disadvantage and might even be seen to challenge the idea of distinctive categories altogether. They have certainly contributed to undermining profoundly the essentialisation or culturalisation of difference, despite some elements which can lead, potentially, to new essentialisations, found in the construction of hybridised categories as distinctive (such as 'black women'). Treating difference and power in a multilayered, situational and nuanced way, intersectionality has become an increasingly hegemonic framing within feminism, and some have made proprietary claims on it (Nash (2016) calls this originalism, which asserts that it has travelled illegitimately beyond its 'founders'). Such a view is far from that of Collins who provides a masterful narrative that goes beyond such concerns.

To put this in context, it's important to note two important and often stated characteristics of intersectionality, which has a long history (Crenshaw 1989; Denis 2008; Collins and Bilge 2016). *Firstly*, intersectionality is embedded in a long tradition of activism and intellectual labour which engages with the multiplicity of oppressions, faced by black or minoritised women (generally within the Global North but see the discussion later). Whilst its history is open to different narrations, it is generally acknowledged that the impetus for intersectionality came from a feminist anti-racist *politics* and was spear-headed by black feminists (e.g. see Combahee River Collective 1977/1982; hooks 1981). As such, it is underpinned by a social justice framework, and cannot be divorced from the political project of such a framework that is not devoted to the task of theory alone. If we treated intersectionality merely as an approach that connects various aspects of difference, there would not be a necessary fit with such a social justice framing. It could be attached to a fascist, neo-liberal or eugenics project (as in the discussion by Collins 2019). However, no self-proclaimed intersectional theorist would frame their work in this way. On the other hand, not all intersectional scholarship has a strong political orientation which is explicitly framed in terms of social justice, and much research is devoted to charting and understanding inequalities, for example in the areas of work, education or health (Romero and Valdez 2016; Nare 2013; Bhopal and Preston 2012; Hankivsky 2012; Levine-Rasky 2011). I believe that this is perfectly legitimate (and could be used towards a justice framework even if it is not explicitly dedicated to it). For the sake of historical accuracy, it's relevant to note that terms like 'intersectional' and 'intersections' were already used in earlier work, including my own (e.g. see Anthias 1982; Anthias and Yuval-Davis 1983). Crenshaw (1989) focused particularly on the injustices propagated in the legal system where the non-recognition at the legislative level of the intersections between gender and race made the specific injustices faced by black women invisible and outside legal protection.

Secondly, intersectional framings go beyond the additive approach found in ideas of double/triple burden/oppression or multiple jeopardy, although these ideas were important precursors of intersectionality. In 1983 Nira Yuval-Davis and I warned against a mechanistic and additive approach (but see my later discussion) before the term 'intersectionality' was first introduced in 1989. Such a critique, also made by many others, was instrumental in giving rise to frames which attempt to go beyond the additive, using terms such as 'mutual constitution', 'interlocking systems of oppression', articulation, assemblages, overlapping systems, simultaneous oppressions, entanglements (as well as the term translocational). The idea of mutual constitution underpins many of these formulations and has been widely used to capture the processes involved. However, this term can mean many different things, from refusing categorical separation to the idea that each one coexists and affects the others (but which ones, given the potentially infinite number of categories that can be played with?). A strong version of mutual constitution gives rise to profound issues about the relationality of social categories and indeed their potential erasure as effectivities in their own right. This is a position found in Carastathis (2016), for example, who takes exception to the view that categories can be separated. We can say what mutual constitution does *not* mean with greater certainty: it is antithetical to an additive model, as well as the view that *one* of them is always the most determining, a position that characterises class reductionist accounts of gender and race or race and class.[2]

Whilst not an exercise in theory alone, intersectionality is embedded in very important theoretical as well as political questions about the social organisation of difference and inequality and the workings of power. It should, therefore, not be restricted to any particular object (such as the inequalities faced by black women) or any particular constituency of those who wish to draw on it and develop it in other directions (for an opposite view see Bilge 2013). On the other

66 Assembling places

hand, the voices on the 'margins' should not be erased, nor racism side-lined (Bilge 2013; Carastathis 2016; Tomlinson 2013).

A variety of positions

The recent book by Collins and Bilge (2016) talks about intersectionality as a broad field of study, recognising the diversity within it. As they demonstrate, there is a long tradition of black feminist thought that has been concerned with the links between the major categories of difference, and particularly gender and race, and I cannot engage with this literature although I would like to underscore the struggles, on the ground, that have generated it. In terms of work coming from within the academy, but motivated by a social justice framing, Kimberle Crenshaw wrote her important first article in 1989 and Patricia Hill Collins her inspiring book on black feminist thought in 1990. Within the UK, the article by Anthias and Yuval-Davis in 1983, one of the first of its kind, was followed soon afterwards by the important Black Feminist issue in *Feminist Review* as well as a critical argument by two socialist feminists, Mary Mcintosh and Michelle Barrett (1985). We were particularly concerned to question the assumed 'sister-hood' of women as it was constructed by western feminists who were blind to the specificities of the oppression of different women placed along the axes of race and class. We located (as did Avtar Brah 1996) the intersection of social divi-sions (as we called them) within the context of power relations and the state, and this was central to the entry of intersectionality approaches within the European context. In Anthias and Yuval-Davis (1983, 1992) – for further developments see Anthias 1998b, 2001a, 2001b, 2008, 2009, 2013a; Yuval-Davis 1997, 2011 – we explored different ways of thinking about the intersections between the social divisions of gender, race/ethnicity and class, as well as problematising the notion of 'sisterhood'. We also questioned the priorities that white feminists gave to issues of reproduction and patriarchy. We developed a position delineating the ontological basis of social divisions, which is revisited and revised substantially later in this chapter.

Crenshaw, using critical race theory within a socio-legal framework, argued that individuals suffer exclusions and subordinations based on race and gender, or any other combination (Crenshaw 1994), which legal provisions for correct-ing injustices around race or gender do not attend to. It is argued that the com-bination of two minority traits gives rise to specific and often acute forms of disadvantage and there should therefore be legal provisions in place to deal with this. A more sociological approach, within an equally anti-racist framework, and a more broadly based engagement with knowledge and power, is found in the important work of Patricia Hill Collins whose writings on black feminist thought have been profoundly important within feminist theory and method. In her work, she treats gender, race and class as modes for the exercise of power (Collins 1990, 1993, 1998), and as historically contingent, proposing the notions of 'interlocking oppressions', and 'matrix of domination' (1990, p. 276) organised through structural, disciplinary, hegemonic and interpersonal power relations (see also her latest magnum opus (2019). Other approaches include a more systems theory framework, treating gender, race and class as separate systems of subordination with their own range of specific and distinctive social relations (Williams 1989; Weber 2001; Walby 2007).

It is impossible to give a full list of the important contributions since the 1990s, some critical to this debate. Apart from the ones above, they include McCall (2001, 2005), Denis (2008), Davis (2008), Brah and Phoenix (2004), Bilge (2010), Dhamoon (2011), Choo and Ferree (2010), Levine-Rasky (2011), Carastathis (2016), Nash (2011), and Hancock (2007). The greatly flagged triad of gender, race and class clearly does not exhaust the range of social categories for an intersectional lens to engage with, and sexuality, faith and disability amongst others (e.g. see Taylor et al. 2011; Meekosha et al. 2009) have been discussed and researched. Indicative of the wide variety of approaches signalled by intersectionality is found in the distinction that Choo and Ferree (2010) make between group-centred, process-centred and system-centred framings.

The path to intersectionality's venture has not always been laden with rose petals and perceived thorns in the path have prevented some people from embracing its potential, whilst others have provided 'loving' critiques in order to augment its heuristic value (see Nash (2011) for an engagement with some of the implications of this). This is despite the astounding theoretical and political rewards that people have claimed for it – for example, McCall (2005) regards intersectionality as the most important theoretical innovation within feminism, and others have talked about its brilliant career (see Lutz 2014). Yet others have argued that it is precisely because it lacks its own distinct concepts or methods that it has been taken up so widely (Davis 2008). On the other hand, this also allows so many different interpretations that it risks becoming a kind of mantra, an empty signifier or functioning as a tabular rasa, as it lacks a theoretical undergirding (e.g. see the critique by Gimenez (2001), from a Marxist position).

On the other hand, there has been a tradition of intersectionality using the prototypical exemplar of the subordinations faced by black women. However, we must be careful that the construction of such a category is not yet another homogenisation and essentialisation, mirroring categories of woman and Black as monist and inscribed with dominant assumptions about women being prototypically about white women, and Black about black men.

Quandaries

I will now discuss some of the central quandaries and difficulties involved, as a cautionary exercise rather than a criticism of the intersectional enterprise, with a focus on obstacles to avoid.

1. Not just intersecting categories: engaging with broader relations of power

Focusing on the primary modes of differentiation (i.e. gender, race, class, sexuality, disability, age) and their intersections can fail to attend to broader social relations of power and their dynamics. Moreover, how the social, structural and cultural context intersect and indeed produce, reproduce or transform categories of difference needs to be incorporated. The tendency to focus on social categorisations and explain their workings through their intersections leaves a whole lot of the social out of the playing field. It treats the divisions themselves as causal in relation to one another rather than interrelating in a playing field whose rules and actions come from the field itself rather than the players in the field alone, such as colonialism, capitalism, the state, governmentalities and institutional structures.

2. A lack of theoretical framing

The permissive nature of the idea of 'intersectionality' means that it has no theoretical anchor within a broader analysis of social relations. It has been criticised for theoretical vagueness (Knapp 2005), that it underemphasises *class* and fails to look at the social relations of capitalism (Skeggs 2005). It has also been accused of under-theorising power and that it can function as an umbrella term, as a rhetorical device and a *consensus signifying term*, particularly in feminism (Carbin and Edenheim 2013). For others the heterogeneity and theoretical vagueness indicate an openness which accounts for its success (e.g. Davis 2008).

3. Conflating different levels of analysis

Whilst this will be discussed in more detail later in this chapter, the issue of levels can also be linked to the need to be clear about the object of analysis (what is intersecting: Anthias 2013a). This means being clear about different foci and methods, noted by many writers (including McCall 2001; Choo and Ferree 2010; Anthias 1998b, 2013a). These might produce different understandings of what is intersecting in terms of the object of analysis. In addition, there is also the issue of how they manifest themselves in different societal arenas such as the organisational, the representational, the intersubjective and the experiential (Anthias 1998b, 2013a) in terms of their simultaneity and co-production. It needs to be attentive to distinctive discourses and practices of representation within legal and other systems (such as auditing, policing and disciplining systems), and how they change.

4. Proliferating and individualising oppression: erasing systematic inequalities

This raises the issue of a potentially endless list of 'hybrid' crosscutting categories (such as black working class, young white lesbian, white working-class young man, poor racialised disabled woman, etc.). One unintentional effect might be that producing potentially endless configurations of difference could erase from view systematic forms of oppression. In addition, it is difficult to see how mobilisation can take place with an individualised focus on difference or oppression. This relates to the political level (see Chapter 7). It's important therefore to look at how outcomes are produced in time and place for specific categories of regulation by the state, and not just at the proliferation of sub-categories – mirroring the problems found in the notions of diversity and super-diversity (see Chapter 2). Attending to structural and discursive processes, whose targets may shift and change, and which are taken up in different ways by subjects, will not individualise. It will help uncover the processes and outcomes at work over time and place. A focus heuristically on distinctive fora of social control and power, as in Collins' idea of the matrix of oppression (1990), and somewhat differently in my own work on the different societal arenas that can be identified as requiring investigation in terms of their role in relations of subordination and hierarchy making (Anthias 1998a, 2013a), can avoid individualisation and homogenisation. Some of these ideas will be developed further in this chapter.

5. The problem of equivalence or flattening

This relates to treating socially salient categories of difference as equivalent domains in terms of power and as always equally important. Avoiding homologising and flattening them (Erel et al. 2011) also raises the question about differences that matter, when, where and how. There is a need to look at their salience in a temporal and contextual way. Not all social categories are equally salient, all the time. Ferree (2009, p. 8) too notes that

> It is an empirical matter in any given context to see what concepts are important to the configuration of inequalities in discourse and in practice.

Treating them as *emergent* rather than given would be the correct way of dealing with this. But even here there is the issue of the potentially invisible categorisations at play once we start the analysis with categories rather than processes. Therefore, the methodological principle of starting with place and context, as I argue later in this chapter, is one way to uncover such invisibilities.

6. The listing of a priori and taken for granted differences

This involves treating categories as ahistorical and taken for granted, leading to their essentialisation (rather than seeing them as constructed in social practice). These are often reduced to identities that intersect (potentially infinite). It is important not to fix these as they would mimic the essentialised categories we seek to overcome with an intersectional lens. However, such hybrid categories may be required in any social policy interventions which apply to groupings of

70 Assembling places

subjects. The challenge here is to retain an intersectional lens in addressing them rather than taking them as given across time and space.

7. Universal applicability or only applicable to marginalised groups?

It's not possible to retain the view that an intersectional lens can only be applied to specific disadvantaged groups (such as black women in the Global North), which in any case is already crosscut by sexuality, generation and class (amongst others) across time and space. A framing must also be able to look at how relations of power are manifested in the production of privilege as well as disadvantage and therefore be applied to dominant groupings. I believe a concern with intersectional relations as contradictory *as well as* reinforcing is important – in other words we need to look at what categories *do*, when they coalesce, in nuanced ways, which I take up with a translocational lens (discussed already in Chapter 1, and which I will return to later in the chapter).

This is by no means an exhaustive list but indicative of some of the important issues raised in both sympathetic and less sympathetic commentaries.

Intersectionality: a heuristic?

The view that intersectionality is a heuristic device (see Anthias 1998a) rather than a theory is now accepted by many writers in the field, as noted earlier. Some have taken issue with this on the grounds that it demotes work produced by black women, mentioned earlier. However, to my mind, treating it as a heuristic device flags its strength. It signals the formation of concepts in process and that they are never finished – a position most forcefully made by Carastathis (2016), drawing on Crenshaw's idea of intersectionality as provisional. In the light of this, the position raised earlier about the lack of a theoretical undergirding is demanding a particular conception of intersectionality. It also demands a conception of theory characterised by a set of systematic and connected concepts (as a given apparatus) that can deliver understandings of the world. This retains a view of theory as being already made, rather than evolving. Prima facie, intersectionality doesn't have a set of distinctive concepts which point to a modus operandi, that is, the social dynamics at play, in any uniform or agreed way. As such it does not *require* any specific theoretical or political position, nor any specific research methods (although see my discussion later).

We can draw on a range of traditions of analysis, such as those found in the work of critical theorists, critical race theorists or post-colonial feminists and the utilisation of Marx, Foucault, Bourdieu and many others, depending on our own theoretical preferences. It can be married to Marxist social reproduction theory (e.g. see Ferguson 2016), as well as, more problematically, to liberal notions of diversity (Dhawan and Varela 2016). For example, Pat Hill Collins (1990, 2019) synthesises a situated knowledge approach with a Foucauldian framing, and Dorothy Smith

(2005) develops a Marxist and phenomenological synthesis with her 'institutional ethnography'. There is no prescriptive foundational theory of social relations that can be glued onto every intersectional analysis. Using Marxism, for example, intersectional research might seek to address specifically issues of the intersections between the mode of production, relations of production and the kinds of ideological representations and categories these relate to. This requires, however, a form of Marxist or political economy analysis that refuses the types of economic determinism of early third wave socialist feminism (e.g. found in the domestic labour debate). It can also be aligned with a more hermeneutic and social action centred Weberian or phenomenological analysis that looks more at how individuals produce and reproduce social, symbolic and normative systems of difference at the intersection of categorial differences and practices, in terms of the types of subjectivities or identifications produced (see Staunes (2003) for an argument about the need for a theorisation of subjectivity within an intersectional framing). Versions that refuse the existence of separate categories, and therefore treat them always and at all levels as mutually constituted (e.g. Carastathis 2016), cannot then look at the work that they do as forms of governmentality, or treat some as more salient at times than others. Intersectionality also requires the adoption of a situated gaze which does not privilege one standpoint, is relational rather than relativist, and which is anti-essentialist and anti-determinist as well as concerned with forms of inequality. The idea of a field of study (see Collins and Bilge (2016) for a view about what characterises this field of study) marries well with this view.

The question of the importance of context and the need to attend to broader relations of power, avoiding a diversity paradigm and the listing of differences (even hybrid ones), which might repeat the essentialising categories intersectionality seeks to undermine, I take to be prima facie elements of all intersectional research, whatever its theoretical preferences or undergirding. Hence, I would argue that it sits diametrically opposite to diversity paradigms, such as diversity management and super-diversity (see Chapter 6). Intersectionality requires a minimal acceptance of these principles.

The whitening of intersectionality and coloniality

Intersectionality has been particularly rooted in a decolonial exercise, contesting hegemonic forms of power production and seeking to make the voices of the oppressed and their situated knowledge central, giving them agency. The pioneering work of Collins is central here drawing already on a tradition of situated analysis which goes back to Marx (1859), Mannheim (1929/1936), phenomenology, and found in the work of feminists such as Harding (2004) and Smith (2005). With this in mind, it's important to attend to those voices which claim that intersectionality has been 'whitened' on its 'travels', that there has been a colonisation of the work of black feminists and writers (e.g. Bilge 2013), and that it has become a liberal framing for academic knowledge production that betrays its more radical anti-racist and transformative origins and potential.

72 Assembling places

Accusations have been levelled against some 'white' academic feminists that they have 'colonised' the concept so that it has become unrecognisable (e.g. see Tomlinson 2013). A particularly powerful critique is that there has been a neo-liberal commodification of the concept, so that both in the academy and in the political arena (Jibrin and Salem 2015) intersectionality has become partly another way of talking about 'diversity', itself a very troubling framing for social correction (see Chapter 6). However, the idea of its 'whitening' has often been conflated with the positions and identities of those who use intersectionality. Whilst the argument of neo-liberal commodification is powerful, to single out feminists based on their positions as academics, or their theoretical/philosophical interrogations of the concept, or as inhabiting white skins, is another matter altogether, which would make intersectionality an identitarian prerogative.

Questions can be raised, such as: has it been colonised by the white academy? Does it act as an obfuscation and marginalise the forms of subordination faced by black women? Do European versions erase the power of race and racism? Should it be restricted to work by and about black feminists? My view, and I will be brief, is that all these questions require an examination of the ways in which intersectionality is being used and the authoritative voices within it. In relation to the latter, if the work of black feminists has been side-lined, there is very little evidence that can be found at the public level. Celebrations, particularly of the contributions of Crenshaw and Collins abound in special journal issues, conferences, symposia and citations. It may have travelled to the European academy and left its own mark with a concern with a range of policy and conceptual issues whose roots lie within a more European tradition of thought and struggle, but I see this as inevitable and welcome. Those arguments that focus on origins (Carastathis 2016) I believe to be misplaced (see also Nash (2016) on intersectional originalism) since all concepts must and do transform over time and different contexts. Indeed, the history of the notion of intersectionality is not a clear cut or unilinear one, with many different beginnings that can be 'invented'. I will therefore not engage with the issue 'who started it' or 'who has the right to use it' and 'who it should be about' that I see as actually inimical to intersectionality itself.

Indeed, one could point to how the contributions of non–US based scholars, particularly in the Global South, have been relatively side-lined. Accusations have been made that intersectionality reproduces forms of coloniality through failing to attend to the contributions of Latin American and post-colonial feminists. The second arm of this critique is that the whole intersectional canon is itself problematic given its Americo-centric focus on black women in the US constructed as the paradigmatic subject of intersectional oppression. This neglects black women worldwide, where they occupy a range of positions in different countries. Dhawan and Varela's (2016) accusation about its *post-coloniality* centre on the argument, precisely, that contributions from the Global South have been ignored. The concern with class, gender and race issues amongst feminists has a long history in the Global South, as they argue, concomitant with, if not

Assembling places **73**

before, US black feminists began developing intersectional framings. However, as they rightly state, referring also to its liberal appropriation, this should not mean the rejection of intersectionality but rather that we rethink it, acknowledging its post-coloniality and moving away from theoretical identitarianism and political non-performativity. One problem with their analysis, however, is the equation of diversity with intersectional approaches and they wish to salvage both from the teeth of liberal knowledge production. Whilst I believe that 'diversity' notions are particularly problematic (see Chapter 2 and Chapter 6), as intersectionality is concerned with the relationality of difference and power, and unequal social outcomes, it is quite different. However, it is true that intersectionality has difficulties relating to its dominant groupist and identity-based focus. The 'categories' it plays with are laden with such difficulties. Clearly it has also suffered from a nation-based and Westo-centric focus (as indeed has much social science and feminist knowledge production).

Translocational intersectionality

Whilst I have drawn attention to some key pitfalls and quandaries, this has been done in order to begin to demonstrate how we can bypass them. It's important to recognise the increasing development of intersectional approaches, characterised by a sensitising and heuristic lens or prism. Whilst the political programmatic of the intersectional framework, from its inception, has critiqued hegemonic knowledge production and sought thereby to give a voice to the complex inequalities faced particularly by black and minority ethnic women, and intervene in public policies, it is impossible that this project lies outside further engaging with the pursuit of analytical tools. This can be done in many ways and from different situated gazes and cannot be restricted to any category of person or group. Indeed, one of the backlashes against intersectionality is that it has been accused of failing to engage with oppressions faced by women who are exposed to anti-Semitism, and in some public social media it has been accused of being anti-Semitic because of this.[3] The equation of Jewishness with whiteness and privilege has meant that the anti-Semitism faced by Jewish women has often been disregarded, and more than this, refused. For example, in a recent article there is a claim that Jewishness and whiteness have become so imbricated in each other, that many feminists argue that by definition Jewish women cannot be oppressed, and can only be seen as 'white' oppressors (Schraub 2019).

The prime conceptual innovation of intersectional frames lies in the idea of how oppressions are not only multiple but that they are mutually constituted. If this is the case individual subjects experience them in highly contextual and situational ways in all their simultaneity and co-constitution – this is but a starting point for the shift against positivistic and essentialised positions. Such a position requires greater specification as this can erase separate categories or collapse them into each other. To what extent is it possible to talk about intersections without already working out the role that separate categories of difference play

74 Assembling places

at different levels of analysis? Methodologically it asks us to interrogate identities and inequalities in a nuanced and complex contextual way. The critique presented earlier signals how *not* to undertake this exercise rather than being a critique of the intersectional enterprise itself. With this view in mind I will present what I see as a way forward.

Translocational intersectionality (contextual, situated, historicised, temporal and scalar) builds on my work on translocational positionality (2002, 2008, 2009, see also Anthias 2013a, 2013c) and was introduced in Chapter 1 as a tool of analysis that focuses on *places* rather than identities in the dual sense of *place as locale* and *place as hierarchical location*. It also offers an analytical and methodological lens distinguishing different levels of analysis and different societal arenas. I regard this as a frame for addressing the problem that I set out with in this chapter: how to reconcile the engagement with separate categories alongside the idea of their mutual constitution. In the following sections, I will provide what I regard to be a way forward through presenting a multi-level framing, discussing different levels of analysis and different societal arenas for investigating the operations of power around categories and their intersections.

Mutual constitution and categorial separation: a multi-level approach

I already noted that one of the central dilemmas of intersectionality lies in the idea of the *different modes of oppression* at play requiring the analytical distinctiveness of the social locations of gender, sexuality, race and class amongst others, and concomitantly, in the central idea of their *mutual constitution*. How can the two ideas – of simultaneously recognising the separate effectivity of each division *and* their mutual constitution be upheld? Defining intersectionality in terms of the 'mutual constitution' of social categories seems to be a formulation that lends itself to this problem.

I argue that it is difficult to deny that separate categories *operate* in the social landscape in socio-spatial and temporal ways. I do not think that intersectionality or any heuristic can dispense with the recognition of the saliency of categories since these, as argued in Chapters 1 and 2 are not only terms used in day-to-day life that inform our understandings of the world, but they involve specific discourses and systems of control and governmentality. A recognition of the specific technologies of power relating to the categories of difference is central. However, at this level there are aspects which they share, and which set them apart. They involve configurations that mark our bodies and our lives, albeit in different ways, using different stigmata as they unfold in time and place and as they collide, and in terms of what they *do* to each other. They are ways of marking and hailing (or interpellating to use Althusser's term (1971)) that derive from the socio-political nexus. They construct, hail, tarnish and violate different bodies even when these are singular physical bodies. As such these categories come from *somewhere, which co-produces them, but this somewhere is multifaceted and may* produce contradictory effects; one marking may efface or be overlaid on the other(s). But they are produced with *different* figurations, and different imperatives, on the one hand, and *similarities* on the other. In Chapter 2, I argued that the commonalities can be found in the ways they naturalise, collectivise, binarise, hierarchise and inferiorise; they are building blocks for unequal resource allocation which operates intersectionally. They come from the same underbelly. But their marks (and masks) are different. The mark of the location of gender and the mark of the location of race or class entail different modalities of power constructing simultaneously the gendered and racialised body which then emerges as a phantom out of this panoply of effectivities: it was never already there. This artefact – of the phoenix arising from the ashes of the constellations of determinations – is a powerful tool for exploitation, ordering, containment and regulation. It works simultaneously on the person, marking them in all these ways at the same time, and in different places and times. Such a cacophony of signs given off by the marks produces specific and changing effects.

In order to explore further the notion of mutual constitution, and as a way of resolving the dilemma of recognising the effectivity of the separate categories, on the one hand, and stipulating how they are mutually constituted, on the other, I explore the issue of different analytical levels: the level of social ontologies; the level of social categories and the level of concrete social relations (see also Anthias 2013a).

I propose that 'mutual constitution', where the determinations come together, pertains primarily to the level of concrete relations. The other levels – social ontologies and categories – operate as different but related technologies of power (see Chapter 2 for the commonalities of central categories of difference). Refusing gender, race and class categories as distinct is incoherent if you do not also refuse hybrid ones (such as white or black women). Thus, mutual constitution can mean that we unlock what they do in the field of power and resource allocation, simultaneously entangled in space and time. In concrete relations they cannot be disassembled in terms of their effects, but we can research the processes involved. The social relations always produce subjects which are both strewn across the places and can be also looked at through the grid or lens of any one of them, at the same time, depending on the level of analysis. Social relations are never *lived* separately as classed or raced, although subjects can point to the effectivities separately. For example, domestic violence perpetrated by a man may be regarded as gender violence, race violence or a combinatory depending on the dynamics at play, the positionalities involved and the situated gaze.

This position is not prescriptive but a starting point for investigation. The issue, therefore, is not that social divisions are always mutually constitutive in the same way. Instead, *mutual constitution is itself a heuristic* that enables investigation: it asks '*what do they do to each other and what does this reveal about the operations of power?*' The salient work of each one of the categories in addressing specific issues such as income levels, violence and so on needs to be looked at contextually and situationally.

76 Assembling places

As Nash also argues they

> utilize differing technologies of categorization and control, disciplining bodies in distinctive ways, and coalescing (or colliding) in particular formations in certain historical, social, cultural, representational, legal, and technological moments.
>
> *(2008, p. 13)*

Whilst we can identify narratives, policies and technologies around the different categories, it's also true that at the level of human experience they are embodied in the individual in their combinatory, and there is differential treatment on the basis of how they interrelate. For example, black women and white women are treated differently in employment and they are subjected to different forms of valuation and violence, as are refugees, migrants, those subjected to trafficking (for sex or work), and domestic workers in interplay with their other imputed characteristics.

The important question then becomes not 'what is intersectionality' but '*what is the problem that intersectionality addresses*'? It seems to me the problem relates to the broader field of social stratification and social hierarchy (see Chapter 4) which is the problem of inequality, inferiorisation and subordination. I have been particularly concerned to reinforce earlier arguments (e.g. see Anthias and Yuval-Davis 1983, 1992) about the problems with an additive and mechanistic model that merely points to pluralist accounts of divisions and identities. However, the 'additive' could denote the discrete workings of each dimension of power alongside others, and could also reference how they act to *reinforce each other in terms of their effects*. Neither of these two possibilities can be presupposed or rejected. This is to recognise that holding marginal or subordinate positions in a range of locations often does lead to the amplification of inequality, and that holding more dominant positions in each one may lead to an amplification of dominant position and power. Thus, whilst the notion of translocational that I presented in Chapter 1 opens the way to understanding how both subordination and hierarchical power can be contradictory, it can also point to how subordinations across categories (and privileges across categories), can be reinforcing. These might appear additive or it may be that what each does to the others appears more complex and variable. For example, whiteness combined with class and minoritisation may at times lead to the invisibilisation of the oppressions faced by East European, Jewish or Roma women. Blackness may lead to the erasure *or* the invisibility of class privilege, and whiteness to the erasure or invisibility of class subordination: since class may 'whiten' or may 'blacken'. In combination with gender, it may exoticise in some cases and demonise in others, depending on the discursive and systemic framework and which category is more socio-temporally salient and powerful. In this way I turn the lens away from what might now be regarded as a sterile argument.

The object of analysis

The first stage in any analysis is a preliminary delineation of the *object* of our analysis – in this case, social ontologies, social categories *or* concrete relations (see also Anthias 2013a). That is, it asks the question: what is that which we see as intersecting – is it the social ontologies – *the different existential spaces in social life* that provide a mapping of 'the order of things', such as sex/gender, ethnicity/race and class as well as others; is it the social categories related to them, and how they specify particular *types of human subjects and their attributions and characteristics as a marking of the bodies that fill them*; or is it the ways these play out at the concrete level of analysis in terms of *experiences, intersubjectivities, organisational forms and representations*, where the relationality of the categories *is lived and embodied*? In other words the levels of ontologies and categories are part of the fabric, and appear as more doxic. However, both these levels are articulated within each arena of the concrete also, but the ways they become effective for individuals or groupings of individuals is through their combinatories or 'articulation' in the sense that Stuart Hall (1996) used the term, that is, as non-essential and situated relations at conjunctures, where there is a meeting point of effectivities *in concrete relations of practice*.

Most self-conscious intersectional research is done at the level of the concrete, that is, the work is concerned with delineating the practices and experiences of people and the operations of representations and procedures in organisations – such as factories and schools. In my work I have stressed the importance of analysing at the processual level (e.g. see Anthias 1998a), within concrete relations and therefore the *processes* of inequality making (which is always a work in progress) within what I refer to as different but interrelated societal arenas (the organisational, representational, intersubjective and experiential), *collecting narratives of people, investigating procedural rules, unpacking representations and examining practices*. This modifies Dorothy Smith's ideas about institutional ethnography which is more ethnomethodological in focus than the one I am suggesting. In all these ways we can interrogate *broader social relations of power*. This also entails attention to temporality and to *historicity* which looks at them as processual and changing within a time and scale framework, recognising that, whilst emergent, they bear the traces of the past (allowing us to ask *how*) and give a nod to their future. Such a focus does not displace the idea of a contextual or situational analysis but adds a focus on the diachronic and the dynamic, rather than remaining at the level of synchronicity. Methodologically, this suggests the importance of *historical* research as well as building into the research the collection of narratives and representations *about time and place*, and also looking at practices and procedures *over time and place*. One important aspect is that we avoid reproducing the categories of governmentality by starting with them at face value.

In the following sections I distinguish between three different ways of constructing the *object* of an intersectional analysis: the level of social ontologies of difference, the level of social categories of difference and the level of concrete

78 Assembling places

relations of difference. *Social ontologies* construct places in the 'order of things' and underpin social categories of the population and boundaries of differentiation. *Social categories* determine the ways places are to be filled by *specific* subjects using changing criteria for the purposes of governmentality, exploitation and differential exclusions. They are in a dialogical relationship with *concrete relations of practice*, in different societal domains or arenas in interplay with systems of economic power, political strategies by powerful social groups, and their resistance on the ground.

1. Social ontologies of difference, and doxa

Postulating social ontologies involves a *heuristic device* (Anthias 1998b). Social ontologies, in my use of the term, can be distinguished from the presupposition that there are actual ontologies (that operate at a pre-discursive level), and distinguished from phrases such as 'the ontological turn' (found particularly in critical anthropology and geography). The notion of social ontologies allows us to examine the construction of *places of beingness* which are *distinct* from one another in relation to gender/sex, ethnos/nation/race and class, for example, as historical products of social relations. These relate to different spheres of practice in social life that come to be seen as *sui generis* – this is particularly the case for sex and gender (see Chapter 5). At this level of abstraction gender, ethnicity, 'race' and class, for example, relate to practices and conceptions about different realms in the world, or ways the world is organised. As such they act like maps, pointing to where sets of relations are situated, manifested in categories and materialised in concrete relations (Anthias 2013a).

Social ontologies are not necessarily fixed and may shift over time with changing configurations of power and struggles, and in relation to contestations and negotiations within which they construct the spaces or grids of difference. In other words, they too are subject to the effectivities of struggles and the agonistic nature of social life. However, such social ontologies, although not static, are relatively stable. For example, although recent developments in relation to transgendering in the West (discussed further in Chapter 5), reflect changing norms about the crossing of gender boundaries, and destabilise the social ontological basis of sex/gender, they have not dismantled its hegemonic framing (see the discussion later in this chapter).

Although social ontologies may have a common grounding in sociality, as well as being tied to the hegemonic Weltanschauung of different historical periods, they can be regarded as analytically distinct, rather than mutually constituted. As social ontologies of gender/sex, ethnos and class hail different spaces of the social they can be referred to as *doxa* in the ways that Bourdieu (1980) uses the term (i.e. as taken for granted understandings of the world), and as dogma, inhabiting in the Freudian sense also the unconscious operations of difference as power. Examining the doxa around social ontologies can enable us to analyse how these emerge out of forms of practice.

Assembling places **79**

Gender/sex references the social ontological space of the social organisation of sexual identity, sexuality, biological reproduction and sexual difference (for the present purposes I have placed gender and sexuality together as I see them as occupying the same social existential base but see Chapter 5).

Ethnos constitutes the social ontological space of collective life as it demarcates the social organisation of sociality related to the production or reproduction of originary groups (on the basis of origins or destinies or as breeding groups see St. Louis 2014).

Class at this level is much more difficult to pinpoint. Class is very much a modern social ontology that has its roots in modern capitalism, with some carrying over of previous modes of production (for an examination of some of the difficulties of the class category see Chapter 4). It relates to the sphere of the organisation of economic life and to the production and reproduction of the means for life itself; at the most basic level modes for subsistence and beyond (see Anthias 1991, 1998b, 2013a; Anthias and Yuval-Davis 1992 for other versions of these delineations).

2. Social categories or 'groupings' of the population

Where the object of analysis is social *categories* of difference, this leads to asking questions about how the places relating to social ontologies are to be filled by embodied subjects who are deemed to possess the appropriate competencies or characteristics. It is here that 'groupings' of the population are embryonically hailed, that is, through the specification of attributions (characteristics are needed to occupy the gender category which sets up *internal* (usually binary) boundaries). Attributes are specified for inhabiting the categorial places, thereby constructing naturalised and collectivised subjects. This relates to notions of being male or female, a 'proper' man or 'proper' woman, trans, queer, bi and so on; never mind that people never actually belong to any *one* group since they are also ordered in different ways into the other groups that are undergirded by the social ontologies. Social categories *naturalise, collectivise and essentialise* social relations. The difference postulated by the categories is not value free. Indeed, the construction of difference is usually accompanied not only by a relative value, on a pole of negative to positive. The categories mark and brand *people who fill the places and hierarchise them within the places*: the social order of things, already laid out by social ontologies becomes converted or translated into an ordering of attributes, and the bodies of those who are to fill the places become marked and hailed. Sometimes this involves the allocation of specific social roles, such as occupational (caste and class) or familial (gender) but, generally, these are accompanied by a pecking order of roles and places within each of the categorial formations.

Categorial formations of difference are being challenged increasingly by changing notions of gender or race fixities, however, or who can fill the places. Therefore, it's important to recognise that these also can shift over time. For

80 Assembling places

example, *gender* constructions, treated as emanating from biological differences, are part of common understandings. This can be challenged by the idea that gender doesn't require biological accoutrements but rather is based on identification, pain and desire, or even self-declaration (something the transgender movement has argued for). Here, there is the question about how people are allocated to a category, that is, the criteria involved (such as sex difference, sexuality, ethnicity, race, age, height, educational achievements, appearance, colour of eyes, etc.), as well as the mode by which this is done. We might want to explore not only what incipient groups are hailed, but also how they take up identities as well as how these change over time.

Social categories are at one and the same time mimetic of social ontologies but fluid and changeable in their meanings, as well as being more apparent. Some more specific categories may be attached to ontologies of ethnos or class For example, refugee and migrant categories are specific ways of constructing national borders and boundaries, as well as class boundaries relating to roles in production. Alternative narrations can produce different allocations of people to categories. As such they can be changeable; for example, the binary nature of the categories of gender and ethnicity is currently being challenged and there are evolving ideas about who can fill specific gender categories as well as the emergence of new ones. In the first case, we can cite the example of transgendering (discussed later) and, in the second, we can refer to multiculturality such as those found in ideas and claims relating to diaspora, hybridity and interculturality (see Anthias 2009).

The categorising of people should not be elided with population categories/ groupings as they relate to concrete social life. For example, the claims that people make, and their practices, may be different to the ways they have been sorted out in terms of auditing systems of the state, or regulatory technologies, or in terms of social representations at any particular point in time and space. A person may claim they are British but may be regarded as a member of an ethnic minority that is not eligible to be British. Placing people into categories involves a sorting exercise which can be done in different ways, and people themselves may not always act or identify in ways denoted by these.

Sex/gender categories, in addition to marking particular bodies, also set out the *social organisation and reproduction* of sexual difference (a specification of the social ontology), in terms of an internal binary (male/female), and inscribe the relationality in terms of intimacy and mutuality, involving desire, procreation and cohabitation. Sexual and gender relations of the two halves of the binary divided are constituted as dependent on a common purpose given by the centrality of the organisation of reproduction, and sexuality. Never mind that in concrete relations, forms of political identity and commonality amongst both men and women have emerged, and the antagonism and hostility (as well as violence) has been as central as that of mutuality and harmony.

Gender has, in fact, constituted a particularly biologically driven social category in the modern world, where sexual difference – that is being born with

Assembling places **81**

particular sexual characteristics such as genitalia – becomes the originary point for the formation of a particular sphere of social life relating to reproduction and sexuality. The category is not based around a homology between sexual difference and sexual preference (e.g. in Ancient Greece, there was an expectation of homo-erotic relationships as 'normal' within higher social groups) but *heteronormativity* is central in the modern world.

In the case of *ethnos* or ethnic, national and racial categories, there is a specification of shared characteristics and solidarity of the persons within a 'group'. Between groups such relations are often based on closure, avoidance and contestation. To put it simply, gender assumes a binary difference that is essentially intimate and profitable to people as individuals, whereas ethnic and race categories assume a binary which is essentially threatening and antagonistic if the people are constructed or construct themselves in terms of belonging to different collectives. The ethnic boundary can be quite permissive or porous as people might be able to marry into it or gain acceptance if they can demonstrate the right credentials for membership (e.g. by adopting the religion or way of life). These credentials have to be evidenced, unlike for those who are born into the group through either matrilineal or patrilineal descent.

We should distinguish between ethnic and race categorisations although these are opportunistic and changeable. The first is focused more on ideas of a shared past and future, organised around ideas about territorial or cultural origin as an important solidary-making foundation. The second is organised more around ideas of generic biological or cultural difference (which itself is imputed to biological difference), or inherited characteristics (relating e.g. to ideas of racial types or the proclivities of different 'groupings'). The ethnic category is not always dependent on an idea of the physical properties of the potential individuals that will come to occupy this existential basis, but rather usually where and to what they were born and on related commonalities of culture and language. This can become deterministic and biologised under different conditions (e.g. in struggles between ethnic groups that lead to genocide or violent conflict, or through economic and political interests). Although there is a tendency to biologise ethnic categories which have emerged as part of this process, exclusion and distinction/difference are the characteristic premises of both ethnic and racial categories with the latter being particularly inferiorising, dehumanising and violent (see Chapter 6).

Class is essentially collective like ethnos and involves closure by the more privileged, and usurpation by the less privileged. Who fills the places of class is also less prescriptive and the border guards more plastic. As discussed further in Chapter 4, class references a state of being at a given point in time (if you acquire an education you can more easily change your class), and as 'achieved', unlike gender and race/ethnicity that are treated as more fixed and stable. Class is usually not a juridico-legal category, like gender and ethnicity. Concomitantly, although in modern societies gender and race inequality and unequal treatment are rife, there are discourses and practices which are dedicated to correcting such

82 Assembling places

inequalities (despite their problems). However, it is perfectly legitimate to discriminate in class terms (in terms of wages, wealth, educational access – private schooling – and so on). Indeed, such discrimination is written into the very category. As pointed out in Chapter 1, a crucial difference between class and the divisions of gender and ethnicity lies in the *acceptance of inequality outcomes* as a prima facie characteristic of class, often even by the people themselves. In other words, class is directly dependent on inequality whereas for gender and ethnicity the difference or boundary is what matters, and inequality is treated as an outcome of an essential binary, but not embedded in the boundary as a matter of definition.

Although class, ethnicity/race and sex/gender categories (as well as others such as ability/disability) are not equivalent they have commonalities (as well as differences) which I discussed in Chapter 2. They all involve boundary-making and hierarchy-making features. They have tended to construct binary versions of difference and identity (e.g. you are either male or female, ethnic insider/ outsider, white or black/brown, rich/poor (noting of course that in practice this is more complex). They homogenise within and they construct collective attributions: traits, tendencies, proclivities and so on. How the categories appear in discourse and practice will differ over time and how they manifest themselves as categories of action in local and specific contexts and in terms of peoples' lives will also vary. Investigating categories over time and place draws attention to context, meaning and variability. For example, the categories produced in social policy and in auditing bodies of the state will differ according to political projects. Different ethnic categories are found in censuses, or in migration law, for example, in terms of who counts as an economic migrant or a refugee, or who is entitled to citizenship. Pat Hill Collins (1990) has also pointed to gender, race and class being discursive means in the exercise of power, using a Foucauldian framework.

As with social ontologies, categories function separately as salient aspects of discourse and practice (i.e. they operate at the concrete level also, and these categories can also be synthetic e.g. 'black women'), for example in auditing systems of the state or state provisions relating to taxation or welfare. Ethnic categories, at the concrete level, are policed in relation to citizenship more explicitly, unlike gender categories, although there may be specific gendering in intersectional ways in terms of family reunification, motherhood or different policies and outcomes faced by black or migrant women. Therefore, in *concrete relations*, the policing of ethnic minority men may be different to that of ethnic minority women (see Yuval-Davis et al. 2005). This means that *hybrid categories* are already always being *made or unmade* out of the foundational work of social ontologies and discrete categories. These 'hybrid' categories are already found within the governmental apparatus, on the one hand, and in the more corrective dispensations of the state apparatus as modes of control, management and regulation, for example, through tax credits for single parents in part-time work or nursery provision for poorer women. These categories also exist in intersectional ways already in people's minds and within everyday rules and assumptions, made by the police, social workers, teachers, employers, the media and so on.

This last example does not detract from the fact that the categories involve distinctive technologies. Some at different times are formal juridico-legal categories (such as ethnicity or race, for example) or gender. Others are not, such as class. However, their irreducibility does not mean that they operate as stand-alone categories in the realm of social practice. A *dialogical* formulation of the categories can provide a specificity to the categories whilst recognising their interpenetration at the level of practice.

3. Concrete social relations and the everyday

I will now turn to the issue of concrete relations that involve the production of social outcomes of hierarchical social location and inequality in concrete relations of the everyday within different *societal arenas* (see later in this chapter). Sex/gender (and associated heteronormativities and sexualities), ethnicity/race/nation (and associated parameters of migration and otherness) and class (and associated processes of precarity and vulnerability found e.g. in surplus populations of labour) constitute systems of power/domination (Collins 1993; Spivak 1994). They are facilitated through technologies of hailing and naming (such as those imposed by states and legal systems). However, none of them function in a coherent manner, are fully effective or mutually exclusive. All individuals occupy places in each one of them, although there is a question mark about whether the class category can be applied to the long-term unemployed or those outside the labour market (found in ideas of the underclass). However, although social categories are analytically distinct, within concrete social relations they produce their effectivities intersectionally, that is, they operate in relation to each other and broader social processes, but not in any a priori fashion.

The level of the intersectional, therefore, relates particularly to the level of concrete social relations. Categorisations, however salient, cannot be immediately translatable in terms of the *concrete relations* that people find themselves in. These are not outcomes only of the salience of these categorisations, but of their intersections and of their embeddedness within a complex array of social relations, located within different arenas of social life and within temporal and spatial contexts. At the level of structural/organisational outcomes, as well as outcomes for human subjects, relating, for example, to forms of identity, it is difficult to unpack where they originate from because in *practice* they are mutually interactive. To be able to point to the differential saliency of one over others and what their '*doing*' entails, requires an excavation through narratives and practices within different societal arenas. This involves *the doing of intersectional work*, not just to describe inequalities as end products, but to point to what systems of power are propagated through social categories in time and place.

In addition, in concrete relations these categorisations may be taken up by subject positions in different ways. The claims that people themselves make and

84 Assembling places

their own resistance to the processes may vary greatly. For example, some of the claims and identifications may be seen as *forms of resistance* – for instance, claiming ethnic difference for purposes of solidarity or for special treatment, or claiming being 'black' as a mode of struggle, or using the disability label (Oliver 1995). Therefore, these claims by people in their political struggles are not only the product of external constructions and social attributions which lead to what Bourdieu (1986) calls habitus or a set of predispositions. Identity claims are not only forms of closure and inclusion but are also modes of organisation and resistance which belie the deterministic nature of the 'habitus'.

Concrete relations of hierarchy are always intersectional, but, as discussed in Chapter 2, are underpinned by social categories that *naturalise, collectivise and essentialise* social relations, and through the workings of processes of *inferiorisation* (stigma, disgust, devaluation, disrespect), as well as *unequal resource allocation*, entailing multiple forms of inequality of access and inequality of outcome. Positions in each modality of difference articulate (both in terms of their constitution and effects) in relation to given places (i.e. in terms of their spatiality) and times (in terms of their temporality) in a variable way. Social placement in the categories, single axis or hybridised/synthetic, produces fissures and contradictions. Intersecting categories and the concrete relations they appear within do not always lead to either greater subordination or its resolution. They are therefore translocational in two ways: in terms of *locales (combining place, time and scale)* and across them, and in terms of *social location (such as gender etc.)* and across them. For example, in the category of race, the White is dominant over the Black. However, modalities of power relating to class and gender *do* things to this category (and vice versa) which produces hierarchical outcomes for individuals and particular 'groupings' of individuals within broader relations of power in spatio-temporal terms.

What gender, ethnicity, class, disability, citizenship, age and so on *do* to each other is variable, depending on the salience of each one at points in time and place. I gave the example earlier about how White, woman, middle class and Jewish interact in ways that invisibilise racism. It's not possible to break up people in terms of such discrete positions. In some cases, one of these may be more central: for example, where there is an employment penalty for women as opposed to men, or in cases of race hate crimes, or where racism leads to very reduced quality of life. Whilst there are intersections, the effects and the strength or salience of each will vary for individuals. As Guillaumin (1995, p. 107) says we may dispense with categories (referring to the category of race) but they still kill us (quoted in St. Louis 2014).

The level of experience impacts on subjects particularly through material inequalities but also practices relating to moral valuation (Sayer 2005), disgust (Lawler 2005), stigma and so on which are intersectionally constituted. The overall effects for individuals and groups is a result of the ways the separate categories fuse and shape each other at determinate points and in relation to economic and political effectivities. Through these processes, there occurs a

Assembling places **85**

construction of places or positions in the social order of things. These may lead to complex forms of hierarchy across a range of different dimensions, allowing for a range of at times contradictory locations and translocational positionalities which may be transformative. Spaces are opened in this manner for contestation and transformation (see the concluding chapter). These operate in terms of power dynamics in the social field more generally but also in terms of struggle and contestation. They not only pertain to domination but also to contestation and the building of agency. Leah Bassel (2015) has recently reframed this aspect of Pat Hill Collins' work, to show how it engages with a more agonistic intersectional position which can help us to understand the struggles of the 'Sans Papiers' women in France.

When we look beyond individuals to changes in *the places themselves* rather than who fills them, we may find that as women perform more of certain kinds of jobs (as has been historically the case with teaching and clerical work), the spaces of gender become re-aligned. Overall domination by androcentric or heteronormative processes may diminish, or it may be that performing such jobs has the effect of reducing the value of those jobs (as, again, when women became clerks and teachers). It's important when looking at concrete relations, to make a separation between *how* individuals are placed in the intersections, and the *ways* in which the places or the locations are valued and rewarded.

Societal arenas of investigation with different technologies of power

My position involves the methodological principle that concrete social relations involve positionalities and hierarchies as they are embodied and articulated within different societal arenas at specific conjunctures, as noted earlier. Specifying such arenas constitutes a useful methodological principle for an intersectional framing because it sorts out a range of analytically distinct questions that can be addressed in contextual and temporal terms. A researcher can choose which of the societal arenas to focus on depending on the research question. Whilst, as noted earlier, Pat Hill Collins distinguishes different domains of power, such as the structural, the disciplinary, the cultural and the interpersonal, which is concerned with theoretically distinguishing the forms of power, Winker and Degele (2011) argue for an approach which focuses on

> interactions between inequality-creating social structures (i.e. of power relations), symbolic representations and identity constructions that are context-specific, topic-orientated and inextricably linked to social praxis.
> *(p. 54)*

Although these delineations are useful and necessary, I use the term 'societal arenas of investigation' (Anthias 1998b, 2013a) in order to map out some foci for investigation. Each arena acts as a context (or 'social field', Bourdieu 1990)

86 Assembling places

for the others. However, unlike Bourdieu's notion of field, the notion of 'societal arena' is a heuristic (Anthias 1998b, 2013a). It enables a comparison of how the social categories operate and intersect in terms of different foci. This is also not equivalent to systems or domain-based approaches (e.g. Layder 2006; Walby 2007).

In brief we can delineate the following societal arenas:

Organisational: This focuses on forms of organisational structure: for example, family structures and networks, employment, educational systems, political and legal systems, the state apparatus and systems of policing and surveillance. For example, how are population categories produced and organised within institutional frameworks? In relation to the organisation of work, what are the *procedural* rules of hiring and firing people and different relations of employment, such as for professionals and those in precarity such as within the gig economy?

Representational: This focuses on the images and texts, the documents and information flows around social categorisation/division found within different fora, for example the media, school texts, legal documents, Google searches, film and so on. What are the modes by which these appear? How are they manufactured and disseminated? What are the contents and assumptions in the texts and images? What are the representational rules that are being followed and whose voices are being heard?

Intersubjective: This focuses on encounters: everyday socialities, practices in relation to others, including non-person actors such as the police, the social security system and so on, as well as friendship and social networks, sexuality, bonds of sociality. How are categories produced and reproduced in encounters? How do people struggle against the categories in their social interactions? What are the rules relating to encounters and how is knowledge produced and distributed about the 'rules of the game' in different encounters, some of which are hierarchical (e.g. in the job interview)? Who and how do people get excluded from certain encounters, and how do they act to overcome these forms of closure or exclusion?

Experiential: This focuses on meaning making and the level of the sociality of the affective and the emotional (including the body), and the ways experience gets translated into knowledge. It focuses on how experience is marshalled and produced in specific locatable contexts (say in the workplace, in the neighbourhood and other social spaces). This includes forms of identification, distinction and othering as individual responses and imaginings by individuals relating to perceptions of threat, gain and intimacy.

The markings of different types of human bodies and persons, such as citizen, migrant, refugee, male, female, queer, trans, old, young, abled, disabled, Muslim and so on, have different salience in different organisational settings, and different intersubjective, experiential and representational features in spatio-temporal terms (e.g. see Burikova (2019) on temporality in care work). This has methodological implications for looking at the operation of difference within and across societal arenas, to elicit the complex and at times uneven and contradictory ways in which bordering and hierarchisation occurs. This is an exercise which acknowledges not only the possibly discordant modes in different societal arenas – thus potentially destabilising governmentality as a guarantee, or at least querying its functionalist underpinnings. It also points to the difficulty of treating knowledge production as an innocent exercise. Moreover, it requires going beyond the structure and action framework towards uncovering processes and outcomes in different spatialities or arenas of the social. The narratives yielded by actors when looked at through different organisational structures, and with the lens turned to experience, intersubjectivity and forms of representation, may differ. It is therefore not just a question of acknowledging the importance of a situated gaze (e.g. with the gaze of a black or minority woman, or black working-class man), but also a question of the exigencies found within different organisational and other societal arenas at different times, and how people are positioned within them. For example, talking to an employer of migrants who worries about his or her role in ascertaining their legality will produce a different narrative on the state than when talking about taxation and what should be done about income tax levels, or talking about the levels of migration or diversity they find acceptable. Similarly, the outcomes of inequality as told by subjects in relaying their experiences can be understood, through the lens of the narrational, as an embodied social effect arising partly out of cultural repertoires of meaning, but also framed from within intersubjectively framed power relations and organisational structures. Therefore, intersections work at the level of the societal arenas too since these arenas are never mutually exclusive either in terms of processes or in terms of outcomes for persons.

The arenas, as noted earlier, do not denote separate spheres of relations in a typological way, but are presented as prisms for social research and for social intervention. As tools they signpost social spaces which give rise, potentially, to different and at times competing and contradictory discourses and practices around social categories of difference. But these themselves intersect or inter-relate within broader and shifting conditions and coalitions of power and their contestation in terms of projects and struggles for resources of different types in situated ways. For example, juridico-legal categorisations are particularly important in producing discursive and practical effects within all these spheres. In addition, importance is given to embodied social practices and the narrations of people themselves, as a way of capturing their lived worlds and experiences. The level of the representational, for example, can be analysed both in terms of social practices which entail the production of texts, media, knowledge and so on and in terms of how actors narrate, assimilate, respond and agonistically challenge these in their everyday understandings and actions. Both at the level of theory and the level of political practice such forms of 'mapping' to borrow Crenshaw's

88 Assembling places

term – but going *beyond the margins so we can also look at the centre* – constitute necessary means of entry into understanding and social change.

Since the methodological principles can be outlined in terms of a focus on relations and practices within given places and times rather than on a priori categories, this includes resisting an ethnic lens whilst allowing for the effectivity of ethnicity along lines relating to *how* it is organised, experienced, practised intersubjectively and represented. This means not starting with sorting people into ethnic groups as though this yielded a necessary breakdown of human subjects. Similarly, with gender, it requires looking at how gender operates organisationally, experientially and so on without bracketing women off, in the first place, as objects of investigation although the narrations, say, of women (or/and men) would be objects of investigation. However, some constituencies of disadvantage (or advantage) which are manifest in any given moment (such as migrant domestic workers, or black unemployed women or white male elites) are categories which clearly demand that we investigate, bearing in mind the danger of essentialising and homogenising. The situated knowledge of these women and men gives rise to 'partial truths' that can aid in informing our understanding of the operations of power (Mannheim 1929; Collins 1990, 2019).

At this methodological level, categories become emergent as are their operations, rather than pre-given or starting points of analysis, thereby instantiating the refusal of a priori categories for investigation. This means *we do not start out with studying categories of people* but start with what Dorothy Smith (2005) calls an 'institutional ethnography' at the level of the organisational or other levels, depending on one's problematic, *or* we start with the practices within organisations and their procedures (as Charles Tilly's 1998 work suggests). Here I argue that categories of difference are *emergent* within material social relations and economic and political projects tied to social formations and their forms of governance and governmentality. Not only are they changeable but they are complex and uneven. They have ever-present traces (or hauntings) and configurations with a long historical effectivity that cannot be reduced to an ordering governmentality imperative alone.

Concluding remarks: a translocational lens for intersectionality

A translocational lens aims to enhance a transnationally based intersectional framing that goes beyond a concern with static categories within what has been called a container model of the state (Amelina 2016) or a neo-liberal intersectional framing (Gimenez 2018). It also goes beyond a situated or contextual approach. As argued in Chapter1, the notion of 'translocational' references the level of the *processual and the reinforcing or contradictory articulation of locations* across axes of difference *and* spatio-temporalities. In this way it considers the simultaneity and entanglement of the *places signalled* by categories (such as gender, race, ethnicity, class, sexuality, legality and so on) as well as the ways these become

Assembling places **89**

encoded differently *in place*, that is, across space, time and scale, with a concern with *historicity*.

This clearly goes beyond the situational and contextual, recognising the traces of the past as well as orientations to the future. In such an approach, categories operate at different levels, both analytically distinct (given their different formations as doxa and as technologies of ordering), and they are socially embedded in concrete relations and in terms of social outcomes. Categories therefore cannot be overlaid onto individuals in any singular way since they are simultaneously effective and become salient in their intersections. Nonetheless the *different categorisations* have an important role as taxonomic devices and ordering and bordering processes. Such categorisations are often binary, naturalising and homogenising. They function as modes for resource allocation, hierarchisation and inferiorisation, thereby doing much of the work of inequality making as they become translated within social life and social action. A multi-level analysis moves again beyond a concern with the *contextual* to further reinforce the importance of the diachronic and *historicity*. In my concluding chapter on theory and politics I attempt to look at the politics of translocation.

The ways categories assemble and re-assemble, articulate and entangle is variable. Subordinations can be reinforced but they may also be mitigated. For example, class disadvantage may be mediated by ethnic or race advantage in the experience of everyday life. Whiteness acts relationally to construct feelings of belonging even where there is class exploitation. Co-ethnicity at the level of work can mitigate the experience of subordination or place a gloss over the class relation involved (this is found e.g. where co-ethnic employer and worker construct ties of mutuality despite class exploitation). However, a different note may be found if one is an ethnic minority employer with a white workforce, or a female employer with a male workforce, or a white male worker working for a minority female employer. Similar processes can occur in different ways when social location shifts over time and space, for example with deskilling and with upward or downward social mobility, but these are not merely cross-categorial disparities, they are enmeshed as forms of experience and practice.

The approach I have outlined makes it necessary to rethink traditional approaches to stratification as it treats at its very heart gendered, ethnicised and racialised relations; the experiential, intersubjective, organisational and representational features of these are themselves constitutive of the stratification system. These are spaces where the production and reproduction of valuational and material resource inequalities take place and where relational and antagonistic social relations are embodied and performed.

Recognising that there are new emerging constellations of invisible intersections, it corrects the tendency to single out some at the potential expense of erasing other boundaries and inequalities which might exist but have not been articulated or claimed. It is also able to acknowledge some social locations that are particularly violent and dehumanising, such as those that Agamben (1998) calls 'bare life' referred to already in Chapter 1, with the proviso that individuals

90 Assembling places

cannot fully be reduced to this; even in the direst circumstances they seek ways to contest and challenge.

My next chapter looks particularly at the issue of resources through the lens of the interrogation of class and social stratification. The aim is to further explore how we might want to consider a different and intersectional approach to stratification that doesn't fall into the pitfall of mere multidimensionality, diversity or classification. In the following chapter I therefore interrogate the notion of class and then turn to rethinking class within an intersectional stratification framing.

Notes

1 An internet site on testing intersectionality can be found at www.intersectionalityscore. com/.
2 For what appears an early additive form of intersectionality see Jeffries and Rumsden (1980). See also a recent attempt by stratification theorists to look at categorical inequality interactions (Segal and Savage 2019) which try to take on board some of the arguments made by intersectionality scholars.
3 For a view that intersectionality is anti-Semitic, see e.g. Jewish Journal (2019).

4

HIERARCHISING PLACES

Dilemmas of class and stratification

Introduction: the problem of inequality

As Imogen Tyler notes, 'What is class?' is the wrong question. Instead, she prefers 'what is the problem that "class" describes?' (Tyler 2015, p. 496). Her answer is that it describes inequality. Although this is exactly what it does, it is also exactly what it doesn't do as the risk is that it would thereby reduce all inequality to the workings of class, thereby negating the role of gender and race locations. The same is true of Savage (2015, p. 224) when he says,

> there are numerous ways of examining stratification and inequality which do not require the concept of class. [Yet] it is important for sociologists to retain the term 'class' in order to draw out the way that economic inequalities are implicated in wider social, cultural and political divisions.

Here an equivalence is made between class and economic inequalities whilst alluding, possibly, to forms of stratification analysis that are concerned more with sorting people into already made classification schemes, an accusation levelled at stratification theorists (Adkins and Skeggs 2005). Whilst I am concerned with inequality beyond (but not outside) class, I do not interpret this as meaning a mode of classifying people but rather a way of understanding the social relations of hierarchical ordering and inequality. Bourdieu, on the other hand, flags struggles over classification in relation to class. Although this is a component it is not the primary modality of class. Struggles over redistribution are key to class formation. However, this does not mean retaining the dualism implicit in Nancy Fraser's distinction between representational and redistributional struggles (1997, see also Alcoff 2006). This is because struggles over representation are also struggles of redistribution if we treat representation as a component of resources: how

92 Hierarchising places

a social group is represented is a modality of distribution and resource allocation. In Chapter 1 and Chapter 2, I talked about the marking of places and the branding of places (some prefer to talk about stigma e.g. Tyler 2015). However, the notion of branding that I use allows privileged places also to be marked rather than stigmatised (however, note the Greek word *stigma* means marking or branding, and does not necessarily carry the same negative connotations as in English).

Currently there is a great deal of discussion around class and inequalities. Thomas Piketty (and his colleagues) has referred to 'the current malaise of extreme and worsening inequality' (Piketty 2014). Similar concerns are also voiced in the work of Tony Atkinson (2015), Joseph Stiglitz (2012) and Danny Dorling (2014), amongst others. These concerns have reopened the debate on class inequalities and capitalism with much at times heated discussion on how to redress such inequalities at the policy level. There have been some important attempts to chart new social groups and inequalities, particularly economic, and offer ways in which they can be corrected in capitalist societies, to some extent using Marx's analysis as a starting point, if not an end-point (e.g. Standing 2011). Class discussions are prominent in public debate around the work of thinkers who have been prompted by austerity and its consequences, but also because of growing understandings of the failures of policies to generate higher forms of social mobility and equality. This is at odds with the decline in interest in class over the years and the proliferation of work around gender and race inequalities. In this chapter I try to locate class within the understanding of inequality and stratification in a translocational intersectional way. This is particularly important as class has been a relatively ghostly figure in such work.

The work of Pierre Bourdieu (1979, 1986) has been important for some time in broadening the debate away from the purely economic with a significant and influential corpus of academic work in sociology which uses his framework. This has centred particularly on different forms of capital. Important concepts include 'class habitus', and cultural forms of social distinction. This corpus of work includes the work of Mike Savage and his associates in the UK, who have devised a heavily debated new class schema (Savage et al. 2013) which uses various non-economic indicators (with a focus particularly on cultural capital) to assign people to different social strata. This has both its admirers and detractors (e.g. see Bradley (2014) for a critique). Bourdieu's work has also inspired others such as Michelle Lamont (e.g. see her article on Bourdieu (Lamont 2012)), who develops a focus on cultural and symbolic boundaries within research on inequality.

At the same time, it's important to note what is happening to economic and social divisions. At the political level, the Trump phenomenon in the US, Brexit in the UK and the rise of far-right parties across the European landscape and worldwide have complexified the links between class and political identities and allegiances. Many people, sometimes referred to as the 'left behind', have been attracted to the populist rhetorics of these political positions. The fuelling of mass hysteria over migration has been one of the elements involved, as well as the attempt to retrench what privilege the white working class has had traditionally over racialised groups, as austerity has hit them hard (as it has the non-white working class). The moving of manufacturing into the Global South has partially removed capital's interest in employing a migrant population, either as cheap labour or as a 'surplus' or 'reserve army' (see debates in Anthias 1980; Farris 2012b; Vickers et al. 2019). Nonetheless, migrants still occupy sectors that indigenous workers have or are evacuating such as agricultural, service and care work, as well as health and medical work, although they are, more often, than not, treated as displacing indigenous workers in the debate on controlling migration. Migrants have been perceived as having been given unwarranted privileges (as far as populist leaders and their followers are concerned), advantages through provisions at the policy level, and been addressed with a (failed) concern at more equal work and pay conditions (as with that other subordinated group, women). Ideas about entitlements on the basis of autochthony have coalesced to divide the working class (manifested in Brexit in the UK) forming a gash in the heart of traditional labour heartlands.

In addition, new configurations of precarity (Standing 2011, 2014) have emerged or been intensified with the growth of zero hours contracts and the gig economy. Not only is the working class no longer a category with a distinctive role in production or indeed the service sector but it is multiply differentiated in terms of conditions and stability of work as well as pay and precarity. Many jobs, sometimes under the guise of self-employment or the guise, euphemistically, of flexible employment are becoming more common today, as are those within the gig economy leading to extreme forms of precarity. The Trades Union Congress, ahead of its annual conference in September 2019, reported that there were 3.7 million people in insecure work, and 1.85 million self-employed people in the UK, earning less than the minimum wage (Guardian 2019). Such developments require a re-writing of class classifications and a rethinking of class in terms of the way it intersects with other forms of division and precarity – for example, precarities relating to links between juridico-legal position and employment (or lack thereof).

This chapter tries to develop a more integrated and intersectional approach to social stratification, which I have already spent some time writing about (see Anthias 1998b, 1992a, 1992b, 2001b, 2002, 2013b), and which Chapter 3 alluded to. As part of this exercise, I not only argue that an approach is needed which differentiates between class and social stratification beyond the classical way of focusing on stratification as relating to an interplay between class and status (e.g. see the discussion in Flemmen et al. 2019; Chan 2019a). Social stratification theorists (e.g. see Crompton 1998; Scott 1994) usually conceptualise the non-class elements within social stratification, following Weber, as a matter of 'status': focusing on lifestyles, values, social distance and association, and the prestige given to different jobs. Where gender or race is included it treats these in terms of the empirical question of how the status of being a woman or a minority impacts on class position. The distinction between class as an economic category and

94 Hierarchising places

stratification as involving additional non-economic forms of inequality, arguably, involves tagging the latter onto class.

I argue for rethinking the relationship between class and the level of the economic, and the need to avoid reducing non-class categories to cultural or symbolic ones, since such categories are also material. In addition, the cultural or symbolic facets of class go beyond the notion of 'symbolic boundaries'. Whilst the latter are important, I argue that class and other major categories are inflected by both the economic and the symbolic which constitute *the economic/symbolic or material/cultural nexus* in social life. I treat the social relations around category-making and their effectivities as forms of political economy, where the economy is culturally embedded (e.g. see Jessop 2009). I also argue that unequal life *chances* (as opportunity structures) and *outcomes* (as hierarchical locations) are products of an intersectional process, which constitutes social stratification. This also means partially accepting the Bourdieusian route of delineating various capitals (mediated through the symbolic), but not accepting that their importance only lies, in the final analysis, in their conversion to the economic. Like Nancy Fraser (1997), I regard symbolic struggles for representation, for example, as intricately woven with resource struggles. However, rather than retaining a dual systems approach that distinguishes between struggles for representation and struggles for redistribution (broadly the cultural and the economic), I treat representation itself as a mode of resource struggle, as noted earlier.

In the formulation I prefer, class becomes a *process* that enters into social stratification analysis as one partner in the construction of hierarchical or inequality outcomes (in terms of resource allocation). These cannot be regarded as formations produced through specific processes relating to production, employment or labour market relations alone, which I see class to be characterised by. On the other hand, class is the mediating node or pathway for broader inequality outcomes, that is, it is a *necessary, but not sufficient, component of inequality processes*. This allows us to retain class as an ever-present effectivity for resource allocation and hierarchical outcomes without reducing these to those of class, nor reducing the other social categories of difference to those of status or the symbolic.

Thinking with and beyond class

Recognising that 'class' can be defined in different ways and often is a working concept and summary term, one of the tasks is to delimit the category, locating it within a range of inequality-producing relations thereby refusing to equate it with social stratification or hierarchical location, a tendency found in both sociologistic and everyday uses of the term. For example, in a discussion of class found in the contributions to an important issue of Daedalus in 2019 (e.g. see articles by Lamont and Pierson 2019; Jensen, Polletta and Raibman 2019; Newman 2019) there is very little attempt to distinguish class processes from the understanding of hierarchy or stratification more broadly.

Hierarchising places **95**

It is too easy to ask class to do all the work of inequality and stratification. Harriet Bradley was able to avoid this in saying:

> Class is a social category which refers to lived relationships surrounding social arrangements of production, exchange, distribution and consumption.
>
> *(1996, p. 19)*

However, she goes on to say,

> While these may narrowly be conceived as economic relationships, to do with money, wealth and property, . . . class should be seen as referring to a much broader web of social relationships, including, for example, lifestyle, educational experiences and patterns of residence. Class, therefore, affects many aspects of our material lives.
>
> *(1996, p. 19)*

Whilst Bradley was referring to how the class category is more than economic, there is an easy slide into it becoming a synonym for social stratification, and being conceptualised as the *only set of relations* which affects lifestyle, education and so on.

Sometimes social stratification and class are treated as homonomous. For example, this idea is found in the following Wikipedia entry defining social stratification:

> Social stratification is a kind of social differentiation whereby a society groups people into socio-economic strata, based upon their occupation and income, wealth and social status, or derived power.
>
> *(p. 1)*

To equate class with stratification (found particularly in its use as a category of practice) is problematic because it disables the role and effectivity of other categorisations and ignores or side-lines the work they do as inequality-producing processes, both in and of themselves but also in combinatories, where they form an assemblage of axes of power.

The idea that people's class explains their social location within hierarchical relations, *even at the economic level*, simply does not work in modern capitalist societies. This is a point recognised widely (e.g. see the discussion in Atkinson 2015), and yet the implications for class theory have not been fully addressed. For one thing, it doesn't explain why persons, who are ascribed particular characteristics, fill certain places within the productive process, and on the other hand, why they occupy particular positions in relation to overall hierarchical social location. Nor does it explain how such places are reproduced as well as why there is such a

96 Hierarchising places

fixing of the types of persons who fill the places, based on the social categorisations of gender and ethnicity/race.

I argued in Chapter 2 that the existential basis of class is found within the sphere of production and that class involves the placing of subjects in the relations of production and the labour market. But *how* such a placing of people occurs cannot be understood purely with reference to production relations, and yet those production relations are heavily dependent on differentiated and collectivised human subjects and not merely abstract labour. Nor can broader inequality outcomes relating to citizenship and representation be linked solely to class place. In other words, if we are concerned with the question of resources and their uneven distribution (i.e. inequality, which according to Tyler (2015) is the problem that class engages with) we cannot find answers purely with reference to class relations, unless all inequality-producing relations under capitalism are subsumed under this umbrella term, in which case it becomes tautologous. Nor can the valuation of the places themselves in production (i.e. the income and other resource allocations related to jobs) be determined purely through relations of production (or the market, to use a more Weberian formulation). The valuation is influenced, over time, by how *those who fill the places are valued*, as suggested earlier, and concomitantly how the *valuation of the places* affects how people are valued: here dialogical relationality is central. So, in this sense class is always already inflected by race/ethnicity and gender. To think with class is to also think with gender and race in particular, and with their many articulations, including sexuality, migration and so on, and vice versa. This requires looking at the ways in which salient categories of difference take on both material and symbolic/cultural forms.

Resources of different types are generated through the relations of class, gender, racialisation, ethnicity, migration, sexuality and others in intersectional and translocational ways. This removes from the idea of hierarchical position the fixity always assumed across time and space, as benefits accruing at the intersectional level are always mediated by time, context and scale. For example, looking at a person's position in the hierarchical order needs to be done with reference to 'where' and 'when' we are doing this. A transnational focus may deal a different hand to a national or local focus. Position in relation to one's ethnic group or country of origin may be different to position in the society of residence. The spatial and temporally relative security and safety of the resources, and their durability, is also important, requiring that we cannot think of them through a still shot view.

Fuzziness and normativity

Like the other concepts discussed in this book there are no generally agreed ways of thinking about class. It is a highly contested term analytically, and as a category of practice it has variable meanings to individuals and groups. As a concept which points to a particular object of reference, whether it is a set of relations, or a grouping of people, it is particularly plastic and indeterminate. The boundaries of class are themselves fuzzy rather than bright, although they are dazzlingly apparent at the extremities – within the upper and lower echelons, with extreme privilege and extreme poverty. It is also complicated by the issue of whether everyone can be included into the analysis of the class structure or only those who are part of the production system. Various terms have been used to describe those who are on the periphery such as the lumpen proletariat, or the underclass and more recently a particular category that spans both employed and non-employed, the precariat (Standing 2011), which can be seen as particularly but not exclusively filled by migrants (Schierup and Alund 2018; Papadopoulos and Tsianos 2013; Pajnik and Campani 2009). Similarly, there are issues around the categories of surplus populations or the reserve army of labour, allocated specific roles within capitalism (surplus populations being a term used to denote some categories of migrant: see the discussion in Vickers et al. (2019) and Farris (2012b), for example).

In everyday language, class is a multilayered and diverse signifier of social rank. Class tends to stand, inter alia, as a shorthand for outcomes relating to status, wealth, lifestyle and social worth. The kind of criteria used for ranking vary from visible marks inscribed in the body such as accent, weight, 'style' or manners, to ideas about 'breeding' or inheritance and centrally to income, wealth and access to economic resources. As an everyday term not only does it have differential meaning to actors themselves but also, because of its moral overtones, it involves much personal investment or refusal. It has been, and remains, a normative concept and very often implies a moral judgement or the valuation of individuals or groups of individuals as found in notions of 'white trash' or the 'underclass'. As Bev Skeggs (1997), amongst others, has shown, people often are at pains to refuse class labels, precisely because of these moral judgements. Class also has emotional overtones relating to belonging and self-valuation, and involves what Tyler (2015), following Bourdieu, calls classification struggles around the stigmatisations involved.

It is not my intention to run through the many different frameworks that use the term class, premised on different theoretical traditions. For such a discussion Atkinson (2015), amongst many others, provides a tour around some of the main perspectives and their difficulties. Class is, at one and the same time, a theoretical concept or at least in the sociological canon has been required to do major theoretical work in explaining and understanding the 'social', but it is also used as a descriptive term in a very taken for granted way to signal economic or social position (usually based on occupation). The usage of notions of class in academic work is littered with fuzziness and a concern with *typologies* of class groupings. Much class analysis effort has been expended on the classification of social classes, based on a range of criteria, as in the Goldthorpe classification schema (1980/87, Goldthorpe and Heath 1992)[1] which relies on employment relations, or the more recent schema developed by Savage et al. (2013) which also ends up classifying occupational strata albeit on very different principles. Unlike

98 Hierarchising places

the Goldthorpe schema, the latter schema is based on the possession of cultural capital as well as benefits accruing to occupational positions.

Class has been understood in a variety of ways drawing primarily on the work of Marx and Weber: as structural location within the economic system (i.e. as an objective feature of social relations) linked to either production (via Marxism) or distribution and the marketplace (via Weber). The broader sociological tradition has been in large part concerned with how and in what way forms of consciousness, identification, culture, solidarity and action are linked to class and/ or economic position (e.g. Hall 1978; Lamont 2019; Chan 2019b). The political support for Trump and for Brexit amongst the working class also reinforces the non-deterministic nature of the relationship between class position and political allegiance. On the other hand, those who work with Bourdieu to look at cultural capital, taste and distinction tend to overdetermine the link between occupational categorisations, acting as a short hand for class groupings, and cultural capital and habitus. Overall the notion of habitus has been used in a deterministic or tautological way – as arising as a phoenix or phantom out of economic or class position (tautological because class position itself is defined by the habitus). Much of their work is concerned with mapping class (primarily through capitals) onto lifestyle preferences and cultural tastes (e.g. see Savage et al. 2013). There is also a significant body of work that is concerned with rethinking the distinction that Weber made between class and status (e.g. Beteille 1996; Flemmen et al. 2019).

The habitus is a key notion in Bourdieu's oeuvre and arose out of the attempt to resolve the dilemmas posed by the spectre of economic determinism, on the one hand, and intersubjectively constituted class subjects, on the other. In his work, arguably, the focus is on the individual since habitus is neither a Weltanschauung (Mannheim 1929) nor a discourse produced in the public sphere as found in the work of Foucault. It is forged through the lived experiences of people, creating dispositions and taken for granted ways of thinking. As argued in Chapter 2 this individualises the habitus, instead of locating its formation in the discursive, institutional or intersubjective. Nor is *social* capital a class collective property. In this frame, although class position influences the mobilisable networks that an individual can access (social capital), it is the individual who draws class benefits (or not) from social capital (see Anthias 2007). So arguably Bourdieu's emphasis on habitus and on cultural and social capital constitutes class as an individual property that is an outcome of these processes. Although class habitus is shared with others who occupy similar class positions, it does not operate to unite them, as classification struggles are those where individuals seek to enhance their own capital. The deterministic nature of habitus leads to a political impasse, and this makes it difficult to think about how such entrenched predispositions can be changed (discussed already in Chapter 2).

This has not deterred researchers who draw from his work, which has grown in importance in the last two decades especially. A whole school of class analysis has developed which can be termed the culturally inflected approach (see Anthias 2013c), for example, found in the work of Mike Savage (2000, 2010),

Beverly Skeggs (1997, 2004; Reay 1998) and many others. His work has also deeply influenced the 'symbolic boundaries' approach found in the work particularly of Michelle Lamont (e.g. 1992, 2000). A Bourdieusian lens has been applied to investigating the ways in which cultural and symbolic inequalities play a fundamental role in the structuration of class position and the very nature of class boundaries themselves. Bourdieu's work on social capital has been, more recently, a central plank of debate, in the discussion of migration and social networks (e.g. Anthias 2007; Erel 2010; Ryan et al. 2016).

Other concerns in the literature include charting the cartography of class places and membership, with discussions about the decreasing importance of class in modern societies. Pakulski and Waters (1995), for example, declared the (premature) death of class. Issues about how to define class, the major social classes, the changing boundaries of class formation, the changing forms (and indeed perhaps demise) of class solidarity and action have been long-standing important features of class debates (see Atkinson 2015). The extent to which class movements have been replaced by other social movements has also been a feature of these debates. It has been argued that other forms of solidarity-making around ethnicity and race, for example, have replaced mobilisations based on class commonalities and claims (e.g. see Bottero 2004).

One of the quandaries that the notion of class faces is that it lies between description and explanation, and tries to do too much in delivering an analysis of hierarchy and inequality. It is used as an explanation, as a description and as a grouping. It can refer to class places or class subjects. At the analytical level there is a merging of the theoretical and everyday uses of the term, and it both constitutes a mode for explaining or understanding economic and positional inequalities and stands as a shorthand for economic and positional inequalities (Anthias 2001b). The latter mirrors perhaps in more scientistic ways the everyday usages of the term, thereby sociologising it (an argument ethnomethodologists make about theoretical concepts being dependent on everyday meanings and interactions). As with the everyday meanings of the term, criteria used for delineating class places and who fills them are often taken for granted and include wealth, income, rank and status or the type of work people do, and often rely on occupational categories. This means that 'class' is deployed as a theory about the production and reproduction of economic inequality and hierarchical economic and social position, on the one hand, but is also actually used just as a *descriptive* label for such differences. Indeed, the use of the term as a descriptor of a range of economic or indeed social inequalities does not necessarily rely on any theoretical consistency about what class relations are. Different cultural markers might be used, where and how people live, who they associate with, what their cultural preferences are, how they talk and so on. This is found particularly in some of the work influenced by Bourdieu's book *Distinction* (1984), and has entered, in some part, in the new class schema devised by Mike Savage and his colleagues, as noted earlier. One of the issues here is the *Eurocentric* way in which class is imagined, drawing from the everyday meanings in western societies, and extrapolating

100 Hierarchising places

from these to a general set of cultural *diakritika*. My argument indeed is that *class at this level can only work in local terms*, depicting social ordering in specific societies. However, because of coloniality, transnationalism and globality there occurs a diasporisation and hybridisation of class meanings that needs to be taken into account.

The difference that class makes

Whilst being mindful of the dangers of homologising categories, in thinking through an intersectional framing, we can also ask whether class should be treated as having a different kind of saliency to other social divisions. How do we place it in the kaleidoscope of inequality that is generated through the working of categories and the role they play in social ordering and place making? Whilst I argue that there is a need to rethink class, as well as delimit it, I also argued earlier that we should retain its central role as a pathway or mediating grid within which the categorisations of human persons pass. *In concrete relations class makes effective the workings of race and gender as inequality regimes, but the workings (and naturalising properties) of race and gender enable the workings of class.* In order to develop such an intersectional approach to stratification, whilst recognising the specificity of class, we may need to begin by taking the class category *outside* the landscape of categories of difference (like gender, race, ethnicity, religion and so on) and consider its possibly unique modus operandi in the sphere of the social, whilst not necessarily treating it as a master category and putting all our inequality eggs in this basket.

At the risk of overgeneralising, as a category class works in symbolic and material ways which makes it rather different to those of gender, ethnicity, race and nation (and others), although they all have distinctive modes of operating. Firstly, class has been given much more prominence in explanations of the social order than other social categories, for example in the work of Marxists, Weberians and those working with Bourdieu. Secondly, class is more *directly* linked to economic resource acquisition in terms of income and wealth. Thirdly, it is a modern social category and lacks the clear originary elements found in gender and ethnicity, particularly since class is accompanied by the idea of individuals being able to achieve their class position, rather than being born into it. In the modern period, it relates to the possession of individual skills, educational qualifications and competencies which are acquired rather than ascribed in an a priori fashion. Therefore people, theoretically, can occupy different places in the class structure at different times and places, depending on the development of these skills and the marketplace.

In common understandings, class attribution involves a complex array of judgements, values and interests which, unlike those that we can identify as gendered or racialised, are more reliant on ideas of achievement and capacities relating to individual personality traits or individual merit. As such, they signal individual embodiments of social relations which become collectivised a posteriori, unlike gender and race where the individualised traits are products of a priori designations. Class also involves the collectivisation of traits and criteria which are conferred on individuals. Collective forms of stigma and attributions are allocated to them. Actors are placed within these on the basis of criteria which are often doxic, although in the auditing and regulatory systems of the state and other institutional bodies they are defined more logistically in terms of occupational and income criteria, also found in the sociological classifications of class which use a range of employment and at times cultural criteria such as those of Goldthorpe and Savage et al., noted earlier.

Some elements of class appear similar to those found in 'racialised' groups – for example, avoidance, housing concentration and so on. There are also collective attributions given to different class categories, such as sharing levels of intelligence, cultural interests and propensities manifested in certain lifestyles (forming class 'tribes', for example). Powerful stigmata are attached to individuals depending also on class origins and not only class positions. Although they can be displaced through mobility, social or physical, it is not so easy to be free of the commonly understood symbolic and cultural features identified with class location or with *parental class position*, in terms of their traces or debris (e.g. see Friedman 2019).

However, in the case of gender and race, at the risk of overgeneralising, visibility (but not deportment or bodily accoutrements necessarily) is more pronounced, as is the greater intractability involved. It's more difficult to move in and out of them (that is not to say that it is so easy in the case of class either, however). In relation to ethnicity, the boundary of the 'other' is marked by a range of elements, more like essential commonalities and solidarities within the 'group', which means that crossing the line is possible but less assumed. Claims to ethnicity are generally policed by the border guarding involved. Claims to class on the other hand are judged in more complex ways. Occupation, education and pay are some of the border guards, but people are also judged by parental background, inherited wealth (where a person may be doing an unskilled job but has an upper middle-class background) and so on. Weight, deportment, accent also act as stigmata on classed bodies. Despite this, in the case of class the crossing of lines from one to the other is regarded as much more porous. In practice, of course, this is oversimplifying matters largely because of social impediments to class mobility and the continuing marks, as noted, left by parental class position even for those who have become socially mobile. This is evidenced in work that looks at the impediments faced by working–class achievers (with formal qualifications) who are disadvantaged in relation to 'elite' jobs (see particularly the work of Friedman (2019), noted earlier).

As they combine with those of gender and race, judgements of class may be particularly stigmatising and hierarchising, or alternatively can be 'whitening'. Indeed, some of the effectivities of class emerge out of the *naturalisations* of gender and race which overdetermine class ascriptions, on the one hand, and the way class can partially '*lift*' ethnic and race attributions in a way in which gender

102 Hierarchising places

and ethnic/race markings do not so easily do to each other. This is because class notions do not treat individuals as prima facie carriers of essential traits, unlike gender and ethnic/racial categorisations, and the latter are modified through class. Class also functions as a valuation of a person's social worth through stigmatisation and homogenisation processes, as with gender and ethnicity/race. However, this relies on markers that are more indeterminate and require educated situational gazes, such as being able to distinguish marks of education or brands relating to clothes, taste, accents and bodily styles. Where these are easily marked, it may be possible to talk about racialised class (Shilliam 2018).

Class, therefore, denotes 'groups' of people formed post rather than pre the category (as they are formed through the acquisition of certain attributes like education, skill and type of work). It is therefore a social category that is not, centrally, biologistically undergirded, although it is inscribed in the body in a variety of ways. As Bourdieu notes in relation to lifestyle expressed in furnishing and clothing (bearing in mind its cultural specificity to France and other countries of the Global North, as well as access to other lifestyles through television programmes and social media forms):

> these properties are the objectification of the economic and cultural necessity which determined their selection, . . . the social relations objectified in familiar objects, in their luxury or poverty, their 'distinction' or 'vulgarity', their 'beauty' or 'ugliness', impress themselves through bodily experiences which may be . . . profoundly unconscious . . .
>
> *(1984, p. 77)*

Class operates as a *distributive* mechanism through the allocation of economic and social value to skills and jobs, as well as through allocating people within this hierarchy of jobs. It also operates as a mechanism of *exploitation* through relations of production. Whilst we can see how the mechanisms of gender and race determine the opportunities of people, which then lead to their position in employment (types of work, glass ceilings, gender and race pay gaps), with class it is the *acquisition* of skills and qualifications which is central. These are affected particularly by the background of the parents (i.e. there is a different and unique reproductive mechanism at work), although it is not the parents that 'done it' (c.f. Phil Cohen 1999). Research has shown the role of parental class on the educational achievements of students and on issues relating to social mobility, that is, the extent to which people can move up (or down) the class structure and what the factors are that can explain (or facilitate) such movements (Halsey, Heath and Ridge 1980; Bernstein 1961). Whilst richer parents can 'buy' better educational opportunities and facilitate the achievements of their children, poorer people's educational achievements are often regarded as the result of inherited traits of intelligence. The capacity to buy means that the children of higher social classes do better, and this reinforces the idea of innate capacities, thereby also naturalising working-class failure. As a category there is much work that class *does* in sorting populations along lines of educational and other technologies. The educational system, for example, has been regarded as valorising the cultural capital of the middle class and divests working-class knowledge, culture and experience of any value, and as sponsoring people to class positions based on parental backgrounds (e.g. see Bernstein 1961; Halsey, Heath and Ridge 1980; Erikson and Goldthorpe 1992; Friedman 2019).

If gender and race are conferred through a biological givenness and ethnicity through a doxic originary culture or territorial space which is essentialist in a different way, then class is conferred through parental inheritance on the one hand and achievement on the other (i.e. it is bifurcated). It is this which makes it such a central element in unequal relations; the inequality is justified and made to seem fair through the predominant discourse of merit and achievement, or through the neo-liberal market relating to incentives and rewards (justifying unequal income distribution). At the policy level, there exist positive action programmes (and in the UK the Equality Duty).[2] Gender and race are amongst the protected equality characteristics in law. However, class is not one of these protected characteristics. In the case of employment, specific kinds of competencies and personal attributes are required, meaning that quotas, for example, are largely absent and there is no anti-classism provision in legislation currently. Concerns for equal opportunities in relation to class are not aimed at eliminating the effects of class distinction (like for gender and race, however deficient these have proved to be). Rather they address the question of equalisation in terms of access to fixed places of class, for example, using terms such as 'value added' for working-class students. Here, universities are urged, for example in the UK, to increase participation levels and admissions for students from working-class backgrounds (but an incipient class position through some level of qualifications is needed already). In other words, there is little disruption to the class order itself.

Beyond equating the economic with class

Talking about women and work Elson and Pearson (1981) say:

> To a large extent, women do not do 'unskilled' jobs because they are the bearers of inferior labour, rather the jobs they do are 'unskilled' because women enter them already determined as inferior bearers of labour.
>
> *(p. 93)*

This suggests that they are already incipient class subjects prior to their entry into the labour market. Already gender and race become part of the social organisation of the economy if this is the case. We can see that economic resources are allocated not only through labour market or class processes but that these allocations take place directly through position in the distinct pecking orders of gender, race and ethnicity and in their translocational configurations. We can turn this

104 Hierarchising places

on its head when talking about class. Class categories, processes and outcomes, like those of gender, ethnicity/race have *cultural* as well as economic features, not only as forms of capital that can be translated into the economic. Cultural and symbolic facets of social life act as resources in their own right, for example in terms of the allocation of citizenship or social welfare (where ethnicity and gender amongst other categories are central). The 'new political economy' as it has been characterised treats the economy as socially and culturally embedded (e.g. see the work of Jessop 2009). Economic processes and mechanisms, therefore, are treated not as explanations in themselves but require an understanding of their social and political conditions of existence (e.g. Gamble 1988; Hay 1999). This suggests that economic forces and processes cannot be situated outside their embeddedness within symbolic, cultural and meaning structures in modern societies and across them in the transnational field, constituting the *material-cultural nexus* of social relations. This relates to how different modes of inequality and division intersect, creating complex articulations which are *patterned* but not fixed or given. People themselves are not fixed into given hierarchical places but will occupy them at specific conjunctures (in contradictory as well as mutually reinforcing ways – see Chapter 3). This does not mean that some people do not experience a homology of location across time and space, some of whom are the very poor and the very rich.

The economic, however, has its own dynamics and functions particularly as a central context for all other value, that is, as a necessary condition of existence. Where Marx made that sphere the determining one, it is also possible to see it as an *a priori condition of existence* for all the others, in terms of allowing for the satisfaction of physically and culturally determined survival needs. However, the economic is but one, albeit a central and necessary resource, up to *a certain level* constituting a condition of existence for the other resources. After this level, economic value assumes a symbolic value (Anthias 2001a).

Although I believe that there is some justification to giving ontological primacy to material needs, I think the inability to think with gender and race has been a result of the ways such material needs have been *delimited to those of the economic.* The importance of economic resource production and acquisition lies largely in terms of people's ability to live a sustainable life, but the yardstick, beyond a certain level (culturally specific), is relational, if only because people's sense of the resources they have is always mediated by what they perceive others to have, and cultural notions of need. The proviso of course is that this must not underemphasise the existence of poverty and denigration where we cannot apply this relational principle. This means that extensive economic resources become valued through their transferability to cultural, symbolic or quality of life value (complicating here Bourdieu's view, so the economic and the cultural are dialogical), and as enabling capitalist activity.

Marx raised the issue of the symbolic (and indeed the psychic) from the point of view of the fetishism of commodities (Marx 1859/1977). Once commodities become fetishised, they no longer function as mere material or economic value, but assume a cultural and symbolic value and, in Bourdieu's terms, become mis-recognised. Similarly, with Bourdieu's work on capitals, we can see that economic (as indeed social and cultural capitals) are only important as and when they function symbolically, that is, in situations where they are socially valued. In and of themselves, economic resources (apart from at the very basic level for human survival), have no intrinsic value – they need to be endowed with social valuation as well as being mobilisable for the achievement of goals.

Without symbolic value, economic resources are like money locked in a bank that has gone bust. Also, like money, they cannot buy all desirable resources for achieving life chances, not only because 'money can't buy you love', as the Beatles song says. Money may buy expensive property, but it cannot buy entry into a social club or a political elite, even if it can buy, in many countries, formal rights of citizenship. National lottery winners become wealthy, but they cannot change the ways in which they may be regarded in class terms, cannot easily acquire other trappings of social position such as cultural preferences, and may not have access to powerful social networks. They may gain power as consumers, or the freedom to live a life of leisure, however. In addition, cultural ideas about consumption values mediate the mere notion of economic value. The value of an item of furniture or fashion clothing is not solely dependent on the economic value they possess. Advertising, digital media and marketing construct the value of commodities; they do not have value in and of themselves. An item of clothing, for example from a budget store like Primark or from a high market clothing store such as Calvin Klein, may be very similar in functionality and lasting power. Their value is gained through display to a knowing audience of such distinctions.

As noted earlier, the term 'status' has been suggested by some writers (e.g. Crompton 1998, p. 127) as 'relating to the overall structuring of inequality along a range of dimensions', going beyond the way Weber relates status to lifestyle or/ and honour-deference. However, the term status here becomes a way of locating everything else, from prestige systems to citizenship rights as they enter into work-based relations. For example, citizenship rights may constitute a place for more than formulating the conditions for access to resources on the basis of work. They are themselves highly gendered and racialised in quite specific ways. Allocating them to the level of 'status' function cannot begin to address these issues.

Not only do women and minorities, on average, earn less and are disadvantaged overall in economic terms (e.g. see Woodhams et al. 2015). We can see the process whereby women get relegated to lower echelons of particular labour markets, and different labour markets. Even where they do the same or similar jobs as men (e.g. as actors or presenters) they are paid less or face 'glass ceilings' (as recently publicised vis-à-vis the BBC in the UK and in Hollywood).[3] Similarly, not only is there an issue about the employment inequalities faced by black and minority graduates, or their access to Russell Group universities, but also in the ways in which they are less likely to be promoted, being disadvantaged

106 Hierarchising places

in a range of ways (Friedman 2019), including not belonging or being familiar with classed white masculine codes (Lamont et al. 2002). This recognition that the material and the cultural coexist within class and beyond requires reassessing the view that some social categories are characterised by cultural, and others by economic, features. It also asks us to revise the idea that culture always has less saliency in the production of inequality than economic factors (as indeed also exemplified by more culturally inflected approaches to class, e.g. in the work of Skeggs (1997)). The simultaneity and entanglement of these in all social spheres is based on *processes and outcomes* relating to *resource production, allocation, distribution and contestation*, which are prime components of all social life. Therefore, boundaries of belonging have both material and cultural elements: for example, providing access to employment or citizenship, on the one hand, and access to modes of knowledge and meaning, on the other.

Beyond the analysis of capitalism as a mode of production (at the abstract level) the focus on the economic alone does not work in the analysis of systems for the social allocation of resources and social relations of hierarchisation and inferiorisation. Even acknowledging the epistemological primacy of 'the economic', in the final analysis, as Althusserian revisions of Marx have done (Althusser 1971), does not require us to maintain this primacy in explaining the social allocation of resources to concrete individuals and groups. Gender and ethnicity involve the allocation of hierarchies of value, inferiorisation as well as unequal resource allocation (on their basis and not through the intermediate relation of production relations), in intersectional terms. For example, women may be paid less for the same job as men, or jobs that women do may be allocated a different economic value. Being a woman or Black (or both) can exclude an individual from access to resources of a group, as is the case with male dominated occupations or those defined as 'masculine', or those defined by the state as only appropriate for British nationals (such as top Civil Service jobs).

If we have deprived class of its singular identification with the economic and its unquestionable pivotal position in the structuring of hierarchy (and inequality, where it must take a position alongside gender and ethnic processes) how does this fit into the position claimed in Chapter 1 about the centrality of categories of difference for capitalism? This requires an analysis of capitalist social formations with their organisational and governmental structures which go beyond and at times against the capitalist class. There are different modalities of power, although in real capitalist relations, those in power have a stake in all of them. These include ownership of the means of production and of wealth, allowing exploitation and subordination of labour market groups. It also includes ownership of gender power, allowing exploitation through specific forms of economic relationship relating to what Hochschild (1989/2012) has called the second shift, emotional labour and the global care chain. Ownership of racial, ethnic and national power allows economic benefits to accrue from the exploitation and subordination of groups based on collective origin differences, and through racialisation, non-belonging and bordering. Examples include male and female migrants who are trafficked, and undocumented migrants living under conditions of modern slavery. Capitalism is therefore more than just an economic system with class as its motor. In this formulation, intersectionally constituted power relations and resource allocations become the motor of capitalist social systems, through the harnessing of categories in potentially plastic and changeable forms.

The logic of capital and unmarked abstract labour: who fills the places

Class analysis has historically been unable to account for the role of gender and race and different modalities of intersection with resource production and allocation (as exist with migrants and refugees). This is not only because there is a failure to distinguish between capitalism at the level of its logic, and as a social formation (e.g. see Anthias 1982; Gimenez 2018). The argument that systems of production have their own imperatives (the imperative of surplus value and accumulation, for example) is at such an abstract level that it cannot deliver explanations for how real capitalisms work nor the organisational forms they take, nor what motivates their particular enterprises or projects. Capitalisms have been particularly adaptable to counterforces and contestations; concessions and modifications have been made over time. Mixed economies, welfare capitalism, moves to gender and race equalisation have all emerged. Despite this, inequality has grown since the 1950s between the rich and the poor (Dorling 2014; Bourguignon 2015).

Even at the level of the logic of capitalism, one could argue there is a missing component in most analyses of the modus operandi of capitalism which is the *flexibility and plasticity* that arises from the marking of differentiated human populations (beyond the abstract labourer and beyond the role of the reserve army of labour). Differently marked populations have underpinned the development of capitalism in its current form – as reinforced in the important work of Cox (1970), Robinson (2000) and Virdee (2014) who point to the centrality of racialisation as a precondition not only for the development of capitalism, but for its continuation. The differentiated social spaces involved in marking populations can sit alongside the reserve army of labour (RAL) in facilitating capitalism's ability to resolve crises. For example, racialisation, migration and sexual subordination all provide means of gaining substitutable cheap labour as many scholars in these areas have already argued (e.g. see Sassen 1996, 2000). These can't be understood strictly as constituting an RAL using a Marxist analysis (see the argument in Anthias 1980).

Whilst the Marxist paradigm looks at class as place in the production system, that is, as a function within production processes, there is little consideration of what and whose bodies get marked. Within this paradigm there occurs a relation of exploitation towards unmarked abstract labour and not particular bodies of particular types of labour. The 'long march of the productive forces' with their

108 Hierarchising places

periodic and spectacular crises leads to their own potential overthrow. Mediating this is the rising consciousness of exploitation, along with the changes in the organisation of production produced by the crises and the contradictions of the capitalist system itself. The way capital constructs different kinds of subjects or groups with different capacities and needs could well have been harnessed to a Marxist idea of 'divide and rule', but this was not part of the Marxist enterprise.

The system's logic is not the logic of real organisations which abide by regulatory regimes, nor real capitalists in any concrete social formation. These are informed by ideas and practices that include the way we categorise people and phenomena, which individual and collective action shapes. Acquiring or mobilising capital in the pursuit of profit is the rationale of capitalism, but in social relations this is mediated by a range of competing regulatory mechanisms and goals. Of course, the insatiable drive to profit can become fetishised as a means for achieving social value and quality of life. This means that it acquires symbolic value within the wider economic and social framework. The argument here is that we cannot infer from the abstract model of capitalism (or its logic) the workings of actual capitalism. As such, an abstract model can only be a comparative one as in Weber's notion of 'ideal type' (1946). As Althusser (1971) argued the moment of the economic 'in the last instance' never comes. Arguably, if we go beyond treating this as more than an ideal type, we risk an essentialisation of capital accumulation as the driver of real economic processes, since this empties it of human subjectivities and intersubjectivities as well as the organisational, representational, intersubjective and experiential elements that are important in all societies. We can look to Weber to provide us with more historicised tools, however contestable they may be in their substance (such as the link between the protestant ethic and capitalism).

The assumption in Marxist approaches is that class processes are subject neutral, that is, the characteristics of individuals prior to entry into the world of production and distribution are irrelevant (apart from ownership of capital or not). However, there is much work now, as noted earlier, which argues that the individuals who fill the places and their valuations and attributions (resulting from inter alia empire, slavery, subordination and control of women) have been instrumental in the development of capitalism itself, as a concrete mode of production and as a social formation. Marx did not consider how the construction of differentiated human subjects relates to roles in the labour market or the production process. However, Marx's statement that 'Labour in a white skin cannot emancipate itself where it is branded in a black skin' (Marx 1976, p. 414) indicates his recognition of the importance of issues of race. Engels' work on the family, private property and the state is exceptional in dealing with the sexual division of labour and the oppression of women (Engels 1884/2004) but it was left to Marxist feminists to develop the political economy of women. Marxist feminists engaged extensively with the role of domestic labour (Molyneaux 1979) in capitalism and have also theorised women as an RAL (e.g. Beechey 1977; Anthias 1980, and more recently Farris 2012b; Vickers et al. 2019). Much of this work has been based on the connection between women's role in biological reproduction and economic subordination, on the one hand, and on notions about a separate system of patriarchal power relations, on the other. Heidi Hartman's incisive work points to what she refers to as the unhappy marriage between 'Marxism and Feminism' (1979) Whilst these contributions paved the way for a fuller understanding of the workings of categories in capitalism and how constructions of discrete population groupings with different capacities and needs is a precondition for capitalism, neither were able to rethink approaches to class and stratification. Indeed, much of this work has remained very much on the periphery of work on class. In addition, the insight that gendered and racialised characteristics of the individuals that fill the places affect the very position of the places in the hierarchical system is not new (e.g. Elson and Pearson 1981) but its implications have not been taken seriously in rethinking class formation.

The material/economic and the cultural/symbolic

It's useful to note the ways in which class (in terms of role in production), gender, ethnicity and race involve an intersection between the economic and the symbolic/cultural (see also Anthias 2001a). Symbolic aspects of work relations include ideas that some jobs are clean and some are dirty, the former often being seen as more desirable irrespective of the economic rewards (found in the different valuation of non-manual and manual work). There are a range of resources that are gained therefore from the performance of more 'desirable' jobs that are relevant for the assessment of an individual's life conditions and life chances (e.g. see the arguments in Pakulski and Waters 1996). Deference is attached to some occupations, such as medicine and law which gives the roles, and the individuals who perform them, authority and to some extent control over others. For example, the medicalisation of childbirth has given doctors power over women's life conditions when they are in a vulnerable condition during pregnancy and childbirth. Some occupations are given value in terms of servicing the community; in this category we can include nurses, possibly teachers, therapists and priests. This gives the individuals self-worth and some degree of power over those with whom they interact professionally. This value, however, is not necessarily translated into high economic rewards, and it could be argued that incentives for these jobs are not derived from the marketplace. The knowledge base of some work is valued in and of itself, although professors, judges, doctors and others may be empowered through that knowledge base. This may give privileged access to knowledge, which can be translated into life conditions, such as knowledge of the best areas for good schools for their children, or the best forms of health care. The work we do may be regarded as an embodiment of ourselves and provide us with self-esteem. Hence those out of work, particularly the long-term unemployed, may lose that self-esteem which, arguably, is a prerequisite to good life chances and conditions. Some forms of work require the objectification and depersonalisation of their incumbents, found in the use of uniforms by

110 Hierarchising places

nurses, priests, judges, policemen, soldiers and others who may have authority. Such symbolic representations of authority or position function to legitimate their behaviour as well as the system that they operate within. Moreover, some bureaucratic jobs are invested with authority to decide how resources should be distributed to populations and individuals, indicating that resource allocation is not only market led (Esping-Anderson 1990). The power of migration officials, security guards, welfare officers and social workers comes to mind.

Individuals may be sponsored to social places. For example, the children of doctors are more likely to be thought of as fit for medical training. Social places are not merely subject to the determination of class but of cultural and embodied social positionalities specifying types of human persons (this is especially the case with notions of gendered or racialised jobs, see Lutz 2017; Anderson 2006; Bradley 1996). Meeting gendered norms is endowed with economic exchange value in the marketplace, as a form of skill or accomplishment, for example for secretaries or waiters. Pop stars, footballers, celebrities, social media stars, and many others, may become embodiments of desire and icons of youth, yielding large economic rewards.

Some jobs and economic rewards are regarded as more suitable for some ethnic groups than for others. For example, there still exists a myth of ethnic entrepreneurship in relation to Jews, Asians, Turks and Cypriots (Anthias and Cederberg 2009). Ethnic resources include ethnic job networks, family enterprises, ethnic niches, and the 'professional ethnic' (e.g. see Phizacklea 1983; Anthias and Yuval-Davis 1992). White or dominant ethnicities (as well as classes) have privileged access to top jobs which may rely on old school networks or other social networks and having the right cultural knowledge or information (see the recent work of Friedman 2019): speaking the 'same language'. A dominant ethnic group may have overall control over resources, for example in their role and hegemony in relation to the state. This includes control over forms of education, or denial of access to groups who lack culturally specific forms of knowledge such as language skills.

The role of women in childcare and in the traditional family constrains their employment. This is a result of cultural assumptions about childcare responsibilities and mothering as well as structural constraints such as inflexible work structures and poor childcare facilities. Sexist definitions of economic value are attached to the work of mothering and domestic labour which are not paid, nor is the job as valued as that of being employed within traditional labour markets (Glucksman 1995).

When work is feminised it becomes less materially valued; the teaching profession and the clerical profession are historically cases in point (see Rubery 2015). Moreover, the class structure and the economy are partially driven by gendered definitions of skill (Phillips and Taylor 1980; Cockburn 1991). The consumption/lifestyles of gender have economic facets personified in the enormous markets for fashion and cosmetics for women, cars and technical equipment for men. Moreover, there is an economic value attached to sexual services particularly of women; both biological reproduction and sex become marketable commodities via surrogacy, prostitution and pornography. The world of work (thought of as an economic or material sphere) is also a cultural sphere that embodies gender and ethnic difference at its very heart and, concomitantly, ethnicity and gender involve material outcomes.

Delimiting class: class as production role and relation

Now we can home in on the delimitation of class relations. I argue for delimiting class heuristically through retaining the idea of class in the Marxist sense to denote positions and relations in the production process, retaining also the idea of class exploitation as a mechanism of class relations. This adheres to a Marxist position but modifies it by arguing that such relations in concrete societies are never only economic. At the level of concrete societies, production is embedded in cultural, historical and symbolic relations to do with deference, with authority, with status and so on. Part of treating labour market roles or production relations as class positions also entails looking therefore at social, cultural and symbolic practices relating to work: ideologies, procedures, contestations, valuations and intersubjectivities. This is a different point to that made by Bourdieu about cultural capital in relation to possessive properties of individuals acquired via education, for example. This relates to the social valuation of jobs, rewards and status rankings in the discursive and narrational field. We can also look at how *the practices and procedures at work are affected by the discourses and practices around the categorial characteristics of those who fill them*, for example in terms of pay scales for jobs that are done primarily by women or by migrant or black people, or any combinations thereof. For example, vulnerabilities relating to insecurities about the legality or citizenship status of migrants, or constraints relating to responsibilities in the family can lead to jobs filled by such categories being lower on the level of pay and other resource rewards. Intersectional analysis reveals how some people fill certain labour market functions that are allocated a specific symbolic and material value (e.g. relating to status of job, rewards, autonomy, income, career progression, requiring levels of education and so on).

In addition to this, intersectional analysis at the level of stratification (broader inequality places) can reveal how ascriptions of categorial difference, relating to gender, age or ethnic and race 'groupings', impact on access to goods, education for children, job promotion, housing access, discrimination practices and so on that link to quality of life in a translocational system of hierarchical social locations along a number of axes. Neither class nor hierarchical social place can be conceived as uniform across time and space. For example, the class position of persons doing the same job will vary from place to place and the hierarchical location of an individual will vary depending on how and whether they are a citizen in a particular country, racialised or what the gender order is (for instance).

Here then the Marxist tradition of treating class as relational rather than a fixed pyramid is important both in terms of how labour market function

112 Hierarchising places

involves relational power (e.g. capitalist–worker, employer–employee), and in terms of intersubjective and experiential factors around actual relations between people with different ascriptions and recognition. However, as a relationship on the ground this relationality is more complex. It operates via an interplay with context bound categorial ascriptions, and the attributions and performativities of concrete individuals. These go beyond Marx's idea of class consciousness (or false consciousness) and the traditional sociological position which makes a distinction between objective and subjective class position, that is, how individuals rank themselves (Giddens 1973). Ideas of affect, identification, stigma, disgust and avoidance are all significant elements in stratification practices and are often treated in status terms within a Weberian or indeed a dominant stratification perspective. But these cannot be encapsulated by the term status or the idea of status groups since they are organised around quite long-standing and ontologically inflected categories of people who are given naturalising and essentialised attributions. Individuals are more than embodiments of class places as they may be complexly related to ideas of danger, disgust and deviance (in the case of race) or desire, mutuality, control (in the case of gender) and linked to othering processes more generally (see Chapter 6 on race).

Class allows us to group individuals in terms of production roles which are themselves imbued with specific economic and non-economic resource allocations (e.g. work status). Although changeable they tend to be relatively stable over considerable periods of time. But once we use a more transnational and translocational intersectional approach it becomes in different cases both easier and more difficult to fix people in terms of life chances and unequal outcomes (depending on how they reinforce, or converge from, each other). This is especially the case if we avoid a methodological nationalist framework (still prominent in class and stratification literature) recognising increasing mobility and transnationalisms. If we move away from methodologically nationalist frames we can identify work categories filled by human subjects who are located in terms of disadvantage, inequality and subordination on a number of fronts (such a category would be, for instance, that of migrant domestic workers – see Chapter 5). Here, translocations produce heightened and reinforcing forms of inequality and subordination. Various categories can be singled out at the front line of mechanisms of inequality, such as precarious non-citizens or trafficked workers, many of whom are women and transnational care workers.

Delimiting class in this way does not restrict the relations to those in production alone since they are embedded in broader systems of power. The determinants of some of the conditions of work and pay, in modern societies, do not emanate strictly from production relations, but the systems of control, procedure, regulation, negotiation and contestation that surround them. These will encompass modes by which resource allocation and distribution are arrived at (which includes the activities of trades unions and professional associations), as well as the allocation of differential symbolic value to the roles or functions in the sphere of production. Marx's notion of the importance of the division

Hierarchising places **113**

between labour and capital is central in the analysis of systems of production, at the holistic level, but the analytical privileging of the economic cannot work in explaining the stratification outcomes for concrete and determinant individuals and groups. This is because other cultural, symbolic, political and juridical factors mediate the abstract level that Marx is concerned with. This also applies to Goldthorpe's analysis of employment relations as being the key to stratification relations. Such employment relations are end products of processes but are not themselves explanations for the allocation of resources of different kinds to individuals and groups, according to the approach that I have outlined. In relation to Savage et al. (2014), the correlation between occupational position and forms of cultural consumption that are central in the production of their class classification scheme cannot yield explanations of the class system. They only point to how symbolic boundaries and material boundaries are connected in specific societal contexts. We must be wary of identifying such symbolic boundaries as necessary in all societies.

Concluding remarks: intersectionality and class

A more intersectional framing (discussed in the last chapter) has been able to transcend debates on class and gender that focused, for example, on the issue of whether women can be treated in the same way as men in the class system, whether their class position derives from that of the family unit (their father or husband), or whether women constitute a class in themselves (for an account see Crompton and Mann 1986). Marxist feminism, with the domestic labour debate and the analysis of women as an RAL (Molyneaux 1979; Beechey 1977) had already made important inroads into this with much heated debate about the role of women in capitalist production and reproduction. But perhaps more importantly, intersectionality has overcome the tendency to treat gender as a 'complicating' variable and enables it to be conceptualised as a central dimension of stratification. However, the theorising of class within intersectionality is very underdeveloped.

Critical race studies and intersectional framings have shifted the debate from issues such as whether all racialised people form a class in themselves, whether they are a sub-proletariat or whether they are class fractions (as migrant labour was seen e.g. in Castles and Kosack's influential book (1973) and in the work of Phizacklea and Miles (1980)). However, there is some important work, some of it recent, that treats race as a central component of the development of class relations and capitalism rather than an additional element that needs to be taken into account (e.g. Virdee 2014). Some of this work is no longer dependent on a full-fledged Marxist paradigm of class relations but draws on it and a range of theoretical positions.

Where social stratification has implied that there is merely a ranking of places, here it takes on the relational and agonistic aspects that class has been strong on. It's important therefore to think of hierarchical positions as relational and

114 Hierarchising places

intersectional within an overall system of inequality. In this way it is possible to enter into the analysis of unequal outcomes, other categorial and concrete relations: around production relations and labour market functions (the basis of class) gender and ethnicity/race, as well as others. This retains the importance given to production relations, as gender and ethnicity and other categories are embedded and operate within that space, on the one hand, and class operates also in the social relations of gender and ethnicity/race.

In this chapter I have argued that the problem which class identifies is indeed inequality, and yet inequality cannot be collapsed with the problem of class. Class relations permeate society but, on their own, do not exhaust the dynamics of inequality making. Class is part of a *process* of inequality making and coexists in a dialogical relation with the other spaces of the organisation of difference, such as gender/sex and race/ethnicity (which I see alongside class as the primary bifurcating and inequality regimes in modern capitalism). I have also argued that we need to rethink a theory of stratification away from the distinction between production relations as material, and ethnicity and gender as solely symbolic or cultural. Within a Marxist framing they are central aspects of the division of labour, facilitating exploitation as economic value is allocated to them. Within a Weberian framing, on the other hand, gender and ethnicity may be given the characteristics of marketable attributes in the marketplace. For example, where there is market value attached to sexual or gender attributes, ranging from explicit sexual services like prostitution or surrogacy, to personality traits or physical traits (such as appearance, using notions of 'attractiveness' or slimness), then gendered characteristics may sit with education or technical skills, that is, as resources which individuals can use for determining their life chances. In terms of ethnicity, knowledge of particular cultures, including language proficiency or the possession of social capital, may constitute conditions for entry into the market.

Within the framing presented here we can centre these categorial formations, and other salient sorting processes of individuals, alongside production and its social relations, as important elements of social stratification, that is, as determining the allocation of socially valued resources and social places/locations. Certainly, other divisions are also important elements in social relations and in stratification (such as age, health, disability, religion and so on). However, I treat the divisions of gender (including sexuality), ethnicity and racialisation as lying at the heart of the social (Anthias 1998b) and being particularly salient constructions of difference and identity, on the one hand, and hierarchisation and unequal resource allocation modes, on the other, within the modern capitalist symbolic/material nexus. This is still so, despite the fact, as argued in Chapter 1, that there have been moves towards fluidities, precariously lodged within spaces of fixity.

Arguably, capitalism, as we know it, could not have been built without the deployment of gender or race categorisations although at the abstract level of analysis Marxism posits an internal logic that is indifferent to the characteristics of individuals. But real capitalisms are not abstract – they are violent and subordinating and built on the exploitation not only of the abstract worker, but the differential exploitation of differently marked bodies. Plantation slavery, colonialism and imperialism, the subordination of women, the cheap labour of the migrant, the insecurity and vulnerability of the precariat, the flexibility of surplus populations are all examples that are clearly charted in the literature. The only conclusion from all this must be that without such categorial distinctions capitalism potentially would face its crises differently, and would have succeeded or failed in different ways. Working out how new social formations can be developed that avoid such unequal effects must be an ongoing concern for all those dedicated to a radical transformation of society, and towards greater equalisation and better quality of life. This involves a concerted challenge against all those categorisations that essentialise and fix, acting as anchors and building blocks for hierarchical distinction, subordination and violations of human life and equality.

In the next two chapters of this book I engage with broader issues of the dilemmas of the categories of gender on the one hand and ethnos on the other, by looking at contemporary debates on gender, intimacy and violence in intersectional ways and at categories of collectivity with a particular focus on migration and racialisation.

Notes

1 The Goldthorpe class schema is based on income, economic security, market situation, location in systems of authority and work situation It arose out of the Oxford Social Mobility Study of England and Wales conducted in 1980 and was later developed by the CASMIN project into an elevenfold classification of occupations.
2 The Equality Duty in the UK is a duty on public bodies to consider the needs of all people in delivering their services and covers the nine protected characteristics found in the 2010 Equality Act. It came into force in 2011. The protected characteristics of the 2010 Equality Act are age, disability, gender reassignment, race, religion, sex, sexual orientation, marriage and civil partnership and pregnancy and maternity.
3 The BBC gender pay gap gained publicity in 2017 when the BBC was forced to publish the salaries of top presenters earning more than £150,000 a year. This showed that many famous men were paid substantially more than their female equivalents. In 2019, the Equality Commission in Britain launched an investigation into the gap between men and women employed by the BBC.

5

TRANSGRESSING PLACES

Dilemmas of gender, intimacy and violence

Introduction: mutuality and control

At the heart of the gender category there is relationality and binarisation, linked to co-dependency and mutuality, on the one hand, and forms of control and violence on the other, both symbolic and physical. However, in concrete social relations, it is not possible to analyse these in terms of gender relations alone as they are always entangled in other forms of ordering, and inequality-making categories, as argued in Chapter 3. The gender order or 'regime' is itself neither given nor constituted in the binary and essentialised conceptions of gender, but gender lends itself particularly as a stigma or branding that translates into the naturalisation of social effectivities. Positing biological proclivities or psychic traits and predispositions functions to legitimise the different roles that gendered subjects play in the fields of the economic, the political and the representational.[1] They penetrate the realms of class and race where, in articulation, they are (further) overlaid by biologistic and collectivised marks, complexly woven in time and place, shifting and fluid, or fixed and entrenched.

As such gender categories facilitate exploitation and differential exclusion in ways that invisibilise the forces at play. This invisibilisation of inequality processes is a central feature of modern societies where systems of representation and legitimisation of power relations can be signalled by terms such as misrecognition/symbolic power (Bourdieu 1984), false consciousness or fetishisation (Marx 1859), reification (Lukacs 1967), hegemony (Gramsci 1971) and the knowledge-power nexus (Foucault 1982). Whilst differently inflected, all these point to the importance of how the social order becomes a given and taken for granted realm.

The forms of domination found in the gender category and its relations appear as forms of symbolic and physical violence. This includes intimate partner violence, familial gender violence and the physical violence inflicted on the bodies of rape victims (where women's bodies 'asked for it' or men's bodies were too excited to resist as they were 'led on'). Domination is exercised through the economic exploitation of migrant women carers, whose supposed proclivities for care and 'choice' function to alleviate the extreme forms of exploitation of their labour. It is found in the abuse and rape of their bodies by their employers, or other members of the dominant group or nation, for whom those bodies are open to violation.[2] Therefore, gender categories reinforce the naturalisation of power; they also reinforce dominant national imaginaries and class relations of exploitation. Feminists have pointed to how gender categories function in the reproduction of compliant ethnic subjects or national citizens (Anthias and Yuval-Davis 1989) and provide reproductive labour for capitalism (found in the domestic labour debate and the debate on applying the notion of the RAL (reserve army of labour) to women, noted later in this chapter. Symbolic power is inscribed onto and into their bodies (fertility and childbirth) and psyches (emotionality, caring, femininity – for women – and others for men) leaving strong imprints, not so much or at least, not only, on predispositions (as Bourdieu (1980) claims) but forms of self-abnegation that can only be resolved within the internal mechanisms of the gendered order of things. This includes demonstration of more and more compliance with the violence exercised on their bodies and selves, through regimes of dieting, beautification and modification (such as violence/mutilation to their breasts or faces through surgery) as ways to achieve a self which is validable and visible through the very invisibilisation of power.

Gender is not the only category that is particularly subject to tropes of the 'natural' and the 'body' – we can see this operating in different ways with 'race' (see Chapter 6). One of the distinctive marks of the category of gender is that of intimacy within its binary formulation, so men and women, for example, and bi and trans men and women, forge solidarities both to their others and to those who share their gender in different ways. This differs from ethnic or class categories where the external boundary is antagonistic rather than solidaristic. However, at the same time, gender establishes prima facie a hierarchically inflected co-dependency between the two halves of the binary divide (e.g. in the dyadic relationship of the modern family form and hetero and homonormativity).

Depending on the life cycle, the family form or stage in reproduction, and in articulation with context, the relation to the other gender in the traditional gender binary is a more important form of identification (e.g. in the hegemonic construction of the intimate couple or family relationship) than amongst men as men or women as women. However, collective group making occurs through forms of sociality which involve solidarity in dealing with abnegation, stigma and violence, expressed in the fight for women only spaces, in LGBTQ struggles as well as political mobilisations over pay, violence and rights. Hen parties and girls' nights out are arguably also forms of solidarity building, although replicating sexist tropes. Many political mobilisations by women seek inclusion on equal terms with men, and others' recognition of the differences of women. Claims to equality cannot tackle long-lasting subordinations which are evident in a gendered division of labour, for example where equal pay for equal work is not applicable. Instead claims to equal pay, even if the work is different, may produce

118 Transgressing places

a more effective rallying cry, similar to the claims that 'we are here, we are queer, get over it' (quoted in de Genova 2010) that are made by the queer community. Forms of solidarity amongst hegemonic groups (including men against women) may take the form of exclusion, or opportunity hoarding as Tilly (1998) describes it, from a protectionist vantage point. Mutuality and common purpose, at the concrete level, are disrupted (some might say underpinned) by what feminists generally call patriarchal social relations.

The relationality of gender is deeply asymmetrical and involves the control and subordination of women, and violence, as well as the construction of disabling femininities and masculinities. Such violence does not only come from men nor, if it does, from any necessary proclivities but also takes the form of violence at work (e.g. where domestic workers may be beaten by their employers) or sex trafficking. But where there is intimate partner violence, this does not eradicate or displace relations of caring, intimacy and solidarity, either within the couple relationship or within the family. The violence that women experience at different levels is overdetermined by forms of intimacy and the emotional and bodily labour that is exacted from them. Intimacy often involves asymmetrical power, as established in the mother–child relationship and much sexual intimacy involves bonds of asymmetrical pleasure, although this is not the place to explore this issue. Certainly, relations of intimacy can be sustained within the parameters of such asymmetries, as the study of the family and sexuality can testify (e.g. see Miller 2010).

Gender categories, like all categories are both analytically distinct with their own effectivities but also intersectional and translocational. The notion of difference in relation to gender is inflected by the ways in which gender constructions and discourses mark the boundaries of the social, and particularly of the nation (see Anthias and Yuval-Davis 1989) and relate to gendered projects of the state (see Pateman 1988). How gender is harnessed to the projects of ethnic and national groupings is one theme of this chapter, which also looks at how women are inserted into the global landscape of inequality, as workers, and within the global care chain. The undoing of gender for many women from the Global North, at the partial level, has been made possible through the continuing 'doing' of gender (often racialised), in the care work of women from the Global South. This also facilitates global inequality, both at national and transnational levels (see McDowell 2014). There is another dilemma that this chapter can only deal with briefly because of constraints of space and this relates to moves towards fluidities, and the undoing of gender, and pulls towards fixities, found within the very heart of such processes. This is raised particularly with different types of gender fluidity, including gender transitioning, and the ways some feminists have responded.

Sex/gender

There has been a tendency (at the risk of oversimplifying quite complex arguments) to see gender as a product of the social organisation of sexuality and to regard sexuality as expressive of gender with differential and varied forms of

Transgressing places **119**

causality implied. For example, for MacKinnon (1982) it is sexuality that determines gender through the social priority given in power relations to heteronormativity which is also then the root of gender inequalities. Oakley (1972/1985) and many others have sought to differentiate between sex and gender in terms of the distinction between sex as biological and gender as socially constructed, using a model of socialisation. More recently, particularly through the work of Butler (1990, 1993), feminists have pointed out that sexual allocation through genitalia and other physiological characteristics is not pre-discursive and reject social constructionist arguments (such as socialisation models). Butler has challenged the binary of sex as natural and gender as social, emphasising sexuality as a form of governmentality and gender as performative (synthesising the work of Foucault 1982 and Goffman 1956). Others (e.g. Bordo 1993) have argued that feminism had pioneered these ideas before Foucault.

Although Butler's is a sophisticated and plausible point of view it arguably fails to consider the meanings which are given to *actual* physical or material aspects of sexual difference, an argument made by Dorothy Smith (2010), for example, in terms of hormonal and other physicalities. The visceral effects are linked to menstruation, the menopause and reproduction. Mediated by the social, through which they acquire their meaning, they inform the very *naturalising* aspect of gender, as an incontrovertible testimony to the existential basis, despite these physicalities not actually being explanations for the social position of men and women. Gender and sex are not just performances, however. They are inscribed in bodies and psyches, in social arrangements, and their performance is not a choice. At the same time gender normativities are not homologous with concrete gender practices. The gap between gives space for change and resistance. This complicates Butler's views that the transgressivity of gender performance, particularly through the performance of queerness, marks the rupture with gender normativities. Such normativities are broken through everyday forms of resistance. Moreover, even with changing conceptions of gender roles, and the transgressivities of queerness, a strong gender ordering in the organisation of society exists at all social levels, testifying to its structural, complex and intersectional basis and to the existence of homonormativities also that are far from socially transgressive (see Richardson 2017; Dhawan and Varela 2016).

Others (e.g. Krais and William 2000) argue that Bourdieu's notion of habitus allows '*doing gender*' as both the action of the individual and as a socially pre-structured practice: the 'gendered and gendering habitus'. In this way the distinction between sex and gender can be overcome. In his essay on male domination, Bourdieu draws attention to symbolic violence, which 'constitutes the essential aspect of male domination' (Bourdieu 1990, p. 11). Although such a notion has proved to be influential in the analysis of domination, asking about the link between gender and sexuality brings into play the problem of categories as well as ontological domains (see Chapter 2) which are not subsumed under Bourdieu's notion of 'habitus'. For Bourdieu, the gendered habitus relates to predispositions that are formed within fields by subjects rather than the ways in which social

120 Transgressing places

categories interpellate them and constitute them. Like the now rather under-used notion of socialisation, habitus implies an active making through a porous self which is open to the effects of location, rather than to the effects of power. Such a position could be critiqued in similar ways to 'identity' (see Brubaker and Cooper 2000; Anthias 2002), that is, as being static and encompassing the totality of the individual (in the case of habitus, their predispositions). Such critiques have challenged binary and static notions of identity (for identity we could substitute habitus), stressing fluidity and multiplicity, and emphasising practices which are contextual and situational as well as performative (see Hall (1996b) also who retains the use of identity whilst arguing for its complexity as it has 'no guarantees').

A particular problem in Bourdieu's masculine domination (2000) is the idea of women's acceptance of sexual domination because of their dispositions, and he gives all women a habitus which is feminine, and by implication universalises gender. The assumption of a fixity to the gendered habitus is at odds, more-over, with his view that habitus functions within specific fields rather than in a broader societal context (see also Chapter 2).

Rejecting simplistic socialisation models does not mean rejecting the role of social relations. Society constructs men and women differently, in terms of notions of passivity, dexterousness, multi-tasking, caring and a range of other supposed attributes which women have in contrast to men. These are con-structions and performativities that have marked effects on ideas and practices (through iteration) by men and women, and of course, about men and women in society. In the case of gender, it is woman that embodies difference. The rules of heteronormativity establish the difference as that which lies on the deviant queer and inferiorised side of the sex and sexuality binary, constituting the other as queer and woman. Although gender is a boundary-making process relating to power rather than a given, it operates within structural arrangements, including those of capital and the state, which produce and reproduce as well as change social hierarchies (Anthias 1998b; Walby 2007).

The cultural turn has dominated the field of enquiry (see discussions in Nich-olson 1994; Sullivan 2003; Richardson 2007). The link to political economy, so prominent in the third wave feminist analysis and in the debates on race, ethnic-ity and class of the 1970s and 1980s has receded. This has been partially a result of some of the perceived failures of political economy. Whilst pointing to material structures of capitalism and its social relations, it was unable to fully attend to complexities relating to identifications and embodiment. However, more recent ideas of femonationalism (Farris 2012a) and the work of social reproduction feminism (Ferguson 2016) are moving in the direction of locating developments in gender relations within economic and political structures and relate them to the economy, the nation and citizenship. Feminist political theorists have been important in discussing forms of gendered citizenship (e.g. Pateman 1988). There has been a shift from a focus on patriarchal relations, considered as the domination of men over women, or alternatively as class domination.

There has been some discussion of the traps of equality talk and practice under neo-liberal governance. As Richardson (2007, p. 468) has argued:

> In the UK and parts of Europe, for instance, one might want to argue that a changed relationship between gender and homosexuality is evident at the institutional level through the operation of a neo-liberal social policy agenda that extends certain rights to (some) lesbians and gay men and deploys 'sameness' with heterosexuals as a central aspect of its argument.

This neo-liberal agenda has been concerned to normalise (e.g. through civil partnerships and marriage) and potentially also to destabilise the radical potential identified with non-heterosexualities, and the challenge of queerness to heteronormativity thus recedes. This may also be the case in terms of their co-optation by new social movements that are not so much concerned with transforming social institutions and structures but with being included within them on equal terms (stressing rights on the basis for equality). Dhawan and Varela (2016) analogously also talk about similar processes with regard to the deployment of equality for queer people in the making of racialisations and nationalisms as homonationalism, and the next section briefly looks at the issue of gender and nation (see also Anthias and Yuval-Davis 1989).

Doing nation: gender, nation and femonationalism

Gender processes are important in understanding how nationhood and belonging are forged and reconstituted, particularly through the role of women as ethnic actors. Ethnic and national practices contain rules and discourses about sex difference, gender roles, sexuality and sexism at their very heart. They are therefore important boundary markers of inclusion and exclusion in conjunction with the ways that class differences produce differential work roles, differences in pay and glass ceilings (see later in the chapter the discussion of migrant women and work). Men and women are particular objects of national and ethnic discourses and policies in terms of the biological reproduction of the group/nation, as well as its cultural reproduction and symbolic figuration (Anthias and Yuval-Davis 1989; Collins 1993; Charles and Hintjens 1998; Wilford and Miller 1998; Mulholland et al. 2018). Women perform different roles (in intersection with class and life cycle) in the reproduction and transmission of symbols, rituals, practices and values. Practices of gender and sexuality often mark the boundaries of the nation. Women are central transmitters of ethnic culture in their chid-rearing role and in migration; they reproduce cultural traditions (having a special role to play in ceremonial and ritual activities, keeping in touch with families and so on) and religious and familial structures and ideologies. They are important as 'mothers' of patriots (Anthias and Yuval-Davis 1989). For example, in both Bosnia and Cyprus, the rape of women involved the project of forcing them to bear the children of the enemy, and

122 Transgressing places

women were violated as 'mothers of the national enemy'. However, it has been argued that women function as objects of discursive practices and social relations, whereas men are its active agents. Anthias and Yuval-Davis (1992) and Wetherell and Potter (1992) argue that men are given the authentic voice to represent their communities. Both are signposted through the essentialisation attributed to sexed bodies. Masculinities are associated with power and force, and femininities with softness and caring.

Women's sexuality and reproductive role are controlled in ways which draw a marked border between those women who have citizenship and those who do not, thus marking the bodies of the first as deserving of protection of their rights, and the bodies of the latter as being legitimately excluded from those rights. So, both migrant men and women are made vulnerable at one and the same time by operations of power relating to allocating different roles to men and women. Men are treated as a threat to women's safety, both native and migrant, and the purported aim is to safeguard women from the sexual violence of racialised and migrant men. This was, for example, found in the discourse against migrant men in Cologne[3] in the New Year celebrations of 2015/16, operating as part of the racialisation of the other.

As Sager and Mulinari (2018) say, concurring with Anthias and Yuval-Davis (1989):

> In nationalist imaginaries women are understood as embodying the borders of the nation, an imaginary that is at the core of a range of forms of violence and threats directed towards women who challenge these boundaries and who are (symbolically) located on both sides of the border (Eduards, 2007). Another central theme at the intersection of gender, sexuality, nation and belonging is the way in which notions of protection and safety act upon the category of woman.
>
> *(p. 151)*

The concern with so-called honour-based violence, discussed later (see also Gill 2010), articulates the need to protect women who are regarded as victims from their ethnic or Muslim culture. This involves stigmatising minorities, and particularly Muslims, treating them as a threat to western values and national interests. It also testifies to the ways in which gender is often at the heart of culturalist constructions of collectivities. Individual cases are regarded as representing collective patterns and there occurs a demonisation of the whole culture (Grillo 2008; Gill 2010), fuelling Islamophobia in particular. As Sara Farris (2012a, p. 184) notes, 'when women migrants are mentioned at all, they are portrayed as veiled and oppressed Orientalist objects'.

In addition, Muslim women become the embodiment of the backwardness of, and cultural danger posed by, migrant and racialised men, particularly through the emblematic figure of the veiled and oppressed Muslim woman (see Anthias 2013c; Farris 2012a). Gender rules may be used to promote racialisation and racist rules may be used to increase sexism. Alternatively, a reduction in one may mean a growth in the other (Anthias and Yuval-Davis 1992). Gender oppression can be hailed as a way of demonising the racialised other and women's protection can be part of a nativist or racialised project. For example, gender equality discourse is used to demonise some racialised categories on the basis of their oppression of women. Farris notes:

> The mobilization, or rather instrumentalization, of the notion of women's equality both by nationalist and xenophobic parties and by neoliberal governments constitutes one of the most important characteristics of the current political conjuncture, particularly in Europe.
>
> *(2012a, p. 184)*

Coining the term femonationalism, Farris puts a name to the attempts of European right-wing parties, amongst others, to co-opt feminist ideals into anti-immigrant and anti-Islam campaigns, echoing Gayatri Chakravorty Spivak's (1994, p. 93) apposite phrase: 'white men [claiming to be] saving brown women from brown men'.

Mutuality as myth? Gendered violence

Violence has been central to gender and sexuality and epitomised in both physical and symbolic violence, and violations of the body and person. Rape and its transnational dimensions, sex trafficking, modern slavery, domestic violence, sexual harassment and sexual violation (the latter taken up very prominently by the 'Me Too' and 'Times Up' movements)[4] are disturbing forms of such violence and harm. An intersectional gaze problematises and pushes further our understandings of different forms of gendered violence, which constitute the other half of the mutuality-violence twin that characterises gender relations. Pat Hill Collins (2000) suggests, rightly, that we must reject simplistic views of violence that assume that 'men dominate women, Whites oppress people of colour, and oppressors victimize the oppressed' (p. 936). The structural underpinnings of violence mean we cannot treat it merely as a gendered phenomenon, and therefore it is not simply a question of what men do towards women. On the other hand, it is often experienced as part of an intimate partner relation, or at work or modern slavery as inflicted by men, and the violence can be treated as part of the patriarchal control of women. Such violence is not only exercised by men (at the level of domestic violence, for example) but it is important to say that it is men primarily who are the perpetrators. Much of the literature on gendered and sexual violence, underemphasises the role of class whilst stressing the intersections between racism, gender inequality and normativity (Anthias 2001b; Gimenez 2001; Anthias 2014). However, women from working-class backgrounds, whatever their ethnicity, are most vulnerable to forms of economic exploitation, domestic violence and work in the sex industry or to being trafficked.

124 Transgressing places

1. Rape

Rape is one of the most devastating violations, and violent crimes, against women and it is treated by the courts in most European countries as a sexual crime rather than a crime of violence against women. Many women do not disclose rape for fear of being branded and because of the ways they are treated by the police and courts. Very few rape crimes end up with a conviction in court as some women withdraw their accusation, but also because the courts very rarely convict the accused.[5] The sexuality of the female victim is often treated as a problem (with the commonplace exhortation to 'dress properly' or the accusation that she 'asked for it') at various stages in the process.

Within feminism, the idea that all men are potential rapists and all sexual consent has an element of force has characterised much writing on issues of rape. For example, MacKinnon (1997) argues that 'women's sexual consent is not meaningful, and rape is indigenous, not exceptional, to women's social condition' (1997, p. 42). Research has shown (e.g. Holland, Ramazanoglou and Sharpe 1998; Ferrett, Herbert and Brodeu 2019) that many young girls submit to sex not because they want to but because of pressure either from their peer group, the male partner or local youth cultures and norms. However, it is not the case that rape cannot be differentiated from sexual consent. Although at times sexual consent can be a product of normative constraints, the violation that women experience, and the physical and symbolic violence of rape victims, has long-term consequences on women's well-being.

As Alison Phipps notes:

> power is written onto female bodies in specific and contingent ways. Violence would be positioned as central but should be seen as a context-dependent structuring principle which has multiple impacts on the experience and aftermath of sexual violence.
>
> *(2009, p. 667)*

The male rapist has been depicted predominantly as the violent working-class or racialised male, and alongside this, a stereotyping and 'othering' of the working-class or racialised female 'victim' takes place. Skeggs (1997, p. 99) has argued that black and white working-class women are also constructed as the sexual and deviant 'other'. This is counterposed to the feminine respectability of the white middle-class woman who has the requisite capital (cultural and symbolic). She argues that there is a form of symbolic violence exercised by the middle classes on the working classes (Skeggs 1997), which involves both fear and disgust (Lawler 2005). This has been one way in which social stratification has operated to hierarchically organise different forms of women.

Rape is also prevalent as part of war and ethnic conflict. The assumptions of hegemonic masculinity become naturalised through social hierarchies and cultural mediums, as well as through force. Rape undertaken by groups of soldiers or ethnically motivated gangs may be part of the reinforcement of ethnic solidarity in times of conflict. It serves to both reinforce hegemonic masculinity and group boundaries and allegiances.

Alison argues:

> part of the reason gang-rape promotes group cohesion may be that it bonds men together in a complicity (in fact a shared awareness of responsibility) that makes loyalty to the group vital. During times of conflict . . . 'our women' are contrasted to 'their women' and 'our men' to 'their men'. 'Our women' are chaste, honourable, and to be protected by 'our men'; 'their women' are unchaste and depraved.
>
> *(2007, p. 77)*

War in the name of *womenandchildren* (as Cynthia Enloe (1998) coined it) reinforces the sexual division of labour and the idea of masculinity as protecting, and femininity as nurturing and submissive. Perpetrating sexual violence against the women of the enemy reconfigures the object of reference of sexual violence away from all women (potentially) towards women who represent the enemy. Indeed 'militarised nationalism' (see Efthymiou 2019) is defined by the normative compulsion to exercise violence against the 'other' as a test of loyalty and commitment to the group. It is also one of the yardsticks of proper masculinity in this context – as heterosexual as well as protective of the group's vulnerable members, seen as women and children.

But, as Alison (2007) argues

> a more complex analysis of empirical cases of wartime sexual violence that examines the interplay between masculinity, femininity, ethnicity and sexuality, is required and serves to bring into relief the problems with accepting this binary *(between men and women)* at face value.
>
> *(p. 89)*

Rape is not merely a manifestation of patriarchy and binary and unequal relations of subordination between men and women. Differentiated masculinities and femininities are constructed through the syncretic working of interlocking power dimensions of gender, race and class, and how subjects take up identity positions. Some of these are opportunistic and incoherent. On the one hand, the ethnic enemy is constructed as uncivilised and barbarian (therefore there is a need to protect our women and children), and on the other hand, the perpetration of extreme forms of violence against the women and children of the 'enemy' mirrors such barbarity.

2. Domestic violence

Domestic violence is also a crime with complex dimensions and has devastating effects on women, indicating how intimacy and violence are intertwined. The

126 Transgressing places

construction of women as 'victims' has been replaced by treating them as 'survivors'. This depiction affirms their agency (Barry 1979; Dunn 2004) and that women resist, cope and survive. The increasing treatment of domestic violence as a proper crime, and therefore requiring criminal intervention, is affected by judgements not only about what constitutes abuse but also how respectable or deserving the women involved are deemed to be. Skeggs (1997) refers to normalised and respectable femininities and the binary it constructs between those who are deserving or undeserving of our sympathy (as with rape). This judgement is both classed and racialised. Dominant tropes come into play about black male masculinities, culturally motivated domestic violence (within families), and women who are to blame through their provocative or unreasonable behaviour.

Many women who have experienced domestic violence do not disclose it. This includes women from all ethnicities and classes. One aspect of this is that 'Individuals may have internalized ideologies antithetical to disclosure of violence' (Bograd 1999, p. 281).

Sokoloff and Dupont argue for the complexities which are part of the reasons for non-disclosure in the following way:

> As a member of a devalued racial identity, some women of colour, particularly African American women, may fear that calling the police will subject their partners to racist treatment by the criminal justice system as well as confirm racist stereotypes of Blacks as violent. . . . Furthermore, lesbians who are not out, or voluntarily open about their sexual orientations, may remain silent about the abuse in their relationships . . .
>
> *(2005, p. 43)*

The traumas of disclosure relate particularly to stigma associated with sexist notions that they 'brought it on' as well as not wanting to be a victim. One of the characteristics of domestic abuse is the creation of bonds of intimacy in the violence. Some abusers vacillate between angry and uncontrollable violence, abjection, persistent claims to 'being driven to it', and promising to never 'do it again', which they cannot keep to. Such behaviour makes it more difficult for a woman to leave her abuser as it generates feelings of self-blame and low worth. Additionally, a sense of protection towards him is aligned with an expectation that his violence can be overcome. In such cases hope triumphs over experience. There are also fears of abandonment and addiction involved in the process.

In looking at these complexities, it is important to avoid an overculturalisation of these phenomena and an underemphasis on the structural dynamics at work. In addition, the primacy of gender becomes unclear as violence and control by a man is not the only form of violence experienced by many women, including racialised women. Lack of support from welfare and other agencies and forms of abuse in terms of racialisation and class are also important (Razack 1998).

Gendered violence in the context of globality and transnationalism

There is a growing recognition of the ways in which globalisation affects women disproportionately and unequally. Women have been most affected by its detrimental effects, such as increasing poverty, forced migration, and sexual and economic forms of exploitation. If we examine, for example, the social location/position of gendered and racialised migrants within a transnationally understood framing, sex trafficking and women's labour in the care sector are important facets of the global reach of this new political economy.

There are a range of forms of violence women experience, such as modern slavery, trafficking, honour killings, and rape, either as part of ethnic or racist crimes but also in terms of the vulnerability of women at work, including as domestic maids, carers and sex workers. There has also been a global inequality that accompanies globalisation linked to the hierarchy of countries in the global world and the increasing exploitation and economic disadvantages faced by many economies and societies in the Global South. The experiences of women in migration are gender specific, many involving forms of violence, both physical and symbolic. These crimes are also racialised as well as culturalised.

1. Honour-based violence/violence against women

Culturalisation and hierarchical difference is found in discourses relating to the veil, honour-based violence and forced marriages. We have seen an emphasis on gender and the female body in depicting undesirable others. Both the debate on the veil and on so-called honour-based violence, including forced marriages, are often framed within a gender equality discourse (e.g. see Roggeband and Verloo 2007; Farris 2012a), which aims to protect minoritised women. There exists a thorough culturalisation of the social issues involved, however, and they are depicted as only related to the 'other'. To critique such culturalisation is not to endorse such gendered crimes or issues they raise about gender equality, however.

It is impossible to give accurate estimates of the number of women who have lost their lives in so-called honour killings. According to the UN population fund over 5,000 women are killed a year in the name of honour, mainly in Asia and the Middle East, but also Europe (World Economic Forum 2016). This is likely to be an underestimate as many women are abducted or disappear (e.g. see Begikhani et al. 2010). The nomenclature of 'honour-based violence' tends to divest it of its gendered aspects, viewing such crimes as the result of cultural values rather than practices of gender-based violence more widely. So-called honour-based crimes are generally differently regarded to other forms of sexual violence undertaken within the domestic or family arena, even though, as crimes, they share some of their characteristics. They are all dependent on patriarchal forms of control and highly gendered notions of appropriate feminine and

128 Transgressing places

masculine roles and practices which of course differ within different social and cultural and national contexts.

In 2017 new legislation was introduced in the UK against forced marriage (see CPS 2019 for update) but there is still no specific offence of 'honour-based crimes' and these are covered by existing legislation. They are regarded as a violation of human rights and seen as particular forms of domestic and/or sexual violence. The Crown Prosecution Service in the UK defines honour-based violence in the following way:

> There is no specific offence of 'honour-based crime'. It is an umbrella term to encompass various offences covered by existing legislation. Honour based violence (HBV) can be described as a collection of practices, which are used to control behaviour within families or other social groups to protect perceived cultural and religious beliefs and/or honour. . . . It is a violation of human rights and may be a form of domestic and/or sexual violence.

The CPS, ACPO and support groups have a common definition of HBV:

> 'Honour based violence' is a crime or incident which has or may have been committed to protect or defend the honour of the family and/or community.
>
> *(CPS 2019)*

Clearly the element of violence against women is being subordinated to the cultural contexts within which it takes place. Of course, unlike domestic violence which is usually conceived as a crime of anger which is uncontrollable, it is usually premeditated and often involves the whole family, rather than just one person. For example, there may be collusion or participation of siblings and maybe even the mother and extended family members. However, this is a particular form of violence against women and is not 'just' cultural. Honour crimes are embedded in broader structures and cannot be seen to derive from either mainly cultural or patriarchal forms alone. Moreover, it is not just Islamic as it is also associated with Mediterranean and Middle Eastern countries (some of which are Christian). Indeed, because of this, it has been argued that they should be seen as part of a more general phenomenon of VAW – Violence Against Women (Gill, Begikhani and Hague 2012).

The culturalisations involved draw on hegemonic versions of religious faith or 'ways of life' of the 'other'. They are also prominent in ways in which forced marriages and genital mutilation are often hailed in public debates and discussions in order to argue that there is a limit to ethnic diversity and multiculturalism. Such debates also include those of the headscarf or the chadur. Muslims and other racialised groups are regarded as unable to integrate because they are unwilling to conform to the supposed universalist principles of western democracies, partially because their culture is seen as backward and incompatible with gender equality (see Chapter 6). The contradictory ways in which the plight of women is constructed is important to note. Whilst racialised women are seen as victims of culture (and not just individual men), non-racialised women are seen as victims of individual men, who are thereby pathologised.

Reactions to practices of body covering (such as the use of the hijab and the chadur) have been intricately woven with the demonisation of Muslims in Europe. Although there is no prohibition in the UK, there has been a great deal of debate on the veil (see Meer et al. 2010) and particularly on the burqa, which is seen as a manifestation of the unwillingness and/or inability of Muslims to integrate and as a security threat. For example, it is argued that it allows terrorists to act as imposters, pretending they are devout women (e.g. see *The Sun*, April 11, 2011, the day when the burqa was banned in France). The hijab and the burqa are sometimes depicted as archaic fetishes that threaten western society. As Edmunds (2012, p. 7) notes

> The 'clash' is neatly crystallized at border crossing points, when the western need for security through surveillance collides with the hijab-wearer's insistence on staying covered. The western press is keen to report stories of male Muslim criminals/terrorists who use the hijab as a disguise.

In relation to so-called 'culturally motivated' crimes, women are supported, but demonisation takes place of the whole group, thereby justifying forms of surveillance and control in the private arena of the home as well as within the private arena of religion, tradition and cultural life. At the same time, girls and women subjected to these forms of violence are often exhorted by anti-racists who may be also members of their group, not to disclose these issues as this would contribute to feeding racism. The contradictions and tensions between political mobilisations on the bases of anti-racism and feminism are here apparent (Anthias and Yuval-Davis 1992).

An intersectional framing here is not just about the recognition of differences of women across lines of race, faith, culture or class. Such a framework must seek also to look at wider discourses and practices as well as structures of dominance and how these feed into the social frameworks involved for tackling gendered violence, as well as the practices and understandings of the actors themselves.

2. Trafficking

Another aspect of the transnational dimensions of gender which link it to violence (and the pursuit of profit) is the crime of trafficking. There is a tendency in the trafficking literature on women to conflate trafficking with sex work. Not only are men and women both trafficked, but women are brought in for particular labour market roles, and not just for sex work, as workers and maids. Treating sex work as work, and as part of the role that migration plays in the formal and informal sectors of the economy is therefore important.

130 Transgressing places

The International Labour Organisation (ILO) notes that

> At any given time in 2016, an estimated 40.3 million people are in modern slavery, including 24.9 million in forced labour and 15.4 million in forced marriage . . . 4.8 million . . . are in forced sexual exploitation . . . women and girls . . . account(ing) for 99% of victims in the commercial sex industry, and 58% in other sectors.
>
> *(2017)*

The ILO developed a Protocol and Recommendation on Forced Labour in 2014, with the aim to eliminate it, ratified by 40 countries currently.

At world level, the 2000 United Nations Convention against Organised Crime in Palermo (United Nations 2000) gives a legal definition of trafficking in human beings and the guidelines for a global approach. Article 3, paragraph (a) of the Protocol to Prevent, Suppress and Punish Trafficking in Persons the UN states:

> the recruitment, transportation, transfer, harbouring or receipt of persons, by means of the threat or use of force or other forms of coercion, of abduction, of fraud, of deception, of the abuse of power or of a position of vulnerability or of the giving or receiving of payments or benefits to achieve the consent of a person having control over another person, for the purpose of exploitation. Exploitation shall include, at a minimum, the exploitation of the prostitution of others or other forms of sexual exploitation, forced labour or services, slavery or practices similar to slavery, servitude or the removal of organs.
>
> *(United Nations – General Assembly 2000)*

Trafficking in women typically involves the movement of women from poorer countries to comparatively richer ones. Women in the ex-Soviet bloc countries, such as Bulgaria and Romania, have been particularly trafficked into the sex trade during the post-socialist transition process. Trafficking lies at the crossroads of migration, gender, policies *and* crime, in the context of globalisation. The GAATW (Global Alliance Against Trafficking in Women) starts from the premise that trafficking is embedded within gendered migration and labour contexts, and women's complex realities. The Trafficking in Persons (TIP) Report issued annually by the US, in 2019 points at difficulties in tackling this crime:

> This multifaceted crime can challenge policy makers. The foundational elements of human trafficking are difficult to grasp, and the real world instances of this exploitation are even harder to identify. Importantly, how governments address human trafficking depends heavily on the way authorities perceive the crime.
>
> *(T.I.P. report 2019, p. 2)*

Transgressing places **131**

The focus on trafficking in the discussion of sex work assumes that all sex work for migrant women is forced and deprives them of agency. Women migrants are actively engaged in using social networks to travel and to advance their social positions, sometimes for pure survival but at times to escape from violent and abusive relationships back home or to flee from political persecution (Anthias and Lazaridis 2000). However, in the process some fall victims to traffickers and yet others may be mindful of the few options for survival they have in difficult circumstances.

Some women are brought in under false pretences purportedly as dancers, 'artistes' or 'musicians' to work in the many clubs or bars (Anthias 2000; Kontos 2009), euphemisms for the sex industry. For example, in Cyprus it caters largely for the indigenous population although tourists also hire sex workers. Migration related to sex work has been very profitable and is an integral part of tourism in many countries in Southern Europe. Sex workers come particularly from Southeast Asian countries, such as Thailand, and from Eastern Europe. These women enter the country within the framework of a legal status as 'artistes'. In their countries of origin, they are recruited either as cabaret dancers or quite openly as prostitutes. Even though the status of 'artiste' is legal, its heavy restrictions create conditions that make the women heavily dependent on their employers. Those sex workers who overstay the permitted period, send a female relative in their place, change employers, or enter on tourist visas and operate illegally are particularly vulnerable to exploitation. Some women are aware that they may be required to do some sex work. Like all migrant workers, they have a degree of agency and work to negotiate and struggle against the economic, social and sexual oppressions they face. Their status usually as undocumented or 'illegal'/ irregular presents problems in terms of escaping some of the degradations and subordinations they face as trafficked women for sex purposes. Their overriding problems are therefore linked to illegality as migrants and the illegal nature of the sex trade itself in many countries, making them doubly vulnerable. Not possessing forms of cultural capital or social capital in their new homes on migration brings to the fore also the class and race issues with which they are confronted.

As Agustin (2005, p. 100) remarks:

> Apart from strategies to make money and structural conditions shaping the labour market, women also want to travel. . . . From Lucía's point of view . . . she knew that selling sex would be an aspect of her first European job . . ., but . . . she saw herself as an artistic dancer and intended to get into 'straight' show business.

However, this discussion needs to be in terms of the global reach of trafficking. This takes place in the context of a global unequal system of countries and people within them, and the migration project of escape and betterment, as a class and at times an ethnic project (relating to forms of ethnic violence and persecution in their own countries). Migration policies mean many migrants are undocumented

132 Transgressing places

and constructed as illegal, thereby making them more vulnerable to exploitative work conditions (including sex work). To privilege gender in understanding sex trafficking fails to consider the ways in which gender, race, ethnicity and class articulate in specific contexts for the specific women involved. There is a need to look at prostitution and trafficking, therefore, in relation to the workings of global capital.

One way of approaching sex trafficking for prostitution, is to question the assumptions that globalisation benefits all women (Elson 2002) and to be aware of the gendered nature of transnational mobilities and processes. As Anderson says (2005, p. 452), there needs to be a framework that is 'grounded in the connections between race, gender, sexuality, and class in the political-economic context of women's lives'. This includes focusing on intersections of power along cultural, economic and political lines. There is a need therefore for a feminist political economy that is globally oriented. Using a gendered framing in relation to globalisation highlights the diverse mechanisms that create vulnerability for different categories of women. These include economic inequalities within sending and receiving countries and the global growth in informal labour markets. This in turn is partially linked to the role of remittances for some economies, particularly from women migrants in the new migrations (Ehrenreich and Hochschild 2002).

Within the scope of the FeMiPoL project (Anthias, Kontos and Morokvasic 2012), we undertook biographical interviews with six trafficked women. There was a variety of experiences of women from a variety of countries – Brazil, Nigeria, Latvia, Guinea, who were now living in four EU member states, Italy, France, Germany, the UK. From these interviews, we found that migration regimes make them susceptible (through being undocumented) to sex traffickers even after migration (Campani and Chiappelli 2012). In the narratives, we found that it is not gendered processes alone at work. It is the interplay between the division of labour, poverty, irregularity, hopelessness and vulnerability on the basis of class, ethnic disadvantage and lack of cultural and social capital.

Violence against women, although suffered differently within different social classes and ethnic and national communities, also cuts across them and women's groups have responded through campaigns, refuges and challenging cultural traditions such as genital mutilation and the stoning of adulterous women or honour crimes. There have been organisations against girl child killings in parts of Asia, trafficking of women and abuses and killings linked to dowries and other economic facets in marriage and familial social exchanges. The local and context-based approach to these gendered and sexualised forms of violence has become a hallmark of the global feminist movement which has moved ahead from debates about multiculturalism versus feminism, for example, that demonised the practices of minority groups (e.g. polygamy, genital mutilation and honour crimes). These failed to be sensitive to the pervasive forms of violence found in western cultures such as dating, romance, heteronormativity, domestic violence, rape and abuse.

Intimacy and violations in transnational work: the global gendered economy

Women's labour is appropriated in diverse ways. In the case of minority ethnic groups, it functions in the reproduction of care work transnationally and forms of economic activity and adaptation which partially enable white women to gain class advantages. There are two sets of gender relations that are involved, those of the minority and those of the dominant majority and the intersection of these in transnational space, demanding and transgressing gender norms and values across them. These gender relations then produce a particular class structuration for different migrant and ethnic minority groups in conjunction with labour market processes and racialisation. Limited rights to citizenship and being constructed as outside the proper boundaries of the nation (and through racialisation) position women in a range of subordinated locations at global levels.

Global capital and global governance produce and reproduce different marked bodies at the meeting place of gender, race, migration, citizenship and class. For example, white western women profit from the exploitation of migrant care workers, which gives them the capacity to enter the labour market. Although this may liberate some white western women from the burdens of child care and domestic work, and enable them entry into the labour market, in the context of poor state provision it does not transform gender relations between men and women. This also alerts us to how different categories of bodies are deployed strategically within the power structures of the modern global order.

The flexibility that global capital needs can harness traditional understandings of gendered bodies as life forms of temporal deployment to be discarded or replaced where the exigencies require this. Migrant women generally fill particular roles in the labour market, being cheap and flexible labour for the service sectors, and in care and domestic work, and in some countries, for small/light manufacturing industries. They have a particularly important presence in doing the care work of the richer world. In this context it is also important to note the ways many migrant women come in as nurses and doctors also (see Farahani 2017; Fathi 2017). Significantly they carry the burden of the honing back and hollowing of the welfare state in many European countries. Many women work in the poorly paid care work sector as nannies and maids doing the work of transnational mothering, constituting a transnational care system or global care chain (Hochschild 2000). Most women are located within a highly gendered and racialised secondary, service-oriented, and often hidden, labour market; their insertion props up and reproduces an ethnic and gender divided system of capitalist relations.

Feminist theorists (Anthias 1992a; Anthias and Lazaridis 2000; Indra 1999; Kofman 1999; Kofman et al. 2000; Morokvasic 1984; Phizacklea 1983; Anderson and Phizacklea 1997) have for some time now highlighted the constraints within which migrants operate. They have also corrected the tendency to divest women of agency, showing how migrants, and in this case migrant women, make choices

134 Transgressing places

and plans for themselves and their families. For example, some of these choices may not be primarily economic and women may be motivated by wanting to escape violent and/or oppressive familial or marital relations. The constraints of gender roles and normative expectations more generally act as powerful factors in many women seeking migration to find greater opportunities (Anthias and Lazaridis 2000; Anthias, Kontos and Morokvasic 2012). Many migrant women's choices are heavily constrained by poverty and instability in their countries and communities. This makes their roles in the global market of production and reproduction particularly complex. Such complexity includes taking account of differences, not only in terms of geographical origin, but also in terms of the differentiated social positions that they occupy in the sending and receiving countries and within globality. It is not just a question of gendering migration, giving agency to migrant women, but also looking at the ways their roles are assigned and the points at which they become dehumanised, over-exploited or disposable (figured most poignantly in the case of the 12 women murdered by an ex-army Greek Cypriot officer in Cyprus in 2019).[6]

Important aspects of migrant women's position globally includes gender and care (Lutz 2014; Hochschild 2012; Kofman 2005); domestic work (Anderson 2000, 2006; Lutz 2017); sex work (Anderson 1997); gender in the manufacturing industry (Phizacklea 1983); and men and women's role in family or 'ethnic' businesses (e.g. see Anthias 1992a; Anthias and Mehta 2003; Al-Dajani et al. 2014). For example, the deployment of women within small enterprises in 'ethnic niches' is part of the use of women as an economic resource which is familialist, reproducing gender relations in the home within the workplace. For example, family labour has been a central pattern for many migrant groups in the post-war period in Western Europe (Anthias 1983) and the survival of many small concerns has depended on the unpaid labour of women and children within them (Anthias and Mehta 2003; Anthias and Cederberg 2009; Song 1999). Other areas of migrant women's work include the service sector and the agricultural and food processing sectors.

Intimacy and care

Sassen (2000) places emphasis on the gendered outcomes of the movement of global capital, stressing also the feminisation of poverty. An increasing number of women from the Global South look for survival by working in the Global North. The greater insertion of women into the labour market in the Global North is partially made possible by using migrant women as maids and carers. The intimacy and affective relations of trust replicate the family form, but outside the purported mutuality of family relations. As Silvia Federici (2006) notes,

> Unlike commodity production, the reproduction of human beings is, to a great extent, irreducible to mechanization, being the satisfaction of complex needs, in which physical and affective elements are inextricably

combined, requiring a high degree of human interaction and a most labour-intensive process.

(p. 13)

In relation to Europe, the lack of welfare provision and cuts to services, that is, the hollowing out of the welfare state in Northern Europe and its underdevelopment in Southern Europe, have led to demand for care and domestic services. This has been filled by migrant women who are often brought in for these roles. Caring roles also include work in nursing and care homes (increasingly privatised), working as home helps for the elderly and in domestic work for families. Majority ethnic women are less likely to want to perform these generally arduous and poorly paid jobs.

Lutz (2014) argues that it is:

> 'not just another labour market' *but* 'a core activity of doing gender. . . . Outsourcing household and care work to another woman is widely accepted because it follows and perpetuates the logic of gender display in accordance with institutionalized genderisms.'

(p. 19)

This is related to what has been called the care crisis with the attendant commodification of care relating to the 'care drain' and the development of the 'global care chain' (Hochschild 2000; Anderson 2000; Lutz 2014, 2017). Women migrants leave their own children to care for the children and elderly in the Global North. Some important contributions in the area include Sassen (1996, 2000, 2014); Parennas (2001) and Ehrenreich and Hochschild (2002).

The specific aspects of the emotionality of care are important. The people performing this care have to invest in forms of affect and intimacy which makes the work quite different to other areas of the economy. Service workers, but to a more limited extent, also perform care, as do schoolteachers or nursery teachers, nurses and doctors, all constituting part of what can be termed the caring professions, again particularly feminised. As many of the women performing the care of mothering have left their own children at home to care for others, this may have complex resonances for them – on the one hand, fulfilling, but on the other, inducing feelings of guilt.

We can illustrate some of the issues by examining the small country of Cyprus. In the 1990s, Cyprus became a country that receives migrants from the Third World and Eastern Europe. Like much of Southern Europe, Cyprus has experienced a feminisation of migration (Anthias 2000). More and more Cypriot women have been incorporated into the labour force for some time now, but the gendered division of labour continues within the Cypriot economy and within the home. Migrant women are therefore important in terms of the changing configuration of gender relations for Cypriot women. Following the pattern found in the rest of Southern Europe, there is little regulation of the terms of

136 Transgressing places

employment of many migrant women. In one prestigious new development in Nicosia, I found that 24 out of 26 families had a foreign maid in 2017. This phenomenon is not confined to families where the women work; more and more women within the middle classes are hiring maids as part of a materialist status symbol. Many migrant women provide services not just for the family that employs them but also for the employer's elderly parents; they may be given tasks of cleaning parental homes and looking after sick relatives as well as looking after the children of brothers and sisters. A barter in maids is not unknown, and a particularly pleasing maid may be passed on to other relatives or friends. Many of them are not treated as part of the family, and they eat their meals separately. They have little protection and can be regarded as another form that precarity takes in Europe.

To address such problems, Maria Kontos (2013) argues for the professionalization of care work and Joan Tronto (2005) for citizenship. However, this needs to be seen in the context of the multiple elements involved in citizenship that cannot be dealt with purely at the formal state level, given the degrees of differential inclusion involved and the multiple local, ethnic and contextual issues raised by citizenship in its diverse forms.

The complexity of the care relationship needs to be acknowledged. The carer may have some degree of power over the cared, found, for example, in the relationship between social workers and welfare dependents or in the surveillance which that relationship entails, giving care work a degree of intersubjective power (Fraser and Gordon 1994). However, for most domestic women carers who are migrants the relationship is asymmetrical in the sense that the care giver has little power. It's important to bear in mind that intimacies are complex and care work is not the exception. As Bridget Anderson notes (2006), narratives of mutuality and trust work to obfuscate relations of power and poor treatment.

Although the domestic sector is an important area of migrant women employment, some writers have questioned the disproportionate focus on domestic work (as well as sex work, e.g. Kofman and Raghuram 2006). They stress the need:

> 'to be careful to make sure that it does not obscure other forms of reproductive labour that migrant women engage in or other contributions they make to receiving economies,' *and* '(t)hey should not provide the discursive limits for theorising migrant women's incorporation into global circuits of reproductive labour.'
>
> *(Kofman and Raghuram 2006, p. 287)*

In the UK, migrant labour has been an important source of care for the National Health Service where nurses, trained overseas, provide a central pool of labour. This has been important both in its development and its feasibility (Kofman et al. 2000; Kofman and Raghuram 2006). Like most countries in the Global North there is a growing pressure on the health services, exacerbated by austerity and an ageing population. It has more recently been affected by the debates around Brexit and the anti-migration discourse that prevails. Many doctors and nurses are leaving Britain and others not arriving. There has been an increasing privatisation under neo-liberalism and many care homes have been part of this privatisation of services. In addition, the domestic sector relies on migrant women, although in a different way in the UK to Southern Europe where maids are more likely to live in and enter the country on short-term contracts. There are high levels of exploitation, such as high workloads and excessive working hours (Anthias, Kontos and Morokvasic 2012). Domestic and care workers are especially vulnerable and exposed to high levels of abuse and exploitation.

In addition to the work described above, migrants, particularly women, take jobs in the service sector, in cleaning, hotel work and catering (McDowell et al. 2006; Anderson and Rogaly 2005). This is found in what can be called the flexible arm of the employment market, with dangers of precarity, and those found in the gig economy, where they are very precarious. The gendered nature of cleaning (McDowell et al. 2006) is manifested in men working more in public spaces (like streets), and women in 'semi-private' spaces, such as offices and hotels, or in private homes. The growth of the agri-food sector is also linked to migrant women's work, and their work is low paid, labour-intensive and often temporary. Much of this work takes place in rural areas. This makes it more difficult for migrants to form networks, leading to greater isolation and vulnerability to exploitation (Anderson and Rogaly 2005; see also Anthias, Kontos and Morokvasic 2012). Such areas of work are characterised by poor levels of job security and relative lack of unionisation, as well as lying often between regularity/irregularity. Such situations also relate to au pairs who may take extra work which is undeclared, as well as students who work more hours a week than they are legally entitled to. Some workers may experience more stability than others who are constructed as a 'surplus' population, brought in and out of the labour force with changing economic needs.

It's also important to look at skilled and professional migrant women, as Fathi (2017) does in her work on Iranian doctors in the UK and Farahani (2017) in Sweden. Such roles are particularly important at a time when the need for 'skilled' labour has been part of the argument about 'managing migration' and 'controlling our borders', regarding the types of skills that should be sought for through migration. It's important to correct the image that migrant women are solely found in the lower echelons of the labour market and are only from the lower social groupings from their countries of origin. This also relates to the importance of differential forms of exclusion and inclusion (Anthias 2001a; Mezzadra and Neilson 2013). Many highly educated and professional women can't use their skills fully because their qualifications may not be recognised, as well as through racism and discrimination (also noted by Friedman (2019) in relation to what he calls the 'class ceiling' for professionals of working-class backgrounds).

138 Transgressing places

Transgendering or undoing gender

In this book I noted the dilemma between pulls to fluidities and pulls towards fixities, raised particularly with gender transitioning. The importance of *the experience* of being in a real woman's body, referencing not only hormonal differences but long-standing experiences of subordination and threats faced by women in their lives from male predatory violations and violence, are prominent in the feminist backlash against transgendering. Built, partially, on the idea of authentic gender experiences, there are also mobilisations around women-only spaces, which are set against transgender 'infiltration'. These are currently being fought over the transgender identity issue, with regards to the use of toilets, political representation and sports participation. They have emerged in the wake of what appears a much more fluid understanding of gender, which has challenged its binary construction.

Transgendering has also involved narratives of 'real' gender identities, of people being in *the wrong body*, echoing essentialist arguments about how gender and the body should be aligned together. The transgender movement at times holds on to stereotypes of masculinity and femininity, also, disavowing the role of biology in terms of physiology but naturalising gender in terms of essential psychological proclivities, with again the trope of being a real woman, if not in body at least in gender identity. Reliance on being 'really' (despite or because of genitalia) man or woman is still a significant trope – within the transgendering process it is seen as the inalienable proof that transitioning is legitimate or illegitimate. Within medical ethics and rules, living as a woman or man for a certain amount of time, passing as a woman or man, and so on, are usually regarded as conditions for being given sex re-alignment surgery.

Non-binary gender identities appear much more challenging to the ordering process than sex re-alignment. This may account for people seeking modification of their bodies so that they are able to express their gender fluidity; fixing their gender through fixing their body. To exist in the in-between is much more difficult to accept within the gendered order of things. However, transgendering can be a complex and multifaceted process. Lisa Diamond and Molly Butterworth (2008), for example, show how some transgender persons have a non-binary version of their bodies. In the accounts they give of four transgender women they say:

> none of these women described feeling 'trapped' in the 'wrong' gender, and none sought to irrevocably replace her female body and identity with a male one. Rather, they all articulated experiences of multiplicity regarding their gender identities and resisted selecting one form of identity as inherently primary.
>
> *(p. 367)*

Sex re-alignment through surgery may be regarded by some as a form of brutality towards the body and, therefore, yet another kind of violence in the name of gender. Judith Butler (2015) in an interview opposes such positions herself, but the interviewer cites gender critical feminists who assert that transwomen are merely mutilated men. Butler acknowledges that gender may be important to some and that being allowed to be the gender one chooses is vital. She embraces the rights of people to fix their gender as and how they please. This might seem paradoxical as in her work gender is treated as performative and socially constructed, and she has a non-essentialist view of identity. However, she is articulating the feminist principle of a (transgender) 'person's right to choose'.

Earlier I mentioned that some feminists are opposed to treating transgendered people as their chosen gender. When the UK Labour Party announced (NEC May 2018) that it would allow transwomen to stand in its all-women candidacy shortlists there was a very quick and angry backlash from some feminists. They saw this as a violation of their rights as women and convened an event in Parliament. This was followed by a new wave of hate speech towards trans-people. Another set of public debates in the UK has centred on transgender women taking part in the women–only sports category. Some, like Martina Navratilova, have argued that this disadvantages ciswomen since transgender women have physical abilities on average that are more like those of men. It is sometimes argued that transgender people should compete as a category separately. If so, this requires two new categories: transmen and transwomen rather than one. Or should the categories of gender remain explicitly binary so that transwomen should be treated for all purposes, including competitive sports and using public toilets, as women and transmen be treated as men, or the other way around? This is currently a topical issue of debate. Some degree of transphobia may emerge, according to some commentators:

> The actions of anti-trans feminism gives rise to one of its paradoxes: feminists telling (trans) people that they are not the authorities on their own experience. With feminism being firmly rooted in the view that the best source of knowledge about our realities is our own experience, this is a counter-intuitive stance.
>
> *(Kalayji 2018)*

Concluding remarks

Gender categories are complex and gender relations often transgress the normativities associated with gender, disrupting the homology of gender and the body. Gender relations manifest multiple trajectories as they articulate with those of the other salient categories of difference and ordering. Intimacy and violence are essential components of the patriarchal and heteronormative framework of the neo-liberal state and capitalism. Some 'othered' poor and vulnerable women perform the caring and dirty work that enables more hegemonic women to transcend, if only partially, their own subordination. Intersectionally constituted hierarchies reveal how their 'privilege' along class and ethnic lines is enmeshed

140 Transgressing places

in gendered forms of subordination and violence. The mutualities expected amongst women in honour-based violence include conformity to patriarchal rules which women themselves at times police, whilst they themselves are vulnerable to violence. In terms of the ways these feed into racism, we can see how demonising whole cultures and ways of life takes place using an equality discourse, playing the trumpet of equality but with the tune of racism. A translocational intersectional lens is able to see these practices as fired not just through the 'doings' of gender, however, but also through how they are done and undone by class and overlaid with racism in socio-spatial and situated ways which are at times contradictory, with pulls to fixity and pulls to fluidity. They are useful modes for the pursuit of inequalities and for dealing with the crises of capitalist societies.

Notes

1 Unlike Butler and Foucault who treat sex and sexuality as historicised and constituted in the entrails of the social, Bourdieu tends to treat sex and gender as givens which are then empty vessels to be filled by social attributions and predispositions from the interplay of fields, i.e. as forms of the habitus.
2 Bourdieu, on the other hand, sees male domination as reinforced by classification associating women with the magical and the secret and that women cultivate their own domain of symbolic power on this basis.
3 In the 2015/16 New Year celebrations it was reported that there were mass sexual assaults and 24 alleged rapes in Cologne, reportedly by men of Arab or North African appearance. These attacks sparked criticism over Germany's asylum policy and the sexism of certain migrant groups.
4 Me Too is a campaign started against sexual abuse in the film industry as a consequence of the allegations against Harvey Weinstein. Although the phrase was used as early as 2006, it was popularised in 2017. Times Up is a movement founded in 2018 by Hollywood celebrities as a response to the Weinstein effect and to the Me Too campaign.
5 In September 2019 the Crown Prosecution Service in the UK launched a review to examine myths and stereotypes about sexual violence in the wake of the release of figures showing very low conviction rates for reported rapes. In 2017 only 5.7% of reported cases ended with a conviction according to the Crime Survey for England (CSEW). See rapecrisis.org. uk.
6 An ex-army officer from Cyprus was convicted of killing 7 migrant women and girls and placing their bodies in a lake in Nicosia. This exposed the ongoing abuse of migrant women.

6

TERRITORIALISING PLACES

Dilemmas of b/ordering the nation

Introduction: fluidities and fixities in trans/national space

There is a paradox at the heart of how collective categories transpose onto national borders today. This lies in the transnationalisation of identities, and associated multiculturalities and convivialities, indicating the growth of fluidities, and the challenge posed by newer and stronger fixities of belonging. Ethnic and cultural ties operate increasingly at a transnational level, for example, through cosmopolitanism and diasporic claims, as well as new communication modes, media forms and digitalities. New transcultural forms have emerged, on the one hand, and newer racisms and ethnocentrisms have appeared, on the other. As globality generates new types of power structure and new dominant groups in the global economy, such as multinational corporations and international financial capital, at the same time it generates or amplifies new forms of inequality and, arguably, new forms of coloniality.

Nation, 'race' and migration mark important spaces where struggles about where and how borders are placed for control and management of populations and resources are played out. Borders, both symbolic and territorial, play a central role in the discourse of states and nations. Addressing these issues requires a focus on the control and management of migration both at the border and inside the border. Such a focus also reveals that the racialised 'other' may be a citizen, but still a 'racialised outsider'. As Sahlins (1989, p. 271) claims, borders are 'privileged sites for the articulations of national distinctions', and therefore, of national belonging. Today, the focus on borders has been amplified through the so-called migration and refugee crisis since 2015 (although it predates this), and the growth of populisms around the world that are marked by racist and nativist tropes.

The management of difference and 'diversity' in relation to 'ethnos/nation' is clearly an important facet of the making of inequality and belonging. This

142 Territorialising places

operates in the context of migrants being at one and the same time a necessary part of the labour market and a contaminator of the national project, and at other times a disposable 'surplus' population within the economies of the western world, and an object of humanitarian global governance through various human rights discourses and bodies, and their contradictions (see Chouliaraki and Georgiou 2017).

This chapter looks at a range of bordering processes relating to collective categories and their contestations, and ways in which belonging is politicised and policed in various ways, hierarchising resources of different types. Borders around collectivities and national boundaries throw into play some of the violent and dislocating aspects of the categories of the collective 'other'. I begin by delineating what I regard as a family of concepts relating to collectivity, and then engage with the saliency of the 'migrant' category in relation to the so-called 'migration and refugee crisis' or what Papastergiades (2000) calls the 'turbulence of migration'. I also examine racisms and nativisms, and the projects of racialisations, as both modes of exclusion and modes of exploitation. These become salient at different times, and are essential to the differentiated nature of the reach of the global. I also consider the uses of the discourse of diversity and integration in the management of the 'other'.

The collective 'other': a family of concepts

The categories of collectivity are highly variable. Categories of collective difference or what can be referred to as 'ethnos', a broader category than the English word 'nation', involve a family of concepts which include ethnicity, nation and race. More specific collective categories such as refugees and migrants can also be treated as part of this complex, as they are relational to national borders, intersecting with social relations of displacement and translocation, as well as gender and class. All involve forms of entitlement/dis-entitlement and belonging/non-belonging of different kinds with both categorical boundary and border-making processes, but also solidary and bond-making practices.

I argued in Chapter 2 that the specificity of this set of category making is linked to the ways in which collectivity and generic social bonds are constructed around those who are seen to share a common origin (formulated at times also as a common destiny) in various ways (which can include shared cultural, biological or territorial attributions). I think a useful way of thinking about this family of concepts is in terms of the social construction of an origin as a significant arena of struggle. This denotes their political nature which plays out in experiential/ affective as well as organisational, intersubjective and representational ways. The category of collectivity can be broadened to include groups who are collectivised and demonised on the basis of undesirable and alien beliefs or values where what is shared is seen as a culture of danger and contamination. These include Muslims, and the Roma who become both ethnicised and racialised, whilst not necessarily being attributed or attributing to themselves a common origin or destiny.

Territorialising places **143**

One of the primary aspects of such categories is the setting up of boundaries between those who can be included in, and those who are excluded from, national or political belonging. The primacy of the 'boundary' is central here, as are the ingredients within the boundary (although Barth (1969/1998) regards 'the cultural stuff' as a subsidiary element), which are imbued with valuation. The more these ingredients are understood as essentially different (deviant), the people as a danger (to life or to resources) or deficient (and therefore undesirable and inferior), the greater the likelihood that they will be racialised. But the processes do not emanate from the relations *between* groups, or indeed in discrete social imaginaries, although these are also important. They emanate from broader social relations of power relating to economic and political processes. Some of these categories have a particularly important role to play in economic exploitation. Others are linked more to the integrity of national boundaries relating to an existential threat, or function centrally as constructing the markers of belonging relationally in antagonistic ways. These are highly political, and at times relate to struggles over territory or hegemony.

The paradox I noted earlier is that social relations have tended towards new fixities as fluidities (found in multiculturalism, conviviality, free movement of labour) begin to challenge the order of things. Indeed, this is sometimes manifested in the contradictory pulls of nationalism and capitalism, where capitalism, in the desire for cheap labour, breaks down the barriers of entry to the 'other', whilst nationalism, both through governmental imperatives and contestations, on the ground, by those who feel displaced as 'natives', reins back the breaking of borders, manifested recently as a political ideology of anti-globalisation. Indeed, there is continuing if not growing centrality given to national imaginaries, through the growth of nativism.

A translocational approach flags the highly heterogeneous appearance of these categories as they friction, collide and intersect with those of other major players in the processes of boundary and hierarchy making, across space and time. One instance is found in the ways gender functions to construct the boundaries of the nation in different ways, which I discussed in the last chapter. At the global level, migration is a particularly important set of relations which mark out the boundaries of entitlement and dis-entitlement relating both to national borders and transnational capitalism.

Globality is often accompanied by increased expressions of inequality, uncertainty, ethnic conflict and hostility and new concerns with security and closure: not all nations or social groups have benefitted equally, and the anti-globalisation movement, as well as the retreat to nativism, is one symptom, partially, of this. In short, there may be contradictions that still need to be played out but globalisation and bordering sit as uneasy but tolerant neighbours today. Anti-racist struggles of different types, the growth of multiculturalist and other discourses and practices that recognise (or should I say mark) diversity, increasing hybridisation and transnational relations exist in the context of the continuing importance, situationally, of the national paradigm and the nation state form (manifested also

144 Territorialising places

in what some have called methodological nationalism, e.g. Beck 1999; Wimmer and Glick-Schiller 2002).

At the academic level there have been calls for a transnational lens to accompany the growth of transnationalism. The ethnic lens has been critiqued since it assumes that ethnicity is always central in explaining the practices of minorities and migrants. Certainly, a transnational lens corrects the worst excesses of methodological nationalism (Wimmer and Glick Schiller 2002; Beck 1996). But despite globalisation nation states are still the determinants of juridical, social and cultural citizenship and the ethno-national project remains central. (Anthias 2009; Brubaker 2010). It is clear, also, that the national boundary possesses affective, discursive, experiential and political relations within a global context. This means that a critique of methodological nationalism need not mean abandoning nation-based lenses for analytical purposes; for example, in looking at social policy, migration procedures and controls, health or educational regimes that differ from one national context to another. Nor does abandoning an ethnic lens mean side-lining the role of ethnicity in social life. Therefore, the lens we use should never be predetermined and depends on the types of questions that we ask.

The age of migration

Today, there are 70.8 million displaced people, of which 25.9 million are refugees, many of the latter interned in refugee camps (the largest is in Bangladesh in Kutumpeng with over 800,000) (UNCHR 2018b). A generation of Somali youth were born in the refugee camps of Kenya. As well as official camps run by the UN or the International Committee of the Red Cross and NGOs there are unofficial camps such as those in Idomeni in Greece where people are left without the support of governments or international organisations. It has been calculated that every minute in 2018, 25 people were forced to flee (unchr.org retrieved September 2, 2019). These are deeply disturbing figures that point to the violence of borders as well as the exacerbation of inequalities in the world today. People drown crossing the Mediterranean seas, they die crossing the Sahara desert, or they die at home because they are unable to escape poverty and disease. People have to choose how to die and not how to live. New technologies of bordering have emerged, directed at migrants and refugees as well as settled racialised populations from older migration trajectories (Mezzadra and Neilson 2013; Yuval-Davis, Wemyss and Cassidy 2019).

There has been an increasing emphasis on the role of bordering practices which manage the 'other' and police the boundaries of nations. Migration controls and the withdrawal of citizenship, linking directly to the policing of national boundaries and racialisation, are certainly not new phenomena nor new concerns. As far back as 1991, Miles and Rathzel noted that, since 1974, immigration law and migration processes continue to be shaped by 'racialised conceptions of national identity and citizenship' (1991, p. 23). The cases of Britain, France and Germany raise the issue of the importance of the different criteria used by nations to determine who its members are. In Britain until 1981 when the Nationality Act introduced for the first time the criterion of birth to a parent born on British soil, any person had a right to British citizenship who was born on British sovereign territory. Recent redefinitions of citizenship and increased immigration controls serve to effectively deny full citizenship to black and other migrants, as well as to new migrants from third country states, whilst a now more figurative than real managed migration system relating to the 'needs' of the British economy functions to exclude the poorest and most disadvantaged in the world.

In tandem with this, new bordering regimes have been put in place to prevent increasing levels of people, escaping poverty, wars and disease, entering Europe. There are many undocumented migrants who risk their lives, as well as asylum seekers, who lodge at the 'hot spots' (Tazzioli and Garelli 2018; Trimikliniotis 2020) such as those at the notorious (and now closed) Calais 'jungle' and Lesbos and Chios in Greece as well as Turkey and other countries outside the EU. The 'controlling our borders' argument, in Britain for example, was a central element in the Brexit vote of 2016. Such narratives underpinned Theresa May's introduction of 'the hostile environment' in 2012. They are played upon by right-wing parties all over the world, in Trump's concern to build the wall with Mexico and in the rise of right-wing parties in Hungary, France and Germany amongst others, as well as in Greece and Cyprus (with New Dawn and Elam).

In January 2018, there were over 20 million non-EU nationals residing in the EU (ec.europa.eu/Eurostat, retrieved October 5, 2019) who make up 4% of its total population and this is on the increase. However, in the UK, since the Brexit vote in 2016, not only has net migration declined but there is an increase in the numbers of EU nationals leaving the UK, itself a manifestation of the lack of safety that they feel. This is haemorrhaging the NHS as well as depleting the service and agricultural sectors which have relied on EU workers at all levels. EU nationals, many of whom have been in the UK for many years, have felt uncertain about their position as they are being increasingly required to demonstrate that they have rights to stay. The Windrush scandal of 2018,[1] which made hundreds of British citizens from the Caribbean stateless, is an example of how policies and practices on the ground are increasingly racialised, with more and more restrictions on who really belongs to British society. In 2018, British citizens who arrived in Britain before 1973 were threatened with deportation, deprived of legal rights and in at least 83 cases were deported back to the Caribbean. Other ex-colonials, for example from India and from Cyprus, also feel this insecurity and that it may be their turn next. Questions about the ways full citizenship is being delimited are raised in this context.

Britain is, at the time of writing, in the cusp of the latter days of the Brexit fiasco, after the appointment of a new Tory prime minister, Boris Johnson, who has taken over from Theresa May. New forms of racism, articulated as nativism which has already been mentioned, have emerged in the wake of austerity which has lasted for over a decade. They have also emerged in the wake of dealing with new economic fears. This was the case with the unification of Germany where

146 Territorialising places

new forms of nationalism and racism emerged in the wake of the destabilisation of the old order. In the ex-Soviet bloc and in the countries emerging out of the former Yugoslavia, particularly, we saw the emergence of new claims to nationhood by previously submerged nationalities (groups with an ancient and historic notion of a national, not merely ethnic, claim to their own territory) who may have had one in the past and who resurrected themselves as 'nations' with their own political autonomy.

'Who' has the right to enter and stay within a nation state is a central concern of our times, but such a discussion has taken a more polarising form in the last few years with austerity politics and the growth of the far right (Fekete 2018). It is also a response to the framing of migration in terms of numbers, and types of population (as 'undesirable'). Such migrations have been complexified in the wake of various wars and displacements worldwide. The use of criteria such as possessing the right attributes of birth, descent, religion or culture (or a mixture), or in terms of possessing the equivalent to these (through a process of deracination and reracination, or acculturation and adaptation), are some of the ways this emerges. Such a process demands that some minorities, particularly Black, Roma or Muslim, lie outside the 'normal' boundaries of the nation, thereby being excluded, or differentially included in subordinate ways, their participation as full members of society being denied. Rights to citizenship or even work are curtailed for those who come, for example, as asylum seekers. Those who manage to come and overstay, that is, are undocumented, face problems of vulnerability, housing and work as well as being in constant fear of being arrested and deported, through the various policing policies of states, including the legal duties of citizens to report them.

The purported threat from 'hostile' identities has underpinned migration and integration policies in Europe, which in Britain gave rise to the move towards creating 'a hostile environment', announced by Theresa May in 2012 to disastrous effect, and exemplified in the Windrush scandal, mentioned earlier. This is an adjunct to the conception of 'hostile' identities embodied in the war against terror, but it is also constructed in terms of fears of unskilled, dependent migrants, asylum seekers and refugees whose cultures and ways of life are seen to be incompatible or undesirable within western societies, and the fear of social breakdown and unrest (echoing Enoch Powell's notorious Rivers of Blood speech in the 1950s). In 2013, May said that a tenet of the policy was 'deport first and hear appeals later'.[2] In 2016 the policy included requirements that landlords, the NHS, charities, community interest companies and banks carry out ID checks. Notorious 'go home' vans in 2013 encouraged voluntary deportation as part of Operation Vaken. It is not just a question, however, of a nation-based hostile environment, as there is an externalisation of borders and international agreements which produce it at the transnational and global levels. The United Nations 2018 Global Compact on Refugees and the Global Compact for Safe, Orderly and Regular Migration provides a non-legally binding frame for political commitments to a worldwide approach, safeguarding migrants from point of origin to arrival, committing to 'empower migrants and societies to realize full inclusion and social cohesion'. The UK has committed, along with many other countries, to this framework. However, this doesn't have any muscle and is based on the good will of partners, and some countries voted against it, five in all – the US, Hungary, the Czech Republic, Poland and Israel, whilst 12 abstained, four of them in the EU.

Borders are being continually constructed and reconstructed in the wake of social, political and economic projects. The socially constructed nature of borders and their political nature contrasts with the naturalised view of nations as embodying singular identities and cultures. Many borders of nations today have been imposed by international treaties in the aftermath of wars and do not relate to national imaginings of peoples or cultures. National borders, however, acquire and lose their significance under different conditions, whether in terms of embodying the 'ethnic group', as significant political communities with international legitimacy, or forms of primary social solidarity. They constitute an important, albeit contested, arena where issues of otherness and belonging are played out, reproduced and transformed. However, as I have argued, to understand them better requires paying attention to their location within broader structures of dominance, and constructions and practices relating to other boundary forming phenomena and identities such as those of gender and class. The more recent focus on 'the border as method' and 'the autonomy of migration' (Mezzadra and Neilson 2013) is a significant development in the understanding of borders. However, this has failed to consider the dimensions of governmentality that relate to migrant and racialised women, raised in the last chapter.

Migrant category/ies

With the panoply of movements and processes that both link the world and fracture it through multiform borders, the category of 'migrant' has become an umbrella term for all forms of mobility relating to border-crossings. The term is not restricted to the traditional notion of the economic migrant wishing to better 'him/self' (sic) and is a catch all term, although it is still not generally applied to richer and better off people, or the British, French or Germans abroad.

Researchers and theorists have tended to work with taken for granted assumptions about the supposedly cohesive nature of the social collectivity, and the interference or 'turbulence' caused by migration. Assumptions about a cohesive societal whole (usually still defined by nation state borders) within which poorer or racialised migrants are framed, lead to their problematisation (see the discussion of diversity and integration later in the chapter). The construction of a migrant or transnational social actor category (as a social collective or group) often relies on notions of 'ethnic' origin (therefore using an ethnic lens) or consciousness/culture/identity/religion. The notion of refugee cuts across notions of ethnicity but again is constructed as a 'type' of person, usually male and predatory and one that is threatening to the resources of the nation (as well as 'abject' – Arendt 1951).

148 Territorialising places

The migrant 'other' signifies the border of the nation, as in and of itself it suggests a category of person that has transgressed a border – either as a welcome guest or someone who may not be wanted. This is partially found in the notion of *xenos* (the non-family member in Greek, or the stranger, as expressed in the work of Schutz and Simmel in different ways). For Schutz (1944), the stranger is one lacking cultural know-how and therefore needs to acquire new repertoires which will allow entry or inclusion, and for Simmel (1908), he (sic) is regarded as a deviant and feared for the difference he (sic) embodies, as 'the dangerous' (epitomised, in Simmel's work, by the Jew). However, it is a complex category and involves many statuses legally, and variable social attributions. It is also a category that relates to expulsions of different kinds, more, or less, forced; for example, the migrant worker seeking to find better economic prospects and the refugee or exile fleeing. It can be transient, circular, settler or sojourner. The people may be given differentiated inclusions through full or partial citizenship or insertion into the labour market, or may be 'illegal', criminalised and expelled/deported. Some experience racism more than others or, at least, different specific forms of othering, depending also on crosscutting categories such as class, colour, skills, language, religion or gender. Those migrants who have gained citizenship are not subjected to the same forms of formal regulation as those who have not. They are not ordered by regulations over work entitlements or settlement status. However, they may still be subjected to surveillance and are more likely to be interrogated and asked to provide evidence of eligibility for work and access to health services. Those who are visibly different in terms of language, dress or colour are more likely to be a 'suspect category' and continually interfered with by the border guarding that is being taken to new levels in all spheres of life – called by some, everyday bordering (Yuval-Davis, Wemyss and Cassidy 2019). Racialised settled communities, on the other hand, will be regulated more through culturalist assumptions, internal policing such as 'stop and search', stigmatisation and othering, indirect job discriminations, and other forms of institutional racism (which do some of the work of ordering, exclusion and exploitation) in schools and universities, and criminalisation. These all involve articulations with gendered and classed denigrations. The intersections with gender and religion, as in the case of Muslim women, involve a contradictory articulation between rights and equality discourse and the othering and racialisation of religion. For example, Muslim women are characterised, with a purported interest in gender equality, as suffering gender violence due to cultural norms exercised by their families and their communities, therefore needing to be saved from them. This is part of the specific forms of racialisation of those groupings (see also Chapter 5).

Specificity of 'migration'?

The notion of 'migrant' in academic work of the Global North has been largely formulated as an abstract category, implicitly presupposing an undifferentiated human subject, often relating to the prototype of the economic migrant.

Territorialising places **149**

However, this became unsustainable in the light of the growing recognition of the multifaceted forms of population movement in the Global North: refugees and asylum seekers, particularly from the Middle East, and more temporary workers, which are not always mutually exclusive, and which are highly gendered and racialised.

This raises the issue of the specificity of 'migration' as an object. What are its boundaries, that is, what are the criteria, if so many people are on the move with different statuses and different outcomes? This is particularly the case since we all live in the age of migration (Castles and Miller 2009) even if we ourselves have never moved. Also, in some countries, international migrants are not just confined to those who travelled in their lifetimes, but they are also citizens, and some are second or third generation minorities. When does a person therefore stop being a migrant? (Robertson 2019). When is a person a refugee rather than a migrant? (see Crawley and Skleparis 2018). The answers relate to the ways the category is used and is very context and country specific. For example, visible others are more likely to continue being regarded as migrants, even where they may have lived for generations in a country. This is also dependent on how they are categorised in juridico-legal terms, on bordering regulations and on social policy.

In addition, this object, however we characterise it, needs to be recognised as inhabiting various categories as it is gendered, classed and raced. The classed nature is particularly significant, in terms of the ability of those with money to buy citizenship. In the UK the Tier 1 investor visa[3] requires an investment of £2 million at least, indicating the desirability of capital inflows. Dislocations do not have such a profound effect on the lives of people who can buy such visas, and they are not constructed in marginal or subordinate ways. Gender too is important given not only the differential placement of migrants in terms of a gendered labour market, explored in the last chapter, but the different imperatives and constraints many women face in migration, and their specific vulnerabilities to exploitation and violence, both in terms of country of origin and on their journeys.

In my view migration as an object of reference relates to processes and outcomes that speak to the effects of crossing symbolic as well as physical borders which essentially throws up the centrality of bordering and ordering in the making of contemporary forms of stratification in the modern world. Mezzadra and Neilson (2013), and their associates and collaborators, have developed the 'autonomy of migration' approach, which treats migration as an independent force with the potential to generate social and political change. This is driven not only by political and economic exigencies but by human creativity and resistance to the bordering process. Others prefer the 'mobility' paradigm developed by Urry (2003, 2007) endorsed by many others (e.g. Salazar, Elliot and Norum 2017), which shifts attention to flows and movements rather than national borders and bordering. Whichever of these paradigms we prefer, and they are not mutually exclusive, they require not just looking at migration or mobility but also looking

150 Territorialising places

at broader social relations as well as bordering *processes*, that is, in terms of how they are managed and regulated. This includes processes relating to the internal 'other', such as Australian Aboriginals (who only received rights to citizenship in 1967), and Black South Africans who have gained this more recently. In addition, the entry and incorporation of migrants may be a result of two sets of rules: one those of their country of origin and the other the country of destination. Some countries allow dual citizenship with certain countries but not with others. Differential access to the state and its resources can also exist amongst different ethnic and racial minorities within the same state, just as their location within the labour market can be very different.

Although migration-related crossings (including those of refugees and asylum seekers) cannot be collapsed together, I treat these as related and contextual categories, some of whom are more legalistic (such as refugees) than others. However, sharp boundaries amongst them are difficult to sustain. Similarly, we cannot always draw sharp edges between migrants and citizens, not only because European migrants from the EU have citizenship in Europe but may be treated as migrants in other ways, indicating the differentialist nature of citizenship itself. In addition, some citizens are treated as 'internal others', and may be subject to processes whereby they cease being citizens. Some examples are the cases in the UK of British-born youngsters who are involved in Isis and their 'brides' such as Shamima Begum (already discussed), as well as the case of the Windrush generation. Differential rights are also evident in more informal ways through 'stop and search', criminalisation and housing allocation processes. Activism around the Grenfell Tower[4] tragedy shows the extent to which working-class people, many of them minorities, have felt discriminated and side-lined. Many of these complex categories are subject to racialisation, and this requires an engagement with race and race making.

Similarly, we cannot draw sharp boundaries between migrants and racialised groups, since they are intertwined, and often experience similar regulatory regimes and ordering. On the other hand, a case could be made that they are different analytical objects, despite migrants also being racialised. Not all racialised are immediately thought of, or think of themselves, as migrants. Not all, in their lifetime, have experienced the crossing of a national border. The terms migrant and refugee, despite variations in categorisations across countries, still retain their association with first generation movement to a different country, and they are more or less socio-legal categories (for some but not for all), where policing of borders constructs them as less than sovereign subjects. Perhaps this may explain why the mobilities of those from more dominant groups, where the border is more a pliable door, has not been framed in terms of the category migrant. For example, the British abroad are referred to as expats, as the symbolic borders are less impenetrable and dislocating. Whilst we may want to challenge such a differentiation, it instinctively speaks to the more violent and 'othering' processes and practices that migrants are subjected to. These have increasingly come to the fore, particularly with new refugee flows and migration flows, and the heavy toll

Territorialising places **151**

of deaths in the seas of Europe. Estimates of total deaths recorded in the Mediterranean by the International Organisation for Migration are tragically high – 14,500 in the period 2014–17 (Laczko et al. 2017, p. 6). Those recently arrived migrant, asylum seeking and refugee groups who have managed to survive their frightening and risk filled journeys suffer from social and economic insecurity, instability in their lives as well as increasing victimisation.

Whereas the issue of borders is central for migrants and refugees, the racialisation of categories occurs both at the border and very much inside it. This relates to populations who have already gained rights of citizenship, as well as some who have been born with those rights. In the UK, the Windrush scandal, the Grenfell Tower disaster and its aftermath, and the issue of policing and criminalisation are centrally important. Such experiences and practices can be designated as part of the ways in which categories are produced, reproduced and transformed.

Multiplicity of forms and the fixed/unfixed

Mobile populations include large numbers of people escaping war and disease, as well as more educated people from the old Eastern bloc (Rudolph and Hillman 1997) who constituted the new migration flows from the 1990s as well as newer ones from the more peripheral Mediterranean countries who have been most affected by austerity measures, such as Greece, Portugal and Spain. A significant number have been asylum seekers since the 1990s (Koser 1997) and even more so currently with the so-called 'refugee crisis' since 2015 in Europe and beyond, indicating a 'perfect storm'. As the director general of the International Organisation for Migration, William Lacy Swing states:

> We are in the middle of a perfect storm as many are forced to migrate by an unprecedented number of conflicts, for which no solutions have been found.
>
> *(2018)*

In addition, a large proportion of migration flows is made up of women who often do the 'dirty work' (Anderson 2000) of domestic care, as well as social care. There is a growing use of women (from Thailand, Sri Lanka, Latin America, Vietnam and the Philippines as well as from Eastern Europe), doing transnational mothering (Lutz 2017) and constituting more broadly the 'global care chain' (Hochschild 2000 – see Chapter 5). As a contrast, a potentially less vulnerable category refers to what Mirjana Morokvasic (2004) has called commuter and brain drain migrants, now often coming from the European periphery, such as Greece and Spain (as well as the Global South), and encamped more and more in these positions as austerity has hit their countries hard.

The variety of these forms of mobility and trans-bordering can be seen not just in terms of the proliferation of 'differences' (ethnic, class, gender and their intersections) or 'diversity/super-diversity'. We need to locate them in relation to

152 Territorialising places

the forces and counterforces to movement. These include, on the one hand, poverty and austerity and, on the other hand, attempts to curb mobilities through more stringent regulations about when, how and who can move across borders. For example, in relation to family reunification, there is the requirement that those migrants who want to bring in members of their family in the UK need a minimum yearly income of over £18,600 for a partner and this is increased for children with what seem like deliberate class and gender discriminations.[5] They also relate to the imperatives people face in terms of work or family reunification. The transnationalisation of care, discussed in Chapter 5, has a significant societal impact in terms of the reconstitution of the family form and gendered relations in the wider population.

One of the most important aspects of this set of contemporary phenomena lies in what I called in Chapter 1 the *fixed-unfixed*. This is a transnational 'other', that is not covered by the terms we find in the discourse on transnational identities and belongings today, despite the phenomenon being widespread. This category of the fixed/unfixed is particularly salient as an accompaniment to the notion of the precariat and its link to surplus populations. Migration and associated bordering have produced new categories of the population who sit on borders, trapped in what Yiftachel (2009) calls 'gray spaces'. They are in camps, in the hot spots of Europe (Tazzioli and Garelli 2018), such as Greece and Italy amongst others, living under excruciating and dehumanising conditions. It's important to look at the construction of populations in the buffer zones between national borders and in the many refugee camps where some people, as Agamben notes, become reduced to 'bare life' (2005), deprived of all rights and agency. Despite this, many are able to act strategically, and they struggle against their confinement in various ways. They are therefore never completely abject objects of sovereign rule, and social resilience is built (Hall and Lamont 2013). These constitute the 'other' transnational others who sit in the buffer zones of *life*. This is a new form of transnationalism that lies deep in the heart of transnationalising processes . . .

As Trimikliniotis notes:

> the so-called 'hotspot approach' as a response to 'the migration and refugee crisis' was designed to 'ease the management of external borders and facilitate an integrated response to inflows at certain arrival points, currently five in Greece and five in Italy.
>
> *(2020, p. 102)*

However, what is clear is that these are places of denigration and abjectness as is exemplified by Trimikliniotis's (2020) account of Moria on the island of Lesbos.

Whilst those trapped in the 'hot spots' are not surplus populations in the traditional sense of a pool that awaits insertion and expulsion temporally through regimes of labour market inclusion and exclusion (as the reserve army traditionally in Marx), they are nonetheless a surplus humanity who sit on the border itself, in an almost permanent sense, waiting to be sorted. The individuals (as with the reserve army) may change, as can the category and location in its specificities. In its generalities, however, this is neither in nor out of the border but sitting in the space of the border, constituting a significant development of modern capitalism in its latest phase.

Growth of nativisms and nationalist populisms

Racist boundaries, in relation to national entitlements and citizenship, confront both those defined as immigrants and internal minorities (e.g. indigenous people) worldwide. Racist markers for the 'other' dominate the historical landscape although often hidden behind ideas of 'cultural difference', undesirability, threat and unsustainability, and even at times, humanitarianism and a gender equality discourse. In the UK and many other nations, racialisations are clearly embedded in current securitisation discourses which have not only led to the granting of new powers to the police and to the tightening of borders but also to new requirements that citizens become handmaidens of the state by policing the borders. This framework places legal duties on citizens, institutions and specific roles in organisations, such as teachers and school administrators, university personnel, landlords, employers, and people in civil institutions (i.e. those within ideological state apparatuses, to use Althusser's (1971) term), to police borders by reporting undocumented migrants. These factors have all contributed to 'racialised' othering, albeit differentially. Ideas about inability to belong, undesirability and threat underpin the types of proclamations increasingly made.

Whilst globalisation (alongside different elements of transnationalism, including digitalities) has extended its reach to make borders of nations increasingly small cogs in a larger machine, so have new localisms and populist forms of nationalism and racism emerged. This is manifested in the growth of extremist right-wing parties and movements (see Wodak 2010; Wodak, KhosraviNik and Mral 2013), reinforcing nationalism and some of its ugly relatives, such as nativist forms of racism. The colonial encounter, with its construction of imperial racisms, is the backdrop to European societies today. The more recent identitarian nativism is not such a very different animal, as nativism also speaks to past glories of empire ('we can be great again') and this informs the far right's flag waving tendencies, re-imagining in their countries' '(in)glorious' past a plausible future, resounding in the UK through discourses around Brexit.

The populist discourse used by far-right parties in recent years plays on people's worries with their living conditions and uses tropes that appear to favour the working classes and their rights against the 'others' who are 'invading' and appropriating their fought for heritage. These have called for sending migrants back home and cleansing the nation, with resonances of fascism. In Britain there is, amongst others, the National Front, the English Defence League, the British Union of Fascists, Britain First and the British National Party. Globally too there has been a shift to what has been called the alt-right with its tropes of racism and anti-migration and anti-refugee discourse, manifesting extreme nationalism.

154 Territorialising places

Across Europe, there has been increased support for racist and xenophobic far-right parties such as the Front National in France, the AfD (Alternative for Germany), the Lega in Italy and the Freedom Party in Austria, amongst others. Indeed, it could be argued that the Brexit vote in Britain is a manifestation of how the ideas propagated by the extreme right have become mainstream, and that white nationalism is becoming more normalised. However, a ray of hope is found in the generational frictions over Brexit, as the young voted predominantly to remain. There has also been a decline of racist attitudes amongst younger people and the growth of acceptance of the multi-ethnic nature of British society[6] (also found in conviviality and everyday multiculturalism discussed later).

Growing alt-right nationalisms in Europe have coincided with what has happened in the US since the election of Donald Trump. He has committed to building a wall with Mexico and has wanted to ban migration from seven Muslim countries. Despite his claims that he is equally opposed to white nationalist terrorists there is no indication that his policing of such racist mobilisations is serious. These mobilisations include American Vanguard, the KKK, and the National Socialist Movement. In the UK also, more limited action is directed to the far-right movements despite the acknowledged risks from them by a former Metropolitan Police counter-terrorism chief, who stated that they constitute an organised and significant threat. The widely critiqued Prevent programme, created to tackle radicalisation and terrorism (home grown) has primarily targeted young Muslims (Abbas 2019) and has thereby fuelled anti-Muslim sentiment. Some research shows that it has given rise to much antagonism and re-assertions of Muslim identity as a counter to being branded a suspect community (Pilkington and Acik 2019).

Local particularities and identities, ethnic violence and extreme nationalist ideologies such as neo-fascism may provide refuge for marginalised populations, both 'nativist' and more recent 'nativised' (such as settled populations from the ex-colonies in the UK) who claim rights to territory and national belonging. Over the past decade, within a global context of increased conflict, we have seen alarmingly high levels of racist violence, physical attacks on asylum seekers and electoral support for the extreme right (in Austria, Belgium, Hungary and France, for instance).[7] Economic crisis, failed policies, failed left-wing political parties, the backlash against multiculturalism, a highly charged European discourse on borders and containment, fears of safety and poverty, the Middle East conflict, securitisation discourse and new legal powers to prevent or control home-grown 'terrorists', nationalisms: all these are some of the central factors involved. Ideas about entitlements to belonging, cultural difference, undesirability, criminality, desert and threat underpin the types of proclamations increasingly made.

Nativisms have always formed part of racialised discourse (found in Sheila Patterson's book *Dark Strangers* (1963), for example). Notions of authenticity and indigeneity are used by those who 'were always already here' and who should have more entitlements than newcomers. Indeed, many land claims by indigenous peoples are based on this, but these are part of countering the pillages by colonial powers which have drained such communities of their resources, and therefore cannot be considered in the same way. The reach of nativism shows the complexity of the phenomenon as it manifests itself amongst poorer and more disenfranchised members of communities. In the UK, some British citizens whose parents or grandparents were born elsewhere, India, Pakistan, Africa, Cyprus, have been opposed to intra-European migration, because of fears for their jobs. This was particularly the case in towns that voted for Brexit such as Luton. With Brexit, we have seen the growth of the legitimacy of nativist claims, of the primacy of the rights of the 'original' inhabitants of the land, the autochthonous population, which of course underplays the different constituencies in the history of the making of British society, like those of almost all societies worldwide.

Race making and the multiple targets of racism

There is the question about how the governmentalities of 'bordering' and 'othering' involve technologies which produce race in different forms. Rather than race diminishing we find race appearing in yet more and more different ways involving quite complex algorithms of belonging and non-belonging, marking bodies in essentialist ways: some of those bodies at first glance do not meet the everyday conception of the racialised but appear to be white, classed and gendered subjects, such as East European women in Italy, Cyprus or Greece, or East European agricultural workers. With the so-called refugee and migration crisis, the amplification of Islamophobia (Fekete 2009) and anti-Semitism, the growth of far-right parties in Europe, and new forms of governmentality over migrants, refugees and asylum seekers worldwide, there has been a growth of different manifestations of racism against a range of categories: anti-Black, anti-Muslim, anti-Jewish, anti-Roma, anti-Eastern European, anti-migrant and anti-refugee. Race categorisations and racism spread their wings beyond traditional notions of race as marked by skin colour and the divisions between black and white, or even by using signifiers of racial difference which rely on religion or cultural difference. This is despite, particularly in the United States, the Black-White dichotomy remaining central and despite the legitimate object of White Studies that seek to show how whiteness is inscribed within many different forms of racialisation. In the face of the proclaimed end of race, race and racism rear their ugly head in opportunistic and multiple ways which don't always rely either on biologistic or culturalist forms of understanding of boundaries, beyond both biological and cultural racisms and instead use ideas of desert or integration (see later).

An important debate in the sociological literature on race has been centred around defining race and racism. For some writers (e.g. Banton 1987), racism is linked to hierarchical racial typologies which specify generic biological differences. Other writers argue that racism occurs when racial categories are imbued

156 Territorialising places

with negative meaning (Miles 1993) and that this is tied to class projects. Both these positions, despite their differences, treat racism in terms of its dependency on explicit racial typologies. Some time ago now the 'new racism' (Barker 1981; that is now being called neo-racism and some refer to as xeno-racism e.g. Gidley 2018) was regarded as characterised by ideas about cultural difference, being used as a justification of exclusion from citizenship or other rights, economic and civil, in contradistinction to ideas about the biological inferiority of 'outsiders'. According to 'xeno-racism', migrant ethnic groups, refugees and so on are undesirable or inferior, but not on the premise of a supposed racial categorisation in the biologistic sense, but as cultural, political or national outsiders and as non-entitled to the resources of the nation, in counter-position to those who are 'one of us'. As well as chromatism, linked to imperial and colonial forms of racism, and cultural racisms that rely on position and undesirable cultural difference, there are racisms of different types, such as nativism (which has been on the increase) that discursively points to the rights of autochthonous subjects. The latter is particularly paradoxical since such nativist claims of majorities have depended historically on the expulsions and exclusions of 'natives' within settler colonial contexts. In addition, there is surveillance racism that is based on racialised biometric algorithms that reinstate biologistic racism in new ways. Others have made a distinction between vernacular racisms, with their historical complexities and continuities, and biopolitical racisms that are exercised in ordering populations (see Amin 2010). All these forms, arguably, are underpinned by essentialist conceptions of biology, physiognomy, culture and autochthony. However, it is possible to go even further, notwithstanding the dangers of over-inflation of the concept (see Mason 1994), and see racism as a set of discourses and practices that inferiorise, subordinate and lead to outcomes relating to exclusionary group boundaries and hierarchies (Anthias and Yuval-Davis 1992; Anthias 1992a). These include outcomes of practices that may not intentionally seek to be racist, such as those found in institutionalised procedures for the allocation of housing that require particular lengths of stay in an area which may be impossible for some groups to meet. This is far removed from the idea of 'unwitting racism' flagged by the Macpherson report in the aftermath of the Stephen Lawrence murder in South East London in 1993 (MacPherson 1999; also see the rapid response issue of Sociological Research Online 1999). Unwitting racism implies that actual discriminatory language and outcomes are non-deliberative and are part of an overall culture: however, we can talk of that culture itself as being deliberatively racist (Goldberg 1993).

The idea of *race making*, or racialisation (as Erasmus (2017) following Miles (1993) prefers – see also the discussions in Murji and Solomos (2014) by Brett St. Lewis (2014) amongst others), uses the notion of 'race', but not as something that can be defined since it doesn't exist in terms of real biological race types; it is a discredited notion and yet socially salient. Race making involves a process whereby a social category or population grouping is constructed in terms of collective characteristics that are essentialist and inalienable, whether the criteria

Territorialising places **157**

used are biological, cultural (including religion) or linked to character and motivation. This doesn't mean that such populations will always be defined in this way since the labels, ideas and practices around them can shift and change and the self-definitions of the people involved will also be subject to change. This is found in the idea that class whitens or blackens, for example, or that Jews are a religious or a racial grouping, or the Roma are an ethnic or lifestyle group. Such definitions are therefore not fixed; attention must be paid to time, place, context and meaning.

Despite fundamental shifts in the view that racism is what white people do to black people (a particularly dominant view in the British Race Relations tradition), the terms 'whiteness' (Garner 2007), 'whitening' and 'blackening' have emerged to signal racialisation processes. This is a recognition that the move away from what might be called chromatism (Dhawan and Varela 2016) doesn't mean that it is not still a central facet of racisms worldwide. Recognising the racialisation process as more variable, however, has been partly a product of the treatment and discourses towards newer inflows of migrants and asylum seekers as well as the rise of anti-Muslim racism, using the contested term Islamophobia (discussed later in this chapter), which focuses on Muslims, on the one hand, and Islam, on the other. This form of racism singles out the danger that Muslims pose to safety and security and the way in which Islamic faith and organisation underpins this danger vis-à-vis western society. This is undergirded by terrorism fears rather than 'race' ascriptions. The growth of anti-Jewish (or the more problematic term anti-Semitism) and anti-Muslim racism articulate complex elements which do not directly link to colonialism but nonetheless link to the formulation of the West as Christian and white. The Irish and Cypriots have also been racialised historically in their migration trajectories in the UK (Hickman 2002; Ryan 2007; Anthias 1992a). A paramount discursive element has been related to the idea of conformity to national values, in Britain for example, hailed by David Cameron:

> a belief in freedom, tolerance of other, accepting personal and social responsibility, respecting and upholding the rule of law . . . they're as British as the Union flag as football as fish and chips.
>
> *(June 14, 2014)*

Roma populations have been targets of racism in a long-standing way. This is sometimes linked to anti-Irish and class-based racisms which focus on what are seen as undesirable ways of life. For example, in 2013, one of the architects of the integration regime, the ex-Home Secretary David Blunkett, talking on BBC Radio Sheffield, said that the arrival of large numbers of Roma migrants would lead to rioting and that their behaviour was 'aggravating' to local people:

> You've got to adhere to our standards and to our way of behaving and if you do this you'll get welcome. We have got to change the behaviour and

158 Territorialising places

> the culture of the incoming community, the Roma community, because there's going to be an explosion otherwise.
>
> *(The Guardian, November 14, 2013)*

In the light of this proliferation of racialised targets, some have argued that race and racism are outdated terms that do not capture the complexity of violence and exclusion against the 'other' both internal and external (for a different but related argument see Gilroy 2004). At the opposite end of the pole are arguments that suggest that racism and racialisation are processes that operate in opportunistic ways to underpin many of these forms of 'othering' (e.g. see Anthias and Yuval-Davis 1992). Whichever position we take, however, there is no doubt about the continuing importance of 'race' markers in the construction of inequalities and subordinations in global operations of power as well as within national state boundaries (e.g. given rising hate crimes figures and black people being sub-jected to stop and search). A testament to the persistence of traditional imperial racisms which sit alongside nativisms can be found in much research. In the UK, Ashe, Borkowska and Nazroo (2018), using the Trades Union Congress's 2016/17 Racism at Work survey, found that 70% of Asian and Black workers surveyed had been racially harassed at work in the last five years, with over 10% of Black, Asian and Mixed origin workers experiencing racial violence. This report puts into question, amongst other things, the idea that we live in a post-race society.

Nativisms are not new either. Ideas in the UK about a national threat posed by migrants or asylum holders ranges from Enoch Powell's notorious warning about 'rivers of blood' through to Margaret Thatcher's 'fears of being swamped', to more subtle notions of 'destroying our ways of life' (see Anthias 2016) or 'controlling *our* borders'. Some of these tropes arise out of concerns for 'our cul-ture' being contaminated by the 'undesirable' lifestyles or values of migrants and minorities, a national culture that deserves being maintained because its claims rest on the greater belonging than others to the real nation, based increasingly on ideas of autochthony or nativism, nationalism's more egocentric twin. This has been accompanied, in many countries including the UK, by a concern that migrants 'integrate'. Part of this process includes requirements that they learn and accept 'British' values of democracy, thereby giving an inferior value to those who cannot claim to be 'British' already, particularly non-European and Muslim groups in Britain.

The meaning of a racialised category has shifted in the UK over time from being regarded as signalling visibilities of skin colour, to signalling New Com-monwealth migrants, to including under its ambit populations who are set out-side the boundary of the proclaimed autochthonous population (such as EU migrants – again the category of the autochthonous is itself subject to shifts and changes over time). Although not all constructions of national identity are rac-ist, criteria of belonging, over the last 30 years, have become increasingly rooted in notions of a racialised *desirability* (and not just cultural difference), sameness and *compliance*. It was possible to argue until quite recently that the growth of the European family through the EU, albeit one sliced in terms of centre and periphery, constructs the differences of the dominant ethnicities of the respective European nations (but not the Eastern Europeans) as essentially acceptable and denoting a benign European commonality, despite difference. In the UK, for example, there has been a racialisation of some categories, such as Eastern Europeans in particular, but even more dominant Europeans have been subjected to racist tropes of expulsion as part of the Brexit agenda and the differential rules within the EU itself. Whilst the undesirables are the 'others' from the outside, the Muslims, the ex-colonials (even those who have lived for centuries within, marked out by their different skin colours or their different religions), third country nationals and asylum seekers, some categories of Europeans constitute 'another' internal enemy. However, such racialisation is itself differentiated and some black people are treated as fully British: for example, famous footballers, sportspeople and musicians, testifying to differential chromatisations. Here an intersectional lens in understanding the targets of racism is important as well as a contextual analysis. For example, in terms of mobilisation, we can see the intersectional nature of the ways that migrants mobilise in trade unions and the ways they have regenerated class action. The mobilisations of Latin American workers in the UK bring together a range of both class and migration-related issues around subordinations at work, relating to pay and conditions, with struggles around migration controls and racism (Però and Solomos 2010).

It's also important to recognise the struggles around the Windrush scandal in 2019, and those in relation to the Grenfell fire in 2017 as well as struggles for rights in relation to forms of anti-racism which increasingly have become resonant with the struggles around migrants and refugees. In response to the 2017 Grenfell tragedy, a tower block in west London that set on fire because of inadequate cladding and which burnt 72 people, working-class people became politicised. This was forged through a common experience of the failures of the system to treat many people with respect and decency.

Anti-Jewish and anti-Muslim racisms

Anti-Jewish and anti-Muslim racism abound in this racialised landscape, again with very different articulations to those of chromatism. Anti-Semitism has taken a particularly important place in discussions at the political level. For example, in the UK, it is a stick that Jeremy Corbyn, the current leader of the Labour Party, has been beaten with.[8] Definitions of what exactly constitutes anti-Semitism have been produced and the definition by the Holocaust group is one generally used, despite its problems (discussed later). The UK Labour Party has also endorsed it despite it conflating anti-Israel sentiments with anti-Jewish sentiments. In addition, anti-Muslim racism is increasingly discussed and there has been debate about the notion of Islamophobia, as well as attempts to find acceptable definitions (see later). The links with securitisation, after the Iraq war, in particular, and the terrorist attacks in Europe and America, have exacerbated

160 Territorialising places

concern with Muslims who have become the prototype of a 'suspect community' embodying the 'dangerous other' at the global level, being seen as potential terrorists. In counter-position to the threat posed to life itself from Muslims, Jews are presented as the devious other 'within', who slyly control the economy, politics and the arts, being an embodiment of the intellectual and economic power that threatens the pursuit of the western ideal of fairness and equal opportunities.

There have been extensive debates on the extent to which the concepts of anti-Semitism and Islamophobia are useful in denoting specific types of othering which cannot be encapsulated by racism. Those who want to incorporate them into a broad racism category prefer notions of anti-Muslim and anti-Jewish racism.

1. Islamophobia/anti-Muslim racism?

The Rushdie affair[9] heralded the growth of the racialisation of Muslims in Britain and the importance given to religion as a marker of undesirability. This took even more virulent forms after the attacks of September 11, 2001, in New York and July 7, 2005, in London and the more recent attacks in Paris, London and elsewhere in Europe, particularly since the Iraq war. Anti-Islamism, fired also by the Israel-Palestine conflict and Isis and Islamic State, presents a new face to racisms, no longer dependent on supposed physiognomic or biological difference or cultural difference, but a religious difference defined as an essence and demonised, being identified, however, not only with terrorists but also with backwardness, lack of civilisation and a denial of having equal value or covalence.

As far back as 1997 the Runnymede Trust stated that Islamophobia is:

> a 'world view involving an unfounded dread and dislike of Muslims which results in practices of exclusion and discrimination'.

Miles and Brown (2003) suggest that 'Islamophobia' might only be appropriate where there is a specific and identifiable hatred of the theology of Islam. They say Islamophobia, if treated as a form of racism, risks treating all Muslims as an ethnically homogenous minority. They add that there is no need for identifying, defining or conceptualising 'anti-Muslimism' as this can be incorporated and framed within existing theories of racism or xenophobia. Hussain and Baggaley (2012) follow Miles and Brown (2003) in conceptualising Islamophobia as distinct, but see it as interacting with racism. Bravo Lopez also rejects the notion of Islamophobia as a form of racism, cultural or otherwise, because it is 'devoid of any of the biological or cultural determinism . . .' (Bravo Lopez 2011, p. 559) of racist discourses. Islamophobia may reference somatic characterisations, but typically it refers to representations of supposedly Islamic beliefs and practices. Alternatively, racist discourse about a Muslim minority may not entail any reference whatsoever to their religious beliefs and practices (Bravo Lopez 2011).

In 2019, the All-Party Parliamentary Group (APPG) on British Muslims proposed the first working definition of Islamophobia in the UK. Its report 'Islamophobia Defined' states

> Islamophobia is rooted in racism and is a type of racism that targets expressions of Muslimness or perceived Muslimness.
>
> *(see www.islamophobia-definition.com)*

This was rejected, however, by Theresa May's government on the grounds that it would undermine counter-terrorism activities. It was also criticised by the National Secular Society. The difficulty in definition relates to critiques of the idea of 'expressions of Muslimness'. Given this difficulty, and what would count and not count as Islamophobia, in this regard the notion of anti-Muslim racism (where the targets are Muslims rather than their beliefs) aligns better with racisms in general. In relation to the complex ingredients that go into racism, studies have shown evidence not of one Islamophobia but many (Meer 2013), with sometimes religion being highlighted and at other times cultural attitudes to women and yet other times fear of world control. In the replacement of the derogatory term Paki that preceded the new phase of anti-Muslim sentiment, attitudes relating to the inferiority of the group in terms of the link to forms of avoidance such as smells (of curry) and lack of western forms of knowledge have been replaced by a combination of tropes relating to backwardness, fanaticism and deviousness (in the latter mirroring some old anti-Semitic tropes). In the case of Muslims, colour, in combination with other somatic differences and culture, combine to signal the 'other' as 'the dangerous other'. The mosque and the headscarf or chadur are the markers of difference, carrying more explicit connotations of cultural difference (coded as terrorism) than skin colour alone. Anti-Muslim racism is linked to culture and the political activity of Muslims, depicted as home-grown terrorists. But there is also an element of colour racism.

The old divisions between Christian and Muslim universes of meaning in the narratives of the Christian world, from the Crusades onwards, underpin ideas about the backwardness of Muslims. In the UK people who were branded as Paki (used as a derogatory term for those from India, Pakistan and Bangladesh) have now come to be called (and to call themselves) Muslim, emerging primarily in the coat of their religion and way of life, instead of their country of origin. With the Muslim, unlike the Jew, the assumption is that it would be acceptable if they divest themselves of their Islamic beliefs and practices: they are not a species being but 'the perverse diverse'. Their political agenda, tied to their Islamic beliefs of hatred towards the West, is at the core of contemporary anti-Muslim racism. Securitisation means being identified with danger and deficit – they are seen to lack the civilised sensibility required to integrate and with the demise of multicultural discourse they are accused of living parallel lives. Gender processes are an important part of the demonisation process: singling out honour killings,

162 Territorialising places

genital cutting and forced marriages in particular, using a gender equality discourse. The body covering of women is seen as an example of gender inequality steeped in the Middle Ages and incompatible with civilised life as well as potentially a terrorist threat, with papers like the *Daily Mail* in the UK imputing that the chadur is used as a disguise by terrorists. The Muslim is also non-Caucasian in a more visible way than the Jew and subjected to a complex process that is colour racism; the Jew is also tarred with physiognomic markers, although can 'pass'.

There is no easy division between hostility to Islam in terms of religion and hostility to the people who are defined as Muslims (often seen in stereotypical ways). Therefore, any argument that says that Islamophobia is a bad term because it makes too much of hostility to Islam misses the point. On the other hand, the term Islamophobia is problematic because it could imply that the problem is religion and that it is about phobia, that is, fear that people have of the religion itself. This focuses on the belief systems rather than the people and cannot capture the systemic, institutional, political and cultural processes at work. Anti-Muslim racism I think captures this better.

2. *Anti-Jewish racism*

The role of the Israel and Palestine conflict has made the debate about anti-Semitism and anti-Jewish sentiment particularly complex (Yuval-Davis 2019). Jews may be seen as the dominant other and Zionism as oppressive to Palestinians. Palestinians, on the other hand, are seen as victims but also as a threat to the western world and as terrorists.

Mosley's anti-Semitic[10] statements (and the march he led in Cable Street in the East End of London in 1936) is an earlier manifestation in the UK of anti-Semitism. With the more current focus on anti-Black racism and anti-Muslim racism as well as anti-migrant sentiments or racisms, this had taken a back seat in the panoply of racisms. However, the desecration of graves and the rise of neo-Nazi parties worldwide have made this a particularly important focus. The debate about the ways in which the Labour Party under the leadership of Jeremy Corbyn has been unable to deal with anti-Semitism is particularly prominent in Europe, as mentioned earlier.

Anti-Semitic tropes reveal a cluster of loosely related phenomena, and include Holocaust denial, and views that Jews have become, wrongly, 'the victim' of the Holocaust and have excluded the experiences of the Roma and homosexuals, who were equally targeted by the Nazis. They essentialise and homogenise. Jews are regarded as both sub-human and super-human but not uncivilised: indeed, they are often deemed to be too clever. The figure of the Jew in Simmel (1908) is seen as the embodiment of the dangerous stranger. In the present context there is still the false image of the Jew as the banker and capitalist as depicted, for example, in a mural (October 2018) endorsed carelessly by Jeremy Corbyn (who was gravely attacked for doing this) which he claimed he did in the context of freedom of cultural expression. There is an argument that critiques of Zionism and of the Israeli state's right to exist have been conflated with questions about the actual practices of the Israeli state in the context of the Israel-Palestine conflict (Yuval-Davis 2019). However, how the nationalist project of Israel is depicted may or may not have elements of racism, depending on whether it produces the figure of the essential Jew, expresses hatred or other negative beliefs towards Jews as a people and/or the Jewish faith and traditions. To regard all critiques of Israel as anti-Semitic conflates political rejection of a nationalist project with discourses and practices against Jews. The International Holocaust Remembrance Alliance's non-legally binding working definition of anti-Semitism (2016) has partly contributed to the conflation, but has been widely adopted:

> Antisemitism is a certain perception of Jews, which may be expressed as hatred toward Jews. Rhetorical and physical manifestations of antisemitism are directed toward Jewish or non-Jewish individuals and/or their property, toward Jewish community institutions and religious facilities.

Examples are given:

> Manifestations might include the targeting of the state of Israel, conceived as a Jewish collectivity, or accusing the Jews as a people, or Israel as a state, of inventing or exaggerating the Holocaust or denying the Jewish people their right to self-determination, e.g., by claiming that the existence of a State of Israel is a racist endeavour.
>
> *(https://www.holocaustremembrance.com/stories-working definition-antisemitism)*

Arguably the term anti-Jewish is better than anti-Semitic, as it focuses on the people rather than the state, or the ideology of the state, and its practices. The Palestinian issue at times may have brought them together inasmuch as there is a conflation potentially between Israel policy and Jews and the latter may be constructed as the enemy by some pro-Palestine campaigners. Many Jews are themselves anti-Zionist and pro-Palestine also.

At another level, Jews are globally integrated in domains of power, politically, economically and culturally and large Jewish lobbies exist worldwide. This is used as a trope to feed into the representation of Jews as the deviant other, but also as the powerful capitalist. The latter depiction is found in the infamous mural which was endorsed, as noted earlier, by Jeremy Corbyn. This resulted in extensive media attacks as well as attacks from within his own party. In the imagination of racists, Jews appear often as the cunning embodiment of capitalism and as inscrutable. However, they are not seen as deficient or subjected to securitisation controls. If there is danger this lies in their potential superiority and, from the point of view of Palestinians, their identification with Israel.

164 Territorialising places

The Jew, however, is regarded as a species being, and the religion is not seen as dangerous or as deviant, deficient or disgusting. Nor in terms of racist attitudes is the Jew seen as an oppressor of women, although orthodox Jews practice gender segregation in some aspects of their lives. But the skull cap is banned in France alongside the hijab. Anti-Semitism is a more essentialist construction than Islamophobia and arguably desire and resentment at the intersubjective level play a stronger role.

The Fundamental Rights Agency Survey (FRA) (2013) found that 66% of the 5,000 plus Jewish people it surveyed felt that anti-Semitism was a problem in eight countries, including the UK, and that it was particularly virulent on the internet. There were high figures in Hungary, France, Belgium and Poland. The perpetrators were regarded as those with Muslim extremist views, the left and the right. The most frequent comments in the UK were 'Jews exploit the holocaust for their own purposes and Israelis behave like Nazis towards the Palestinians (both 35%)'. The follow-up FRA report in 2018 found rising levels of anti-Semitism:

> About 90% of respondents feel that antisemitism is growing in their country. Around 90% also feel it is particularly problematic online, while about 70% cite public spaces, the media and politics as common sources of antisemitism. Almost 30% have been harassed, with those being visibly Jewish most affected. Almost 80% do not report serious incidents to the police or any other body. Often this is because they feel nothing will change. Over a third avoid taking part in Jewish events or visiting Jewish sites because they fear for their safety and feel insecure. The same proportion have also even considered emigrating.
>
> *(FRA 2018, https://europa.eu)*

There is also the link to class: the Jew is identified with higher class deviance – business, finance, politics, the professions and the pro-Israel lobby. The Muslim is identified with the uneducated lower class, with 'blackness', insularity and with riots, although some discourses play on the infiltration of better educated Muslims into positions of power.

Anti-Jewish racism presents a complex picture. There is a large prosperous middle class but the rise of anti-Semitic attacks shows that, alongside other minority groups in Britain, they are still not regarded as 'one of us'. We could say that Jews have experienced religious persecution but not racism, and that the basis or hostility for both Jews and Muslims is a religious one. However, whether practices of stigmatisation and discrimination manifest themselves in terms of hostility using religious articulations and discourses or whether they use biologistic or cultural articulations, the people designated as Jews or Muslims, are being constructed as a negative and monolithic category and subjected to hate crimes. Because of this, whatever the ingredients used it's important to regard this as a form of racialisation with racist effects.

Beyond definitions of racism: focusing on practices and outcomes

Questions of racisms are questions, not about definitions, but social problems. Looked at this way we can then look at processes of othering, exclusion, discrimination, violence and hierarchisation. These are some of the elements shared in different ways by all those who are targeted as collectivised persons (in intersection with other categories like gender and class, religion and many other categories). To ask if religion is the basis, or if it is race, assumes that these can be divided. This is not the case because the social relations being articulated are complex, contradictory and changing. Religion or purported racial difference are ingredients that are used at different times for othering populations. Therefore, it is important to focus on the historical and contextual processes which make different ingredients salient.

Instead of asking whether this is racism or something else, it is more productive to ask: how are people categorised, how are they positioned, what are the practices that they experience, what are the outcomes for their lives? We can also ask: how is all this linked to economic and political forces and projects of state-making and contestations of different kinds. A major facet of racisms is that they are constituted through effects, that is, are outcomes of social practices, discourses and social relations at different societal levels, such as representational, intersubjective, institutional and experiential (discussed in Chapter 3 and in Anthias 1998a) and therefore complex. They are intersectionally constituted – it is not vital to see these as products of the articulations of race difference in order that they produce outcomes which are racist – they can be products of the interplay of social forces linked to inequality regimes.

This means we start with discourses, experiences, practices and outcomes and not definitions. It is practices that are imbued with violence towards a collectivised category and this links to a politics of exploitation, appropriation, expulsion, exclusion or subordinated incorporation (or exclusionary inclusion – see Anthias 2001b). This means that it is not just a question of hostility in terms of interpersonal acts, found in everyday and vernacular racisms, although these are themselves complexly interwoven with political (and here I include nationalist) or economic projects. We can think of this in terms of some extreme practices of extermination or expulsion directed against collectivised categories, through eugenics, apartheid (in the US against African Americans and Latinos), the Holocaust (against Jews in Germany), genocides in many places (including Rwanda), expulsions (including Greeks in Asia Minor), ethnic cleansing (including Bosnian Muslims), through exiles and displacements of war (experienced e.g. by Kurds and Syrians). Singling out the object, e.g. Jews or Muslims as the collective other, may involve a more, or less, religious-based conflict (as is the case historically for Muslims).

Generally, today racisms are not articulated specifically as a conflict of religions for power. Jews are seen as Jews, as argued earlier, not because they are

166 Territorialising places

religiously Jewish but because of their purported 'nature' or species being and indeed have been represented historically as a kind of primordial other. Similarly, anti-Muslim practices focus not so much on religion but on the culturalisation and demonisation of the religious followers and their securitisation. However, faith-based attributions operate as more important signifiers contemporaneously for Muslims compared to Jews whilst generic or essentialised 'species' types characteristics are more dominant for the latter. There are complex articulations between claims and attributions of religion, culture, security, race and collectivised othering, shifting in relation to global conflicts and interests. Racism towards Muslims and Jews is not *about* religion, but religion becomes, at different times, a means and main criterion for marking difference and demonising it. One can call the processes racism but also argue that there are particular forms of racism. For example, anti-Muslim racism discursively relates to securitisation and demonisation of the faith-followers, and gender-based practices, using notions which involve totalising the category – fundamentalism, fanaticism, backwardness, insularity, culturalised violence against women and danger.

This discussion of the panoply of racialised objects suggests that the othering that is central to racism can use all kinds of signifiers or markers, and that it is attached to bodies in various ways, articulating borders of belonging and resource entitlement which serve to deny full participation in economic, social, political and cultural life, using various means for the setting up and legitimation of exclusions or subordinated forms of inclusion. These involve projects that are, at different times, informed by nationalist, economic or other struggles for dominance and their related forms of ordering and sorting. Here we can talk about the presence of 'race' as a real phenomenon with real material effects and we can talk about the racial order in ways far removed from the idea of the 'racial order' as depicting innate hierarchies of human beings. To refuse to engage with race is to refuse to engage with the continuing violence exerted in its name, a name that is plastic but always brutal – see also Alana Lentin on the continuing importance of race in a post-racial world (2016), and the work of Shilliam (2018) and Erasmus (2017).

Major tropes underlying contemporary racisms are danger, deviance, deficit and disgust (Anthias 2013b), as mentioned already. These are what I call the four Ds, an easy mnemonic for the discursive elements shared to different extents and in different combinations, by racisms.[11]

> **Danger:** constructing the collectivised other as a danger – either to culture or the national character or identity, or as a threat to life itself and as a security issue.
>
> **Deviance:** the other is endemically deviant and at times evil or their beliefs are such that they cannot be accommodated by mainstream or hegemonic culture or interests, making them undesirable, excludable and expendable.
>
> **Deficit:** the other is deficient and cannot meet the level required by the society (i.e. the dominant social locations) and therefore needs to be

corrected and if judged unable to correct their lack of cultural competence or deficient way of behaving then they should be excluded or segregated: this appears in terms of citizenship tests and requirements at entry for migrants as proofs of integration or capacity to integrate.

Disgust (and desire): the other's ways of life or character give rise to emotions which are characterised by physical and bodily responses leading to avoidance, sexualisation and animality as with disgust over food smells or bodily characteristics and stigmatisation. Disgust involves ideas of contagion, contamination, smells of food and eating, sexuality of the other.

Conviviality and the normalisation of diversity

The 'convivial' turn acts as a counter to the discussion of the growth of racisms and flags the concomitant existence of everyday 'cultural' or 'ethnic/racial' encounters and intersubjectivities alongside a racialised landscape. It also counters the negative connotations given to contemporary multicultures, outside the old multicultural reification (and celebration) of cultural difference. What many writers call 'the normalisation of diversity' and 'living with diversity' (Amin 2002) is partly fired by Gilroy's focus on conviviality and multiculture (2004), involving micro publics (Amin 2002, p. 959) with notions of 'ordinary diversity' or 'unremarked diversity', found in the global city and in urban settings (see Pemberton 2017 for a review of some of this work). This does not mean the erasure of difference in urban settings but rather that the 'getting along' aspect is stressed. Some of this work echoes to some extent earlier sociological concerns with the effects of culture contact on 'ethnic relations' (e.g. Herskovitz 1938). It has been argued for some time, however, that issues of culture are not as important as other problems in local neighbourhoods to do with housing, public policy, local governance and safety (Rogaly and Taylor 2007; Amin 2008; Hickman et al. 2008; Vertovec and Wessendorf 2006). In addition, not all recent studies have stressed the positive effects of living in urban settings (for contrasting research results see Wise and Velayutham 2009; Wessendorf 2014; Piekut and Valentine 2017; Valentine 2008).

Such everyday interculturalities are played out in a racialised and classed landscape with amplified inequalities of position, due to failures of governance, years of austerity, the growth of racism and hate crime since the Brexit referendum in the UK, and the growth of right-wing parties in Europe and beyond. This has produced dis-entitlements, expulsions and border guarding and tightening, and the growth of precarity. There are continuing ethnic enclaves which are in large part a product of disadvantage and differential exclusion. So-called 'diversity encounters' today need to be located with reference to such processes that affect not only the racialised. Such conditions and their impact on the most deprived 'multicultural' neighbourhoods, despite 'living together' or more commonly 'living side by side', have led to the increase in knife crime and other forms of violence, disaffection and alienation.

168 Territorialising places

The stress on conviviality can be contrasted to the critique of multicultural-ism which pointed to the growth of 'parallel communities' living in their own ghettoes, and thereby being responsible for creating conditions for alienation and social unrest. The creation of spaces of everyday engagement that express affin-ities of concern and struggle around local issues of health, welfare, education and housing and anti-austerity is an important reminder of the ways in which assumptions about the primacy of ethnicity have distorted the ways we research social relations, reinforcing the call to abandon the ethnic lens (e.g. Runfors 2016) and to de-migrantise research (Dahinden 2016). At the same time, both on the ground and in public political debate there is a growth of anti-migration and racist discourse, as discussed earlier. So, whilst it is important to abandon a priori assumptions about the primacy of ethnicity or migration as a social and analytical lens, it's still vital to attend to the social relations that produce these as salient aspects of social relations, and disadvantage and exclusion. Recent out-breaks over police violence, such as in Dalston in East London after a black youth was killed in 2017,[12] point to the centrality of events which trigger such violence in spaces that appear convivial. Also 'convivial' can mean 'living side by side' or 'living together' which are quite different; the first denotes lack of interconnect-ing spaces, whilst the latter the creation of bonds and networks. The first is not so dissimilar to the idea of 'parallel communities' or a 'community of communities' (Parekh 2000), again different to each other, whilst the second can be seen to denote transethnicity.

Managing the 'diverse' and bordering practices

This discussion of convivial diversity prompts an interrogation that lies at the heart of the modern-day management of the 'other'. Bordering practices include the policing of borders from those outside and the management and regulation of those inside; these are parallel processes. There are explicit forms of policing of the 'other' which relate to securitisation (in Britain the highly criticised Pre-vent programme[13]), to stop and search powers, surveillance and to citizens being required as part of their civic duty to become border guards.

These developments have been amplified particularly since the 2015 refugee and migration crisis and the numbers of terrorist attacks in Europe. However, another arm of the governmentality involved is found in discourses and practices of diversity and integration. As diversity signals heterogeneity and the multiplic-ity of social life within many progressive discourses (e.g. in the idea of convivial-ity), it is a desirable aim to propagate. It can stand as a coda for those we might wish to incorporate (e.g. when actors and film makers call for more diversity) but it can also act as a code for the 'other' which we might want to reject or eject (fearing that there is too much diversity ruining 'our way of life' found in some Brexit supporting views about our high streets being taken over by Polish or other shops). This relates to what I have called the 'Janus face of diversity' (Anth-ias 2013b) and related practices and discourses that, on the one hand, seek to integrate the diverse (but on the terms of the hegemonic and naturalised nativist

Territorialising places **169**

'self'), and, on the other hand, wish to expel particular kinds of the diverse, exclude them or marginalise and disempower them, because they are seen as incompatible with 'our way of life' or even a threat, constructing them as the 'perverse diverse'. The intersectional and translocational nature of the difference hailed by diversity is largely unacknowledged and therefore leads to some of the problems of the discourse and practice of 'diversity'.

The vocabulary of diversity is a boundary-making vocabulary as it does not merely hail difference, but it constructs it. In doing this it discriminates amongst differences, treating some as good and some as bad (therefore also hierarchising difference), sorting in terms of social worth – see Chapter 2. The notion of diversity can function as a politically correct and neutralising term. However, diversity denotes 'us' and 'them' also denoting the heterogeneity of 'the other' (Anderson 2017) in distinction from the normal and homogeneous dominant 'us'. As a boundary maker, the political use of diversity functions to undermine the very intent it appears to activate (Anthias 2013b). If its intent is to demarcate or to include then it registers the difference that can be bridged, flagging and thereby reinforcing it. On the other hand, if its intent is to exclude then it constructs the demarcation and difference as alien or 'other', occupying a terrain that cannot be crossed. Simmel (1908) illustrates the conundrum, the contradiction or paradox involved. He refers to the idea of the bridge as both connecting spaces but also demarcating a boundary (Simmel 1994).

Diversity and integration discourses and practices are part of the management of the 'other', although they have receded with the emphasis on control of migration and securitisation. Diversity and integration can be seen as spaces which are consensus making and yet are founded on the principle of dissensus (Rancière 2004) in terms of the potential that the 'other' has to disrupt existing hierarchies. This is a manifestation of how structures rely on legitimating diversity talk for doing some of the work of managing dissensus and promoting, concomitantly, differential exclusion and inclusion. The overall non-performativity of 'diversity' policies and 'talk' has been highlighted particularly in the work of Sara Ahmed (2007, 2016) amongst others. Whilst diversity policies and programmes are of different types, equal opportunities, promoting 'cultural diversity', facilitating work and so on, it can also be argued that:

> these diversity programmes function as a specific social technique that employs semantics of inequality reduction while actually reproducing the inequality-generating effects of the respective classifications.
>
> *(Amelina 2017, p. 23)*

Other research has also shown that the emphasis on diversity side-lines inequality (Deem and Morley 2006).

As Lentin and Titley (2008) argue:

> diversity has become a ubiquitous and widely adopted notion and framework not because it synthesises and furthers an array of political projects

170 Territorialising places

and critiques, but because it provides a gently unifying, cost-free form of political commitment attuned to the mediated, consumer logics of contemporary societies.

(p. 13)

We could treat such discourses and associated practices therefore as a form of neo-liberal mobile technology (Ong 2006a, 2006b) whose aim is to rearrange populations and spaces. Such tropes justify differential treatment on the basis that the 'other' lacks the requisite commitment to 'our' values, either because they fail to commit or because they are incapable of acquiring the cultural recipes or values needed. Here there is the idea of the *perverse diverse* (Anthias 2013b), a figuration which slides into racialisation.

Whilst the governmentality of the racialised subject found in imperial domination links to the dehumanisation of the other as 'species', whether articulated through biological, religious or cultural ascriptions and attributions, the figure of the contemporary racialised subject is the 'diverse' and found to occupy a range of spaces of difference. This can operate even where there is the concession of the possibility of assimilation; the 'diverse' being those who are deemed to be undeserving of the fullest entitlements, unlike the 'native'. The proviso here is that these are not the 'native' of settler societies who are instead seen as previous nature children of the land which they could not usefully instrumentalise (this was designated to be the role of the white settler colonialists). Indigeneity and autochthony thus bear different value in terms of entitlements in different discourses around different projects of resource claiming and governmentality. A racialised subject can occupy the terrain of the diverse or can cease to be the 'other' as and when the logics of hegemonic social and economic forces, as well as struggles against these, derail the foundations of imperial racisms and their debris. In the current period the dehumanisation of the refugee (as 'bare life' – Agamben 1998) is also the object of humanitarianism that re-inserts their humanity but as part of a complex and contradictory project of management and containment, involving new forms of ordering (Chouliaraki and Georgiou 2017).

The trope of 'cultural difference' is central to the notion of the ways the 'other' is marked. This is prominent in ideas of cultural racism (see Barker 1981) and neo-racism mentioned earlier. 'Cultural diversity' as a way of managing difference and otherness is explicitly present in the nomenclature of multiculturalism. Multiculturalism is a range of normative and policy discourses and practices that commit to the validation of cultural difference and try to engage with it in ways which foster social harmony. It is not my intention to review the enormous literature on multiculturalism but rather to see it as a precursor, on the one hand, to current diversity talk, and on the other, as distinctive. Within this framing, culture (commonly defined in terms of 'ethnic' culture) is treated as a collective property of a 'group' and as a set of ingredients (or as 'stuff' to use Barth's term (1969/1998)) with the tendency to homogenise members of minority 'cultures'.

Territorialising places **171**

State multiculturalism in the UK was publicly concerned with enabling difference at the cultural level by endorsing the 'cultural' needs of groups, and failed to acknowledge the gender-specific, and indeed at times sexist, elements of ethnic culture or the ways in which ethnic boundaries are exclusionary. Despite its culturalisation of difference, multiculturalism also set out measures to integrate people at the structural level. Sets of contradictory outcomes contributed to the return of new forms of assimilationism (Rattansi 2004) with the new emphasis on social cohesion and diversity. Such policies aspire to a society with homogeneous values, as distinct from multiculturalism which endorses heterogeneity up to a certain level. Multiculturalism puts the onus on mainstream society to understand and tolerate the values and traditions of the 'diverse' (through the much maligned focus on 'steel bands, saris and samosas'[14]). Diversity talk, which is aligned to a discourse of integration requires compliance with so-called British values, and is less concerned with the structural incorporation of the 'other'.

Some of the 'other' are regarded as 'unwilling to integrate' or 'unable to integrate' (Anthias 2013b). An 'unwillingness to integrate' is to be corrected by requiring a demonstration through, for example, sitting citizenship or integration tests. People's own cultural and social resources are thereby treated as *deficient* for the purposes of participating in society. Those 'unable to integrate' are endowed with 'bad' difference which poses a *danger* to society and to western values (regarded as universalistic values). One example is found in the ways in which integration and securitisation discourses are closely linked.

We can see a continuity between the notorious Rivers of Blood speech by Enoch Powell (1968), fuelling fears of carnage and more recent concerns with integration and fears that the 'diverse', or at least some of them, cannot adapt and adopt British values. In his 1968 speech, Powell says:

> The Sikh communities' campaign to maintain customs inappropriate in Britain is much to be regretted. . . . To claim special communal rights (or should one say rites?) leads to a dangerous fragmentation within society.
>
> *(p. 8)*

The fears that New Commonwealth migrants in the UK could not integrate, because they did not regard being British as their primary identity, have long been part of the British paranoia about the 'diverse', depicted by Norman Tebbit's cricket test (Which team would Asians cheer?).[15] In 2014 he said the equivalent for EU countries today would be to ask 'Who did they fight in the Second World War?', suggesting that EU migrants should be asked if their forefathers fought the Nazis.[16] David Blunkett under New Labour marked out the dangers of multiculturalism and living in diversity: building a new assimilationism based on the erosion of difference and incorporation into the hegemonic culture (see the discussion in Yuval-Davis, Anthias and Kofan 2005). This relates, therefore, to political projects of belonging where the 'diverse' act as a code for 'the other',

172 Territorialising places

both as stranger to be accommodated and stranger to be excluded. 'The diverse', whilst a contradictory and normatively framed denotation of the 'other', also references racialised subjects, constructing non-belonging.

Integration: a problem of culture and identity

The politics of social diversity and integration has reasserted the primacy of the 'national' collective. In Gordon Brown's and later David Cameron's concern with British values, Britain has claimed ownership of democratic and egalitarian values of tolerance and caring for others. Social cohesion and integration policies in Europe (Commission of the European Communities 2005), linked to diversity talk, assume that society should have homogeneous values. Citizenship tests require minorities to have knowledge and competencies not required by majority populations. This has also gone hand in hand with tighter border controls in the interests of national security. Such a framing constructs 'the stranger' (who may be a British citizen or even second or third generation locally born) as the root cause of social and political alienation.

At the sociological level, the concept of integration arose out of a concern with the question of social order (Durkheim 1893/1984/2014). In sociological work more generally it refers to the modes by which people become part of society and the multiple ways they participate within the locality, the school, work, family or the political process. In this way integration refers to something that everyone needs to accomplish in order to become a member of any society. However, within the Chicago School (Thomas and Znaniecki 1918–22; Park 1928/1950) of social research it came to refer to a process which resulted from migration and was deprived of its earlier sociological meaning. It came to be used in terms of the specific problems for society posed by migrants and this evolved into its referent being how newcomers integrated into the 'nation state', rather than society. The assumption about the equivalence between the social and the national is part of the ways in which the governmentality of racialised populations is achieved, not all of whom are migrant. Current policies on integration in the UK have been framed as a backlash against multiculturalism (e.g. see Commission on Integration and Cohesion (2007)) and its perceived problems, in the UK for example, particularly as a response to the development of 'parallel communities' and 'home-grown' terrorism, noted earlier. Integration, in its current manifestation, is the latest assimilationist logic framing the concern with the governance of diversity. However, as Trimikliniotis notes in relation to Europe,

> the funding on the actual migrant integration programmes have been cut back after the 2008 financial crisis and after the 2015 'asylum and migration crisis'. Funding priorities shifted towards 'managing migration flows', i.e. curtailing the flows of migrants into the EU via criminalisation and containing migrant rights.

(2020, p. 100)

Indeed, Trimikliniotis notes that the 2018 EU Communication on the 'progress under the European agenda on migration', which is concerned with 'managing migration in all its aspects', makes no mention of migrant integration (see Eurostat 2017, 2018). Despite a continuing commitment to integration this step back is linked to austerity as well as the so-called refugee and migration crisis. According to the FRA, 'the current political climate provides fertile ground for toxic narratives that turn immigrants into convenient scapegoats' (FRA 2018). This indicates how far the emphasis has shifted to controlling migrants at the border, but this doesn't mean that the technologies of 'integration' are no longer in place, such as those of citizenship tests. Such integration measures have always been accompanied by a focus on the management of migration both at the point of entry and in terms of forms of settlement and accommodation. This, however, has been exacerbated through the migrant and refugee crisis since 2015.

The ways integration has been conceived have changed over the years within EU policy. Whilst earlier conceptions were based on the idea of granting equal rights, full residence rights and equal treatment to third country migrants, this changed in 2003 with the Long-term Residence Directive (Anthias, Kontos and Morokvsic 2012). Such rights were now to be seen as rewards for those who have demonstrated that they have become integrated, for example, by learning the language or getting a job. At the same time a tiered citizenship process was introduced with, for the first time, the setting up of a probationary period. The Family Reunification Directive (2003) also permits member states to require compliance with pre-departure integration measures, such as having to take language courses before members of families can be given residence rights (Anthias and Pajnik 2014; Groenendijk 2004), constituting part of an 'aggressive civic integrationism' (Morokvasic and Catarino 2006). Poorer third country migrants and women have been affected particularly by this (Anthias et al. 2008; Kofman et al. 2000). Such policies are geared to the containment of undesirable surplus migrants to the economy and polity, and a desire to preserve national integrity and contain conflict and terrorism. Integration discourse and policies are means for managing and containing the effects of transnational migration, in terms of the interests of nation states and operate at national and European and transnational levels.

As noted earlier, the decline in actual provision for integration has not reduced the emphasis given to the concern with 'shared values'. Indeed, issues of identity and belonging dominate the political landscape in many countries, alongside the issue of the migration and refugee crisis discussed in the last chapter. In the UK recently (April 2019), Tony Blair, a Labour ex-prime minister, has called for migrants to commit to British values, echoing an earlier call by David Cameron, the Tory ex-prime minister.

Concluding remarks

Whilst transnational spaces like multicultural cities and beyond challenge 'national' imaginaries of belonging, greater bordering and guarding against the global movement of people asks us to engage with the enduring and indeed

174 Territorialising places

amplifying of national borders and boundaries, and new ways of ordering populations. The borders of the nation state are being increasingly policed against undesirable others in formal and informal ways, through migration controls, and different technologies for (differentially) incorporating and managing minorities within, whilst excluding others on the outside. This goes hand in hand with impingements by the state on everyday intersubjectivities, requiring individuals in schools, hospitals and other institutions to become handmaidens of the state in the name of public duty, and to police the borders of the nation. The legal duties of people in policing the nation is related to the erosion of the institutional fabric of the state with the neo-liberal projects of privatisation and the dismantling of welfare provision. Some of those affected by these developments include those who in Britain are being called 'the left behind', through new technology and new flexible employment patterns leading to unemployment and precarity. This particularly affects sections of the working classes, sometimes referred to as the precariat and those in the gig economy, which include intersecting categories of racialised minorities and women.

The management of populations through migration controls and related forms of bordering demonstrates how multiculturality and what some call conviviality (e.g. Gilroy) is being undermined. This has led to a central paradox in the heart of the western world, between the growth of multi-ethnicity and the policing or exclusion of the multiple 'other'. In the next, concluding, Chapter I turn to issues of theory and politics and consider how a translocational lens can address contestations of these processes.

Notes

1 The Windrush generation is named after the ship that brought one of the first groups of West Indian migrants to the UK in 1948.
2 Nicola Bartlett, *Mirror*, April 20, 2018 (retrieved February 13, 2019).
3 Investment visa UK Tier 1 requires an investment of £2 million plus. For details see www.gov.uk-tier-1–investor.
4 Grenfell Tower was a 24 storey social housing estate in West London that burnt down in June 2017 due to faulty cladding, killing 72 people, many of them minorities and working class. Subsequently, many of the surviving residents became politicised who were not politically active beforehand.
5 For cost of bringing in family members and income and savings criteria see www.gov.uk.
6 British Social Attitudes Survey conducted by the National Centre for Social Research in 2018 showed a decline of racism amongst young people. See https://bsa.natcen.ac.uk.
7 Figures for hate crimes: see Hate Crime, England and Wales, 2017/18, Statistical Bulletin 2018, www.gov.uk.
8 Jeremy Corbyn and the Labour Party have been branded as anti-Semitic partly because of their support for Palestinians and criticisms of Israel. In addition, there have been cases relating to Corbyn's endorsement of an anti-Semitic mural – see details later in the chapter.
9 The Rushdie affair is a shorthand term used to denote the storm that brewed after the publication of *The Satanic Verses*, first published in 1988 in the UK. A fatwa was issued against him by Khomeini of Iran and there were public burnings of the book. Rushdie

Territorialising places 175

went into hiding for many years to avoid being killed. The events heralded a new era of securitisation and anti-Muslim sentiment.

10 Oswald Mosley was a British politician who became the leader of the British Union of Fascists in 1932. He organised the Cable Street march in the East End of London (where there was a large Jewish community). There were clashes with people who opposed him, and the march was abandoned. He continued to organise marches and the government passed the Public Order Act in 1936 as a response and a deterrent.

11 Alana Lentin (2016) also talks about another set of Ds, deflection, distancing and denial.

12 A black youth, Rashan Charles, died after restraint by a police officer having been chased by the police in Dalston in 2017. This led to protests and anti-police activity. The subsequent inquest, to the shock of many, found that his death was accidental.

13 The Prevent programme in the UK was set up in 2009 as part of a strategy of counter-terrorism to stop people becoming terrorists or supporting them, contributing to Muslims becoming a 'suspect community'.

14 Steel bands, saris and samosas: these are the well- known S's of multiculturalism depicting its emphasis on the cultures of groups rather than on anti-racism. They are quoted usually as criticisms.

15 The Norman Tebbit cricket test arose out of a phrase that the British Conservative politician used in 1990 to suggest that immigrants who supported their countries of origin rather than England were lacking in commitment to Britain.

16 *The Telegraph*, November 28, 2014.

7

EPILOGOS. TRANSFORMING PLACES

Towards a politics of translocation

Introduction: knowledge in the heartlands of power

This book has insisted that concepts are necessary as heuristic tools and that they are always politically inflected. Concepts with all their political inflections cannot be ditched in favour of a phantasmagorical neutral description, since description itself requires using often unconscious theoretical assumptions about the nature of our object of study. Theory is always an unfinished business and knowledge always operates in the heartlands of power. Some of the presuppositions of theory are not far from being a product of applying a political or normative lens to the world.

Although this is not the place to engage with the vast literature on theorising and on method, in a book such as this that advances a particular framing, a translocational lens, it's necessary to say something about the level of the conceptual. I see concepts as heuristic tools, that is, as enablers in a knowledge project which is always partial, always situated and therefore always unfinished. Such a view does not counterpose itself to 'theory', however. This involves a break with positivistic notions of knowledge to treat knowledge in terms of its social basis.

The issue of the situational, as in the 'situated nature of knowledge', is a fundamental premise of much feminist work (e.g. see Harding 2004), drawing on a broader intellectual tradition that looks at knowledge as 'located' and therefore unfinished. The class and political basis of knowledge derives from a Marxist sociology of knowledge, found in the Marxist theory of ideology (Marx and Engels 1932) and the notion of class consciousness (as well as false consciousness). It has been developed further by the Frankfurt School's Critical Theory (see Arato and Gebhardt (1975) for writings by various members of the school). Mannheim (1929) argues that distinct groupings with their own locations develop different ways of understanding the world, or distinct Weltanschauungs (problematically, he excludes intellectuals who, he argues, can synthesise knowledge and do not have a social basis). The insights of the sociology of knowledge have been translated and developed extensively within the work of feminists such as Dorothy Smith (2005), Patricia Hill Collins (1990, 2019) and Sandra Harding (2004), amongst others.

'Situated knowledge' treats all knowledge as an unfinished business, as well as socially located, without seeking to provide epistemological guarantees for knowledge as truth. There is a danger, however, of a cultural relativism that validates equally all forms of knowledge. Alternatively, there is the danger of treating some forms of knowledge as arbiters of others, on the grounds that they constitute more effective ways of knowing, or because of the special knowledge of certain social groups. The latter is the favoured feminist position from standpoint theory (e.g. see the debate around Hekman 1997). However, such an interpretation can result in giving epistemological weightiness to the 'knowing' subject, unproblematising experience and allocating more epistemological value to certain identity constructs over others. Whilst broadly agreeing with the view that those who experience oppression are, overall, better placed to talk about its effects, this does not guarantee that they are necessarily, or always, best placed to understand whence oppressions come from. An example might be the view that women who experience patriarchy are best able to understand or explain it. However, such a view can lead to the origins of that oppression being found in individual men's proclivities rather than systems of social relations.

Theories are essentially a set of tools, or a tool kit as Foucault referred to them, or '*software*' to use a more contemporary metaphor. They enable us to ask particular kinds of questions that we might not otherwise ask. They enable us to identify our objects of study. They point us towards a partial specification of social processes and outcomes. They are relational and provisional, aiming to facilitate comparison. They can help us to construct a model which we can compare with what we discover about the world. Or they can allow us to compare concrete relations and practices across space, time and scale. As such our concepts need to be formulated in such a way that they open up, and do not foreclose, research into the problems we seek to engage with, rather than being concerned with definitions. In the concern with social categories, and their entangled simultaneities, we need to avoid starting with categories as ready-made or given.

In this book I have argued for an approach that considers categories around difference as modes of power which also inform people's sense of belonging as well as relating to processes of differential inclusion, resource allocation and oppression. I have presented a translocational lens that combines a focus on categories as places and how they are filled by subjects at different points in time and place, with a view that these places, in concrete relations, are entangled and intersecting. Whilst this alerts us to the futility of seeking for the origins of differentiated and stratified social outcomes with reference to a single causal principle, I argue that it's important to hold on to the centrality of the agonistic nature of relations of resource allocation and distribution, and to the historicities of

178 Epilogos

social life in terms of discursive and representational forces which also function as resources in agonistic ways. Resources can be treated as both economic and non-economic, and following Bourdieu, given value through symbolic meanings which are themselves changeable. The materialism of this position treats resource allocation in a much broader way than the notion of 'the economic' (found in both Marx and Bourdieu); it suggests an interplay between symbolic and material value and the spilling over of one onto the other without necessarily *always* giving primacy to one over the other at any conjuncture.

This approach avoids the treatment of technologies of power as diffuse, impersonal and monolithic, and instead treats them as targeted and tied to political and economic projects of exploitation, exclusion and oppression. The field in which they play out is highly differentiated and characterised by contradiction, antagonism, contestation and struggle. There is no monolithic power that guarantees the effects of such technologies in their entirety even where they become implemented through authoritarian or violent means.

The politics of translocation: agonistic and dialogical solidarities

Intersectionality has produced, as we saw in Chapter 3, critiques and backlashes concerning its potential 'whitening', neo-liberal agenda, policy framing, its individualisation of difference, and claims and counterclaims about its origins. There is therefore the issue of the form of politics which it fosters, whether it be identity politics or solidarity politics (which I do not see as always incompatible). In this concluding chapter I make some provisional reflections on how we might pursue a 'politics of translocation' which has direct relevance to the issue of the politics of intersectionality.

It's useful to start here with addressing intersectional 'categories', which raises the issue of whether giving recognition to more and more combinatories of difference can be exhaustive, on the one hand, and the degree to which it is efficacious politically, on the other (does it yield more potential for coalitions and solidarity politics?). Intersectionality, on the one hand, opens possibilities for dialogue and solidarity and yet may reaffirm identity politics around more hybrid identity claims, such as those of minority or black women. Although such constituencies of struggle are important today, there is the possibility that struggles built on identity claims around particular constituencies (as opposed to violence or exploitation, may contribute to the essentialisation of newer and more complex categories of disadvantage and their homogenisation. For example, the production of an essentialised and homogenised category of 'black women' is not only unable to look at heterogeneities, but can forget those black women who are the majority in many non-western countries and the hierarchies amongst them. On the other hand, a recognition of the complexities within the category (on the basis of class, disability, place or citizenship, for example) is able to avoid this, particularly in a reflexive coalition with others who share goals of social justice.

In addition, and very important, if categories are aspects of the way governmentality works (one argument in this book), then such newer categories could *enable new objects of governmentality*. I would argue that they sometimes do, and they sometimes don't, and this needs to be judged contextually and situationally. We could argue that intersectional or syncretic categories are already deployed in auditing systems and bordering practices of the state, both explicitly and implicitly, demarcating specific constituencies within categories of gender (such as migrant women or single mothers), for example. If this is the case, this type of 'intersectionality' is already built into power structures. In terms of a social justice framework, delineating such hybrid categories and inserting them into policies of social correction and regulation can backfire in some cases, but this would need to be investigated. Therefore, it's important that any contestational politics avoids this fixing of constituencies of struggle.

In developing 'translocational intersectionality', I have tried to work towards a complex recognition of hierarchical relations which is not reliant on a focus on intersectional *categories* but instead on *processes and outcomes* in spatio-temporal ways. This has a wider theoretical resonance in terms of social stratification. It locates the hierarchical and stratifying process as complexly interwoven with the *different* operations of power and oppression attached to the social relations of categorisation. This approach also involves a plastic notion of what different modalities of power *do to one another*. The issue is not how we say the latter – whether we prefer 'articulation' or 'intersection/mutual constitution' – but the issue is the problem it addresses and the process it engages with. From this point of view, what modalities of power do to one another in spatio-temporal terms is open and emergent and not to be presupposed. This allows a range of connections and saliencies to unfold in the project of knowledge and political struggle.

A translocational lens provides a way of understanding in contextual and yet historicised ways how social categories are subject to the workings of power structures within modern forms of capitalism and its governance, and how they act to mutually reinforce one another, or to set up contradictory and, at times, dissonant locations for social actors (Anthias 1998a). For instance, for racialised migrant women, they may articulate to produce a reinforcing set of practices of subordination. This affirms the violent and exclusionary effects of how social relations play out at the level of lived experience. However, they may also construct multiple and uneven social patterns of domination and subordination. For example, white working-class men have a different position with respect to ethnic and gender hierarchies than with respect to class ones. They are in a position of subordination in production relations but in a position of super-ordination in relation to gender and race/ethnicity. Contradictory and in-between positions construct identities and actions that constitute important points of departure for understanding the dynamics of social stratification, on the one hand, and, possibly, social transformation on the other. Such dissonance, if, and when, it becomes apparent, may lead to a range of politics, usurpationary or exclusionary, progressive or conservative/populist. In the writings of Marx, Foucault and others, there

180 Epilogos

is a concern with the ways in which the 'appearance' of the real functions as a mode of governance. Where this 'real' is put into question then contestation and struggle become more likely. For Marx this was a process relating to the ways the crises of capitalism revealed the common interests that workers had. For Bourdieu it lies in overcoming the sway of the doxic in social relations. In the approach that I have suggested, the visibility of power comes (also) from the light in the gaps opened up by translocational borders and boundaries and the light they shine on violence and oppression.

The approach I have worked with entails a way of thinking about social strati-fication. The debate about stratification as a question of places, and stratification as a question of population groupings, needs to be rethought in the light of the ways the places serve to single out attributes for people to fill them, and the ways in which the attributes of those who fill the places over time will serve to mark out the location of the places within the hierarchical system. The process of structura-tion of positions and groupings is a dynamic and relational one. This is particularly important in a global and mobile world. Recognising complexity and changeabili-ties in time and space is central if we move away from a concern with the nation state and incorporate transnational processes and actors. There is no doubt that both globalisation itself, as well as the grand sweep of globalisation theory, have put into question the understanding of identities, states, classes and communication modes as sociologists have tended to treat them, that is, in terms of singular social systems usually defined vis-à-vis the boundaries of the nation state. Critiques of methodological nationalism have facilitated a pull away from such approaches, at least as an intention even when this has not always been adhered to. The growth of global economic, social and cultural forms should alert us to the problems of treating categories (like social class) as bounded by the nation state and help us to understand the transnational reach of class processes. We should also avoid gener-alising about the link between economic position and lifestyle/cultural preferences (working both with and against Bourdieu), and avoiding a Eurocentric focus.

Movements of people through migration and displacement might mean that class places themselves can only be understood in translocational ways, in the sense that the places of class hierarchy will differ in different national contexts as are the criteria by which people come to fill them. This leads to highly context-specific processes of class formation. For individuals it leads to a very complex set of class positions emerging in the transnational arena (e.g. through deskilling, relational cultural valuations and different economic contexts). However, this does not mean that the hierarchical landscape is blurred – far from it. Within this landscape emerge particularly disadvantaged and oppressed categories at the intersection, despite some of the contradictory locations some of them may occupy in terms of economic, political and human rights. Examples found in Chapters 5 and 6 include the shifting categorisations of migrants and the case of migrant domestic and care workers.

A central component of the argument in this book is that the differentiation of human populations lends itself well to understanding the ways modern capitalist societies have and indeed continue to adapt in order to pursue their inequality projects. Flexibility, mixed economies, concessions to struggles on the ground, unfixing categories, concerns for bounded equalisations are required if they are to survive. Marx himself posited the role of the RAL and its different constituencies at the abstract level. Many writers have tried to fill the abstract categories with categories of people, with women (e.g. Beechey 1977) and with migrants (Castles and Kosack 1973). Such attempts are important but within the framework of Marxist theory do not have a theoretical scaffolding as there is no theory of difference in Marx's work. We need to look beyond the use (and sometimes misuse (see Anthias 1980) of the notion of the RAL. It is important to explore how differentiated populations, allocated different resources, life conditions and life chances, are part of modern capitalism's ability (so far) to respond to the complexities of its evolution and its crises, in interplay with political processes relating to the border and boundary making of the 'nation' in this new phase of globalising economies and governance. Here the construction of differentiated populations, naturalised and 'placed' hierarchically becomes important in fulfilling such needs. In the process bodies are subjected to both fixities and fluidities translocationally, especially in spatio-temporal terms.

Beyond dialogical politics

One of the most pressing theoretical and political issues linked to a politics of social transformation can be bundled together under the rubric of how different cultural understandings and loyalties can be harnessed towards a better life for all (perhaps Stuart Hall's (2000) multicultural question). One set of answers might be found in various forms of dialogic politics (e.g. see Collins 1990; Yuval-Davis 2011), where negotiating differences can lead to changed perceptions of ourselves and others. This is a position favoured in some types of peace and intercommunal initiatives, despite their persistent failings on the ground, worldwide. The failures of dialogue are numerous. Movements in Cyprus, for example, have not been able to address the political intractabilities involved. The prime actors in the political field from both sides of the ethnic divide are invested with contradictory interests and understandings of what is just (e.g. see Trimikliniotis and Bozkurt 2012). However, there are engagements across difference that can go beyond static and antagonistic collective imaginings, also. Such instances are found in many women's transnational groups and their activities across ethnic divides.[1]

Whilst dialogue or free communicative exchanges[2] are an important part of the political at any level, they must be seen in the context of contestation over power. Dialogue between people from different constituencies is always good and potentially fruitful but on its own is rarely enough. This is because effective dialogue requires social conditions which maximise equal intersubjective and representational power, neutralise 'interests' and enable action, that is, the ability to enter the domains of power. Not only does this require that incumbents

182 Epilogos

of positions are able to meet on equal terms but that they can take this forward in terms of mobilisation to action in multivocal ways. They need to gain access to the means of communication and representation, that is, to become effective political constituencies. It is not just a question of the power to speak, but also the power to be heard and the power to act on this basis. Digitalities have enabled these mobilisations but they have also enabled powers of darkness to suffuse people's minds through right-wing extremisms and racisms.

Dialogue can also be a legitimisation tool which demonstrates that all are free to speak to each other, so power is disassembled at the surface level. Whilst dialogue becomes monologue in the colonial or hegemonic/hierarchised encounter, even dialogue on equal terms may mean we are only talking essentially to others who are willing to listen to us, a variant of ourselves. Dialogue is necessary but not sufficient therefore. It is not here a question of cultural difference which is negotiated dialogically, but a question of mobilisation for a movement which aims to be transformative. This is very difficult where there are different economic and political/national interests at stake as we see in world conflicts and in more local wars and conflicts: in Cyprus, in Kashmir and in the Middle East, for example. However, I do not think this is the same when we look at organising on the ground against subordinations, as long as we recognise the simultaneity and co-dependency of these subordinations. Shreya Atrey (2018) gives an account of the political space an intersectionally framed women's struggle can provide, using the case of Dalit women in India and their struggles, in response to Martha Nussbaum's (2016) analysis of CEDAW.[3] Here she counters Nussbaum's assessment of the success of CEDAW which Nussbaum treats as a product of the recognition and the building of *commonalities*. Instead Atrey argues that the women's movement was strengthened not because but *despite* the rhetoric of 'commonness'; that is, by the recognition of *differences*. If this is the case, a dialogue dedicated to reaching a common view may then only speak to those who were engaged in the dialogue but not beyond them.

Dialogical encounters which are built on fostering commonalities, whilst at the same time engaging with differences can overcome some of the problems of identity politics. Nonetheless, an impediment is found in the processes that structure positions taken by groups and their members when they are located unequally in the social structure. These structural contexts often lead to lack of trust or inabilities to understand the experiences of others (or partially if at all). In such situations the best that can be achieved may be compromise and pragmatism. Asserting the right to have rights as opposed to striving for 'commonness' through dialogue might be a better position, that is, claiming the rights to difference and the right to be equal, despite difference, and working towards an agreed goal in terms of specificities at any point in time. This might not entail cultural transformation but the recognition of overall collective interests, situationally formulated, despite differences. Such a position is found in a solidarity politics that engages with the other as a partner but not as a common cultural subject.

A politics that works towards equal rights despite difference, however, can reproduce hegemonic patterns of thought and practice. For example, the right to gay marriage is an assertion of equal rights, but this can function to consolidate existing gender binaries and conventions/traditions, despite the affective importance of the symbolism of marriage within the couple dyad. Whilst welcomed by some, others have treated such victories as potentially hollow and as forms of homonormativity that mirror heteronormativity (e.g. Richardson 2017). Similar themes can be picked up from within the transgender movement, with the possible replication of gender binaries through 'corrections' to the body. Whilst for those persons such transitioning physically may be healing and liberating, it may play to the idea of gender fixities. It is central to frame such struggles as a challenge to gender binary systems, and not only fixed gender identities at the person level. Only when we can dispense with gender as a given identity category with its 'cultural' stuff and economic effectivities and other hierarchies will this occur (but see Butler (2015) for a different view of gender).

The need for strategic alliances across struggles has been much written about (e.g. see Cockburn 1998, 2004) and this is one arm of a politics of translocation which goes beyond transnational and transethnic alliances. The need for commitment to networks and alliances across borders (i.e. transnationally) and across boundaries of race, sexuality, ethnicity, faith, ability and class are central to a politics of translocation. Various global feminist networks signal what some have called transnational feminism or global feminism, found in campaigns around women's human rights where *violence* against women has been a central plank for uniting women's groups across boundaries and borders. As Niamh Reilly (2007) has stated,

> More than three decades of second-wave feminist critiques have underlined the message that no feminist project, academic or practical, can be based on an assumption of women as a monolithic group with a 'natural' common agenda.
>
> *(p. 189)*

Italian feminists coined the term 'transversal politics', endorsed and developed by a number of writers (e.g. notably Yuval-Davis 1994; Cockburn 1998; Collins 2010, 2017). Such a politics emphasises the disparities of social location and social differences in working towards solidarity forms of politics and provides important insights regarding processes which can help to overcome some of the difficulties involved. The ideas of rooting and shifting are important (see Yuval-Davis 2011). However, the idea that feminists come from a particular place of difference (which they root 'within' and work towards shifting 'from') may play to the idea of a 'rooting' that has resonances with a privileging of experience and particular identities. Arguably this may be at odds to some extent with a fully intersectional politics, since intersectionality treats identities as multiplex and situational. Here the issue becomes how to harness the very intersectional nature

184 Epilogos

of difference for political action itself. To root and shift in terms of cultural differences amongst women, for example, does not provide the means for overcoming differences of social location and translocation more broadly, or at specific times, although it is a good first step. Whilst alliances along ethnic lines may be forged within feminism (e.g. in Cyprus, with the feminist group Hands Across the Divide – see Cockburn 2004; Hadjipavlou 2010), this does not consider the other intersecting positions at play, relating to class, for example. Of course, the saliency of each difference will vary in time and place and in terms of the form of political mobilisation. When it comes to issues relating to national conflict it may be that issues of ethnicity become more salient than issues of gender or class, age or disability. Difficulties of dialogue are particularly intractable when some will lose, and others will gain, by particular objectives. Agreeing such objectives is difficult, as the difficulty of finding resolutions to the Israel-Palestine and the Cyprus conflicts show. This is not just because of the politics at the top, but also because of the politics from below. It is only when one's identity with one or another is disrupted through the recognition of commonalities of *purpose*, and working *with* intersectional complexities, that this can work. This requires the dismantling of discrete identity categories towards a translocational imaginary. From this point of view, solidarity politics needs itself to be what Pat Hill Collins (2017) calls flexible as well as situational. The promise of a fully intersectional solidarity politics of the 'oppressed' even in terms of specific issues such as police violence is still to be achieved. It may be, therefore, that constituencies of identity still provide a way into the making of solidarity-based struggles, and that we should not pitch identity politics against solidarity politics in a binary way.

A politics of translocation and the issue of identity politics

Espousing solidarity politics rather than identity politics, and dismantling discrete and unitary identities, does not mean that one cannot occupy them for discrete purposes. To say one rejects a totalising view of ethnic identity does not mean that one cannot think through the prism of ethnicity. For example, talking about the commonalities and differences of Cypriot Greeks and Cypriot Turks requires thinking through the prism of ethnicity, at times, but in a non-binary way (since ethnic affiliations and solidarities are 'social facts', however much we may wish to be rid of them). Identity can function as a mobilising cry, if it is conceived outside essentialised claims to resources on their basis. A politics can *start from* belonging to an attributed or claimed identity (e.g. Dalit women) but need not *end* up as a claim *for* that identity. In this way identity can be part of a solidarity politics, for example where you are struggling for a greater unification of Cyprus which goes beyond Greek and Turkish conflict narratives. This can be mobilised through the identities of people who think of themselves as either one or the other, but *also as united* (through being Cypriot). Similarly, the Black Lives Matter movement, although mobilised on the basis of black identity, not only has pulled in a heterogeneity of social locations relating to 'blackness' but

Epilogos **185**

potentially may mobilise queer, disabled and other constituencies of struggle and work towards more and more coalitions. To start from 'Black Lives' should not mean to end with them, as the struggle against oppression and violence talks to many others too.

Another example is that struggle can be fought by migrant women at the lead that is not just about achieving political gains as migrant women. This is only possible if there is a recognition of the broader implications of single strand politics (say where domestic workers may be mobilising for better pay, this also taps in to claims by workers and by women and enables forging alliances – see also Bassel 2015). The Cities of Sanctuary movement, in the UK, is based on a broad coalition of forces linking different groups, from trade unions to religious groups and associations. According to Squire (2011) such coalitions constitute 'mobile solidarities' and are transethnic rather than ethnic-based mobilisations. The idea of a migrant commons (see Trimikliniotis, Parsanoglou and Tsianos 2016; Parsanoglou and Tsianos 2019; Schierup and Alund 2018) is also based on the idea of commonalities and coalitions across migrant groups which, it is argued, hold the potential for generating radical transformation.

Identity claims and attributions often provide a fertile ground for mobilisations because of the common language of culture, norms and experiences that can be harnessed. These 'strategic essentialisms' (Spivak 1994) do not require the pursuit of identity politics in the sense of making claims politically which relate only to that particular identity. Women can organise for equality without this being a claim only about women. In all these cases struggling as a particular constituency involves coalition building with others, but also a *common target or common enemy*.

We can divide solidarity politics in terms of a focus on shared interests, shared targets or shared goals. Where all three exist, this makes mobilisation more effective even where there are differences of culture or position. However, from an intersectional point of view shared interests are always provisional and situational rather than fixed since interests, like identities, are mobile and translocational. This indicates that solidary mobilisations do not construct permanent constituencies of struggle but are always directed *against* a target which has been formulated and agreed. If solidarity can also be formulated *towards* a goal which is commonly agreed, then differences are less important. Here, a politics of 'the other' and appreciation of values of equality and justice are paramount, but not always achievable. Problems with solidarity politics can be summarised as: dealing with differences of interest; unequal power to voice; and unequal access to the political process. The latter two can be partially resolved by advocacy where some constituents develop a framework of trust. Then those with more voice can speak and advocate for them. It's also possible to find ways in which those with voice can transfer power to those with less voice (through a politics of power-sharing). These are all difficult issues but move the agenda beyond dialogic politics that focuses on difference, particularly ethnic and cultural difference.

186 Epilogos

1. *Access, parity, participation and belonging*

Integration (see Chapter 6) and belonging (Chapter 1) are current buzz-words. The category of integration, as we saw, in tandem with the notion of diversity, is problematic on several fronts. It assumes a holistic community which one is integrated into and does not require us to take account of the terms of integration or belonging. For example, there are disempowering forms of belonging and integration. For women this is found in both the so-called public and private sphere (where women belong in asymmetrical ways to families, networks or organisations). For minorities, of any gender and irrespective of class differences, there are asymmetries in the labour market and in relation to citizenship, especially where they may be included in very exploitative and disadvantaged ways. Moreover, any integration or belonging can be no more than approximate since not every individual and group can, or indeed wants to, be integrated or to belong in all social spheres. Social incorporation relating to citizenship practices and freedom from forms of violence, exploitation and subordination are prerequisites of belonging. Equality of access should be accompanied by mechanisms for enablement, and moves towards equality of outcomes must always be made, however difficult.

Further issues relate to *targeting mainstream hegemonic discourses and practices* rather than merely focusing on policies which are aimed at those who are victims of structures, however they are defined. This means struggle to transform the frame of reference of the very polity and society. This requires a move to a broader based notion of communities, which are not defined by national or ethnic characteristics but by inclusive forms of citizenship and belonging. In such a way, although there remain difficult issues about the ways in which cultural differences between groups are to be reconciled, this allows a greater emphasis on tackling the impediments to full participation through the attack on translocational subordinations on several fronts. In any society the more voices heard and represented from different translocational positionalities, the greater the safeguard against violations and exclusions, although the issue of competing claims remains. But the lines between these are multidimensional enabling more effective dialogue than those that are premised on dialogue from ethnic or racialised positions – a translocational politics brings all these into play.

Telos

I would like to return to the dilemmas posed by debates on the themes addressed in this book about translocational belonging delivered by social categories of difference. All practices that serve to subordinate and oppress are tied to a range of structural processes which include the state apparatus, the socio-legal framework and the dominance of western capitalist interests and cultural forms within which some are relegated to the dustbin of life. Solidarity politics which harnesses the strong mobilising potential of a reflexive translocational positionality politics is part of the struggle against these structures. Often such struggles emerge through personal experience or through personal projection, as in the ways children have rallied to oppose the ecological damage the earth has been inflicted, and to save it.

There is no doubt that we face a crucial moment in the struggles for equalities that I believe are more and more dependent on the rejection of fixed categories of difference, and the need to move towards greater fluidities and multiplicities. Recognising how we are all intertwined in social life and co-dependent on each other is important, and how we also occupy those spaces in between. Those who we construct as 'the other' inhabit ourselves too in many ways and can stand for ourselves: such a recognition of translocation makes the line between self and other more and more blurred. In this difficult time with the crisis of the neo-liberal state and the retrenchment of fixities, the growth of populisms, racisms and rampant inequalities and violence, social correction needs to work on a number of fronts: in terms of socio-material conditions, the discursive apparatus and mechanisms of subjective identification. The role of agency and organisation based on solidarity politics, which can harness translocational identities, is crucial here.

There is a great deal of work to be done in refining the understanding of the operations of power relating to the construction of difference and its social organisation. This work is both ambitious and challenging, particularly given the changing configuration of categories of differentiation and hierarchisation in the modern world, and the economic and political dimensions of the processes. Examining different societal arenas and broader power relations, including the economic and the political and their workings in relation to one another, is important. An intersectional framework that considers *processes* of social categorisation and division also requires looking at how categories operate as forms of governmentality and modes of resource allocation. The spaces where they cross-cut one another shines a light on the workings of the power dynamics linked to economic and political projects within contemporary capitalist governmentality. In this way, what can be called a translocational trans-scalar heuristic addresses not only issues of heterogeneity but the social processes that lead to how difference is harnessed to produce outcomes of inequality.

A number of concerns are central to this research and political agenda, which this book has tried to begin addressing. Firstly, we need to chart what is happening to the saliency of social categories of difference, what new forms are emerging and how these are embedded in resource allocation, hierarchisation and inferiorisation. For example, in Chapter 4 we saw that new types of class categorisation have emerged in the latest phase of neo-liberal capitalism, particularly with austerity. These point to the importance of precarity, on the one hand, and the further fractioning of working-class lives and positionalities. This is expressed through the ways class allegiances have been divided over Brexit in the UK, and over Trump in the US, and indeed over migration and social justice and equality projects. The rise of right-wing populisms of various kinds

188 Epilogos

throughout the world indicate some of the problems faced by treating any specific economic class as having a natural political proclivity. It asks us to look at how class processes relate to those of political and discursive formations and in relation to 'interests' based on intersections with ethnicity, 'race' and gender amongst others. Also, as I have noted, some central categories – like gender – are becoming less fixed, given the growing acceptance of transgendering (see also Brubaker 2017). However, although individuals may be able to change their gender, to what extent is there an undoing of gender as a modality of power? To what extent are the naturalising assumptions of gender becoming less important in determining social location in its broadest sense? Other categories are shifting too, not only with greater recognition of syncretic, diasporic and hybrid formations linked to transnational and multi-ethnic societies. Categorisations – such as migrant, refugee, citizen, asylum seeker – are subject to the different imperatives of the political projects of the state and political ideologies related particularly to nationalism and racism.

We can also ask questions about the changing forms of 'othering' and the governing involved, with extensions of state power, partly prompted by the new face of the 'war on terror' but also the war against migrants and refugees who are treated as illegitimately plundering the goods of European societies, which were explored in Chapter 6. This extends the state to citizens, making us all vigilantes of the state. This raises the question of how these processes can be countered and the forms of political engagement that they instigate. To what extent is the 'autonomy of migration' thesis (Mezzadra and Neilson 2013; Mezzadra 2011) and the idea of a migrant political constituency expressed, for example, in the idea of a 'migrant commons', noted earlier, able to deliver such a politics? More broadly this raises the issue of how identity politics and solidarity politics can be evaluated as motors for social change.

We can also see an increasing individualisation and privatisation of difference, on the one hand, alongside more rigid categories of entitlement relating to the primordial rights of those who are the 'original' inhabitants of the nation and culture. Such categories are those that fulfil the dominant criteria of 'desert': able-bodied, employed, skilled, culturally competent in the dominant culture and way of life, usually white and in the UK English by birth. The notion of nativism, discussed in Chapter 6, perhaps is not an adequate label for the intersectional nature of this ideological camera obscura. It is interlaced with classism, ableism, sexism and racism. Such issues raise questions of solidarity, resistance and call for new imaginaries of social transformation.

Such a call involves going beyond the mere recognition of collaboration based on organising around particular kinds of struggles, rather than particular kinds of identities. It must be fought on the basis of a new imaginary of a world, well-nigh seemingly impossible after the demise of the 'great utopian experiment' of the Soviet world. Such an imaginary needs to promote more equal resource allocation as a basic human and social right, and foster a new vision of human sociality where values of care and co-operation supplant those of competition

Epilogos **189**

and strife. A concern with quality of life sits alongside solutions to poverty and inequality and has an ethical dimension in regard to dealing with the addictions, despair and loneliness we find amongst both the old and the young today. In other words, a vision of equality needs to go beyond equality in the narrow sense of equality of treatment or even equality of outcome, to a refashioning of what we want being human to become. Disrupting categories of difference as modes of ordering and hierarchy making as well as the boundary between the material and the cultural is one challenge (some have engaged with the boundary of the human and the non-human, towards the posthuman, e.g. Bradiotti 2016).

The political economy underpinning the framework of this book is precisely a move away from the economic as homonomous with 'the material', and as a reified set of practices. It involves a recognition that the material is both embedded in meaning structures but also relates to the production and distribution of a range of resources in society, including the commons, our natural resources, the air that we breathe and the earth that is our mother and our place of rest. These must be central to the understanding of how power and inequality are produced and reproduced in modern neo-liberal states.

Notes

1 Such groups include Hands Across the Divide in Cyprus, the Northern Ireland Women's Coalition and Women Wage Peace in Israel/Palestine. Many women's groups are involved in transnational dialogue and include: WIDE (Women in Development Europe); AWMR (Association of women of the Mediterranean Region); DAWN (Development Alternatives with Women for a New Era); WLUML (Women Living under Muslim Laws) and AF3IRM: a transnational feminist organization (the latter inspired by feminist Chandra Mohanty.
2 Mead (1934) saw intersubjectivity or dialogue as the basis for the construction of self and society. In dialogue one is faced with the 'other' and has to negotiate meaning. Alternatively, Habermas's ethics of communicative action (1984) involves rational minds oriented to understanding. Bakhtin's dialogical sociality (1986) insists not on Mead's generalised other but the social as heterogeneous, as having no unified core.
3 Convention on the Elimination of All Forms of Discrimination Against Women, adopted December, 18 1979, Res. 34/180 UN.

REFERENCES

Abbas, M.S. (2019) '"I grew a beard and my dad flipped out!" Co-option of British Muslim parents in countering "extremism" within their families in Bradford and Leeds', *Journal of Ethnic and Migration Studies*, 45 (9): 1458–1476.

Abercrombie, N. and J. Urry (1983) *Capital, Labour and the Middle Classes*, London: Allen and Unwin.

Acker, J. (2006) 'Inequality regimes: Gender, class, and race in organisations', *Gender and Society*, 20 (4): 441–464.

Adkins, L. and B. Skeggs (2005) 'Context and background: Pierre Bourdieu's analysis of class, gender and sexuality', in Adkins L. and B. Skeggs (eds.), *Feminism after Bourdieu*, Oxford: Blackwell, pp. 19–33.

Agamben, G. (1998) *Homo Sacer: Sovereign Power and Bare Life*, Stanford: Stanford University Press.

Agamben, G. (2005) *State of Exception*, Chicago: University of Chicago Press.

Agustin, L.M. (2005) 'Migrants in the mistress's house: Other voices in the "trafficking" debate', *Social Politics: International Studies in Gender, Religion State and Society*, 12 (1): 96–117.

Ahmed, S. (2004) *The Cultural Politics of Emotion*, London: Routledge.

Ahmed, S. (2007) 'The language of diversity', *Ethnic and Racial Studies*, 30 (2): 235–256.

Ahmed, S. (2009) 'Embodying diversity: Problems and paradoxes for black feminists', *Race, Ethnicity and Education*, 12 (1): 41–52.

Ahmed, S. (2016) 'How not to do things with word's', *Wagadu, A Journal of Transnational Women's and Gender Studies*, 16: 1–10.

Ahonen, P. (2014) 'Hidden contexts and invisible power relations: A Foucauldian reading of diversity research', *Human Relations*, 6 (3): 263–286.

Alcoff, L.M. (2006) 'Fraser on redistribution, recognition, and identity', *European Journal of Political Theory*, 6: 255.

Al-Dajani, H., Z. Bika, L. Collins and J. Swail (2014) 'Gender and family business: New theoretical directions', *International Journal of Gender and Entrepreneurship*, 6 (3): 218–230.

Alison, M. (2007) 'Wartime sexual violence: Women's human rights and questions of masculinity', *Review of International Studies*, 33: 75–90.

Althusser, L. (1971) 'Ideology and ideological state apparatuses,' in *Lenin and Philosophy and Other Essays*, New York: Monthly Review Press.

Amelina, A. (2016) *Transnationalising Inequalities in Europe: Sociocultural Boundaries, Assemblages and Regimes of Intersection*, London: Routledge.

Amelina, A. (2017) 'After the reflexive turn in migration studies: Towards the doing migration approach', Working Paper, Gender, Diversity and Migration No. 13.

Amin, A. (2002) 'Ethnicity and the multicultural city: Living with diversity', *Environment and Planning*, 34: 959–980.

Amin, A. (2008) 'Thinking past integration and community cohesion', Presented at 'Integration and Community Cohesion' Seminar, Belfast Castle, Facilitated by Belfast City Council's Conflict Transformation Project.

Amin, A. (2010) 'The remainders of race', *Theory Culture and Society*, 27 (1): 1–23.

Anderson, B. (1997) 'Servants and slaves: Europe's domestic workers', *Race and Class*, 39 (1): 37–49.

Anderson, B. (2000) *Doing the Dirty Work? The Global Politics of Domestic Labour*, London: Zed Books.

Anderson, B. (2006) 'A very private business: Migration and domestic work', COMPAS Working Paper No. 28, University of Oxford.

Anderson, B. (2017) *Us and Them: The Dangerous Politics of Immigration Control*, Oxford: Oxford University Press.

Anderson, B. and A. Phizacklea (1997) 'Migrant domestic workers: A European perspective', Dept of Sociology, University of Leicester, Leicester.

Anderson, B. and B. Rogaly (2005) *Forced Labour and Migration to the UK*, London: Trades Union Congress.

Anderson, M.L. (2005) 'Thinking about women: A quarter century's view', *Gender and Society*, 19 (4): 437–455.

Anthias, F. (1980) 'Women and the reserve army of labour, a critique of Veronica Beechey', *Capital and Class*, 4 (1): 50–63.

Anthias, F. (1982) *Ethnicity and Class Among Greek Cypriot Migrants: A Study in the Conceptualisation of Ethnicity*, Ph.D. Thesis, University of London.

Anthias, F. (1983) 'Sexual divisions and ethnic adaptation: Greek Cypriot women in Britain', in A. Phizacklea (ed.), *One Way Ticket*, London: Routledge.

Anthias, F. (1990) 'Race and class revisited: Conceptualising race and racisms', *The Sociological Review*, 38 (1): 19–42.

Anthias, F. (1991) 'Parameters of difference and identity and the problem of connections – Gender, ethnicity and class', *International Review of Sociology*, 2 (2): 29–51.

Anthias, F. (1992a) *Ethnicity, Class, Gender and Migration, Greek Cypriots in Britain*, Avebury: Ashgate.

Anthias, F. (1992b) 'Connecting "race" and ethnic phenomena', *Sociology*, 26 (3): 421–438.

Anthias, F. (1993) 'Gendered ethnicities in the British Labour Market', in H. Rudolph and M. Morokvasic (eds.), *Bridging States and Markets*, Berlin: Sigma, pp. 163–191.

Anthias, F. (1998a) 'Rethinking social divisions: Some notes towards a theoretical framework', *Sociological Review*, 46 (3): 506–535.

Anthias, F. (1998b) 'Evaluating diaspora: Beyond ethnicity?', *Sociology*, 32 (3): 557–580.

Anthias, F. (2000) 'Metaphors of home', in F. Anthias and G. Lazaridis (eds.), *Gender and Migration in Southern Europe: Women on the Move*, Oxford: Berg, pp. 15–49.

Anthias, F. (2001a) 'The material and the symbolic in theorising social stratification', *British Journal of Sociology*, 52 (3): 367–390.

Anthias, F. (2001b) 'The concept of "social division" and theorising social stratification: Looking at ethnicity and class', *Sociology*, 35 (4): 835–854.

192 References

Anthias, F. (2001c) 'New hybridities, old concepts: The limits of culture', *Ethnic and Racial Studies*, 24 (4): 617–641.

Anthias, F. (2002) 'Where do I belong?: Narrating identity and translocational positionality', *Ethnicities*, 2 (4): 491–515.

Anthias, F. (2006) 'Belongings in a globalizing and unequal world: Rethinking translocations', in N. Yuval-Davis, K. Kannabiran and U. Vieten (eds.), *The Situated Politics of Belonging*, London: Sage, pp. 17–31.

Anthias, F. (2007) 'Ethnic ties: Social capital and the question of mobilisability', *The Sociological Review*, 55 (4): 788–805.

Anthias, F. (2008) 'Thinking through the lens of translocational positionality: An intersectionality frame for understanding identity and belonging', *Translocations, Migration and Change*, 4 (1): 5–20.

Anthias, F. (2009) 'Translocational belonging, identity and generation: Questions and problems in migration and ethnic studies', *Finnish Journal of Ethnicity and Migration (FJEM)*, 4 (1): 6–16. www.etmu.fi

Anthias, F. (2013a) 'Intersectional what? Social divisions, intersectionality and levels of analysis', *Ethnicities*, 13: 3–19.

Anthias, F. (2013b) 'Moving beyond the Janus face of integration and diversity discourses: Towards an intersectional framing', *The Sociological Review*, 61 (2): 323–343.

Anthias, F. (2013c) 'Hierarchies of social location, class and intersectionality', *International Sociology*, 28 (1): 121–138.

Anthias, F. (2014) 'The intersections of class, gender, sexuality and "race": The political economy of gendered violence', *International Journal of Politics, Culture and Society*, 27 (2): 153–171.

Anthias, F. (2016) 'Interconnecting boundaries of identity and belonging within transnational mobility studies: Framing inequalities', *Current Sociology Monograph*, 64 (2): 172–190.

Anthias, F. and M. Cederberg (2009) 'Using ethnic bonds in self-employment and the issue of social capital', *Journal of Ethnic and Migration Studies*, 35 (6): 901–917.

Anthias, F., M. Kontos, F. Kupferberg, G. Lazaridis, S. Mason, S. Papaioannou and W. Privitera (2008) 'Arenas of policy making', in U. Apitzsch and M. Kontos (eds.), *Self-Employment Activities of Women and Minorities: Their Success or Failure in Relation to Social Citizenship Policies*, Berlin: VS Verlag.

Anthias, F., M. Kontos and M. Morokvasic (eds.) (2012) *Female Migrants in Europe: The Paradoxes of Integration*, New York: Springer.

Anthias, F. and G. Lazaridis (2000) *Into the Margins: Migration and Exclusion in Southern Europe*, Ashgate: Avebury, 209p.

Anthias, F. and G. Lazaridis (2002) *Gender and Migration in Southern Europe: Women on the Move*, Oxford: Berg.

Anthias, F. and C. Lloyd (eds.) (2002) *Rethinking Anti-Racisms: From Theory to Practice*, London: Routledge.

Anthias, F. and N. Mehta (2003) 'The intersection between gender, the family and self-employment: The family as a resource', *International Review of Sociology*, 13 (1): 105–116.

Anthias, F. and M. Pajnik (eds.) (2014) *Contesting Integration, Engendering Migration*, London: Palgrave.

Anthias, F. and N. Yuval-Davis (1983) 'Contextualising feminism: Ethnic, gender and class divisions', *Feminist Review*, 15: 62–76.

Anthias, F. and N. Yuval-Davis (1989) 'Introduction' in *Woman, Nation, State*, Basingstone: Macmillan, pp. 1–16.

References   **193**

Anthias, F. and N. Yuval-Davis (1992) *Racialised Boundaries: Nation, Race, Ethnicity, Colour and Class and the Anti Racist Struggle*, London: Routledge.

Antonsich, M. (2010) 'Searching for belonging: An analytical frame', *Geography Compass*, 4 (6): 644–659.

Anzaldua, G. (1999) *Borderlands/La Frontera: The New Mestiza*, San Francisco: Spinsters/Aunt Lute.

Arato, A. and E. Gebhardt (eds.) (1975) *The Essential Frankfurt School Reader*, New York: Continuum.

Arendt, H. (1951/1968) *The Origins of Totalitarianism*, New York: Harcourt, Brace and Jovanovich (1968 edition).

Ashe, S., M. Borkowska and J. Nazroo (2018) 'Racism ruins lives: An analysis of the 2016–2017 TUC Racism at Work Survey', *Trades Union Congress*. www.ethnicity.ac.uk/research/projects/racism-at-work/

Atkinson, A.B. (2015) *Inequality: What Can Be Done*, London: Harvard University Press.

Atkinson, W. (2015) *Class*, London: John Wiley and Sons.

Atrey, S. (2018) 'Women's human rights: From progress to transformation, an intersectional response to Martha Nussbaum', *Human Rights Quarterly*, 40 (4): 859–904.

Bakhtin, M.M. (1986) *Speech Genres and Other Late Essays,* Austin: University of Texas Press.

Banton, M. (1987) *Racial Theories*, Cambridge: Cambridge University Press.

Barbalet, J.M. (1992) 'A macro sociology of emotion-class resentment', *Sociological Theory*, 10 (2): 150–163.

Barker, M.J. (1981) *The New Racism*, London: Junction Books.

Barth, F. (1969/1998) *Ethnic Groups and Boundaries*, New York: Waveland Press, Inc.

Barry, K. (1979) *Female Sexual Slavery*, Englewood Cliffs, NJ: Prentice-Hall.

Bassel, L. (2014) 'Acting "as" and acting "as if": Two approaches to the politics of race and migration', in K. Murji and J. Solomos (eds.), *Theories of Race and Ethnicity*, Cambridge: Cambridge University Press, pp. 96–113.

Beck, U. (1996) *Risk Society*, London: Sage.

Beck, U. (1999) *What Is Globalization?* Cambridge: Polity Press.

Beechey, V. (1977) 'Some notes on female wage labour', *Capital and Class*, 3: 45.

Begikhani, N., A. Gill, G. Hague and K. Ibrahiim (2010) 'Honour based violence and honour based killings in Iraqi Kurdistan and in the Kurdish diaspora in the UK', Final Report, Centre for Gender and Violence Research, Bristol University.

Benson, M. (2019) 'Brexit, British people of colour in the EU 27 and everyday racism in Britain and Europe', *Ethnic and Racial Studies*, online first.

Berg, M. and N. Sigona (2013) 'Ethnography, diversity and urban space', *Identities*, 20 (4): 347–360.

Bernstein, B. (1961) 'Social structure, language and learning', *Educational Researcher*, 13 (3): 163–176.

Beteille, A. (1996) 'The mismatch between class and status', *British Journal of Sociology*, 47 (3): 513–525.

Bhattacharya, T. (ed.) (2017) *Social Reproduction Theory: Remapping Class, Recentering Oppression*, London: Pluto Press.

Bhopal, K. and J. Preston (2012) *Intersectionality and Race in Education*, London: Routledge.

Bilge, S. (2010) 'Recent feminist outlooks on intersectionality', *Diogenes*, 57: 58–72.

Bilge, S. (2013) 'Intersectionality undone: Saving intersectionality from feminist intersectionality studies', *Du Bois Review: Social Science Research on Race*, 10 (2): 405–424.

Blunkett, D. (2013) Cited in *The Guardian*, 12th November.

Bograd, M. (1999) 'Strengthening domestic violence theories: Intersections of race, class, sexual orientation and gender', *Journal of Marital and Family Therapy*, 25: 275–289.

194 References

Bordo, S. (1993) 'Feminism, Foucault and the politics of the body', in C. Ramazanoglou (ed.), *Up Against Foucault: Explorations of Some Tensions between Foucault and Feminism*, London: Routledge.

Bottero, W. (2004) 'Class identities and the identity of class', *Sociology*, 38 (5): 985–1003.

Bourdieu, P. (1977a) *Algeria 1960*, Cambridge: Cambridge University Press.

Bourdieu, P. (1977b) *Outline of a Theory of Practice*, Cambridge: Cambridge.

Bourdieu, P. (1980) *The Logic of Practice*, Stanford: Stanford University Press.

Bourdieu, P. (1984) *Distinction: A Social Critique of the Judgement of Taste*, London: Routledge (first published in 1979).

Bourdieu, P. (1985) 'Social space and the genesis of groups', *Theory and Society*, 14 (6): 723–744.

Bourdieu, P. (1986) 'The forms of capital', in J.G. Richardson (ed.), *Handbook of Theory and Research for the Sociology of Education*, New York: Greenwood Press, pp. 241–258.

Bourdieu, P. (1990) 'La domination masculine', *Actes de la reserche en sciences sociales*, 84: 2–31.

Bourdieu, P. (2000) *Pascalian Meditations*, Cambridge: Polity Press.

Bourdieu, P. and L. Wacquant (1992) *An Invitation to Reflexive Sociology*, Chicago: Chicago University Press.

Bourguignon, F. (2015) *The Globalisation of Inequality*, Princeton: Princeton University Press.

Bradiotti, R. (2016) 'Posthuman critical theory', in D. Banerji and M. Paranjape (eds.), *Critical Posthumanism and Planetary Future*, New Delhi: Springer, pp. 13–32.

Bradley, H. (1996) *Fractured Identities*, Cambridge: Polity.

Bradley, H. (2014) 'Class descriptors or class relations? Thoughts towards a critique of Savage et al', *Sociology*, 48 (3): 429–436.

Brah, A. (1996) *Cartographies of the Diaspora*, London: Routledge.

Brah, A. and A. Phoenix (2004) 'Ain't I a woman? Revisiting intersectionality', *Journal of International Women's Studies*, 5 (3): 75–86.

Bravo Lopez, F. (2011) 'Towards a definition of Islamophobia: Approximations of the early 21st century', *Ethnic and Racial Studies*, 34 (4): 556–573.

Breach, A. and Y. Li (2017) *Gender Pay Gap by Ethnicity in Britain*, London: Fawcett. www.fawcett society.org.uk

Brenner, N. (1994) 'Foucault's new functionalism', *Theory and Society*, 23: 679–709.

Brickell, K. and A. Datta (eds.) (2011) *Translocal Geographies*, Farnham: Ashgate.

Brubaker, R. (2004) *Ethnicity without Groups*, Cambridge, MA: Harvard University Press.

Brubaker, R. (2010) 'Migration, membership, and the modern nation-state: Internal and external dimensions of the politics of belonging', *Journal of Interdisciplinary History*, xli (1): 61–78.

Brubaker, R. (2017) *Trans: Gender and Race in an Age of Unsettled Identities*, Princeton: Princeton University Press.

Brubaker, R. and F. Cooper (2000) 'Beyond "identity"', *Theory and Society*, 29 (1): 1–47.

Brubaker, R. and M. Fernandez (2019) 'Cross domain comparison and the politics of difference', *British Journal of Sociology*, online first.

Burawoy, M. (2018) 'Making sense of Bourdieu: From demolition to recuperation and critique', *Catalysts*, 2 (1): 51–87.

Burikova, Z.S. (2019) 'Au pairs, nannies and baby-sitters: Paid care as a temporary life course experience in Slovakia and the UK', *Feminist Review*, 122: 80–94.

Burkitt, I. (2002) 'Technologies of the self: Habitus and capacities', *Journal for the Theory of Social Behaviour*, 32 (2): 219–237.

References 195

Butler, J. (1990) *Gender Trouble*, New York: Routledge.

Butler, J. (1993) *Bodies that Matter*, New York: Routledge.

Butler, J. (1997) *Excitable Speech: A Politics of the Performative*, New York: Routledge.

Butler, J. (1998) 'Performativity's social magic', in R. Shusterman (ed.), *Bourdieu: A Critical Reader*, Oxford: Wiley Blackwell, pp. 113–128.

Butler, J. (2006) *Precarious Life*, New York: Routledge.

Butler, J. (2010) *Frames of War*, London and New York: Verso.

Butler, J. (2015) 'Interview with Stephanie Berbec', *Versobooks.com*, 6th May 2015.

Cameron, D. (2014) Cited in *The Guardian*, 14th June.

Campani, G. and T. Chiappelli (2012) 'Trafficking and women's migration in the global context', in F. Anthias, M. Kontos and M. Morokvasic (eds.), *Paradoxes of Integration: Female Migrants in Europe,* London: Springer, pp. 173–191.

Carastathis, A. (2016) *Intersectionality: Origins, Contestations, Horizons*, Lincoln: University of Nebraska Press.

Carbin, M. and S. Edenheim (2013) 'The intersectional turn in feminist theory: A dream of a common language?', *European Journal of Women's Studies*, 20 (3): 233–248.

Carchedi, G. (1977) *On the Economic Identification of Social Classes*, London: Routledge Kegan Paul.

Castells, M. (1975) 'Immigrant workers and class struggles in advanced capitalism: The Western European experience', *Politics and Society*, 5 (1): 33–66.

Castles, S., H. Booth and T. Wallace (1984) *Here for Good, New Ethnic Minorities*, London: Pluto Press.

Castles, S. and G. Kosack (1973) *Immigrant Workers in the Class Structure of Western Europe*, Oxford: Oxford University Press.

Castles, S. and M.J. Miller (2009) *The Age of Migration, International Population Movements in the Modern World*, 4th edn., London: Palgrave Macmillan.

Chan, T.W. (2019a) 'Understanding cultural omnivores: Social and political attitudes', *British Journal of Sociology*, 70 (3): 748–806.

Chan, T.W. (2019b) 'Understanding social status: A reply to Flemmen, Jarness and Roselund', *British Journal of Sociology*, 70 (3): 784–806.

Charles, N. and H. Hintjens (1998) *Gender, Ethnicity and Political Ideologies*, London: Routledge.

Choo, H.Y. and M.M. Ferree (2010) 'Practicing intersectionality in sociological research: A critical analysis of inclusions and institutions in the study of inequalities', *Sociological Theory*, 28 (2): 129–149.

Chouliaraki, L. and M. Georgiou (2017) 'Hospitability: The communicative architecture of humanitarian securitization at Europe's borders', *Journal of Communication*, 67 (2): 159–180.

Cockburn, C. (1991) *In the Way of Women: Men's Resistance to Sex Equalty in Organisations*, London: MacMillan.

Cockburn, C. (1998) *The Space Between Us: Negotiating Gender and National Identities in Conflict*, London: Zed Books.

Cockburn, C. (2004) *The Line: Women, Partition and the Gender Order in Cyprus*, London: Zed Books.

Cohen, P. (1999) *New Ethnicities, Old Racisms*, London: Zed Books.

Collins, P.H. (1990) *Black Feminist Thought*, London: Harper Collins.

Collins, P.H. (1993) 'Toward a new vision: Race, class and gender as categories of analysis and connection', *Race, Sex and Class*, 1 (1): 25–45.

Collins, P.H. (1998) 'Intersections of race, class, gender, and nation: Some implications for black family studies', *Journal of Comparative Family Studies*, 29 (1): 27–36.

196 References

Collins, P.H. (2010) 'The new politics of community', *American Sociological Review*, 75 (1): 7–30.

Collins, P.H. (2017) 'On violence, intersectionality and transversal politics', *Ethnic and Racial Studies*, 40 (9): 1460–1473.

Collins, P.H. (2019) *Intersectionality as Critical Theory*, Durham: Duke University Press.

Collins, P.H. and S. Bilge (2016) *Intersectionality*, Cambridge: John Wiley and Sons.

Combahee River Collective (1977/1982) 'A black feminist statement', in G.T. Hull, P.B. Scott and B. Smith (eds.), *All the Women Are White, All the Blacks Are Men, But Some of Us Are Brave*, New York: Feminist Press, pp. 13–22.

Commission of the European Communities (2005) 'A common agenda for integration framework for the integration of third-country nationals in the European Union', Brussels, COM (2005) 389 final (1.9.2005).

Commission on Integration and Cohesion (2007) *Our Shared Future*. www.integrationandcohesion. org.uk

Cox, O. (1970) *Class Caste and Race: A Study in Social Dynamics*, New York: Modern Reader Paperbacks.

Crown Prosection Service (CPS) (2019) *Honour Based Violence and Forced Marriage*. www.cps.gov.uk.publication

Crawley, H. and D. Skleparis (2018) 'Refugees, migrants, neither, both: Categorical fetishism and the politics of bounding in Europe's "migration crisis"', *Journal of Ethnic and Migration Studies*, 44 (1): 48–64.

Crenshaw, K. (1989) 'Demarginalising the intersection of race and class: A black feminist critique of anti-discrimination doctrine, feminist theory and antiracist politics', *University of Chicago Legal Forum*, 139–167.

Crenshaw, K. (1994) 'Mapping the margins: Intersectionality, identity politics and violence against women of color', in M.A. Fineman and R. Mykitiuk (eds.), *The Public Nature of Private Violence: Women and the Discovery of Domestic Abuse*, London: Routledge, pp. 93–118.

Crenshaw, K. (2011) 'Postscript', in H. Lutz, M.T.H. Vivar and L. Supik (eds.), *Framing Intersectionality: Debates on a Multifaceted Concept in Gender Studies*, Farnham: Ashgate, pp. 221–233.

Crenshaw, K. (2016) 'The urgency of intersectionality', *Ted Talk*. www.ted.com/talks/kimberle-crenshaw

Crompton, R. (1998) *Class and Stratification*, Cambridge: Polity.

Crompton, R. and M. Mann (1986/1994) *Gender and Stratification*, Cambridge: Polity.

Cronin, C. (1996) 'Bourdieu and Foucault on power and modernity', *Philosophy and Social Criticism*, 22 (6): 55–85.

Dahinden, J. (2016) 'A plea for the "de-migranticization" of research on migration and integration', *Ethnic and Racial Studies*, 39 (13): 2207–2225.

Davis, K. (2008) 'Intersectionality as buzzword: A sociology of science perspective on what makes a feminist theory successful', *Feminist Theory*, 9 (1): 67–85.

Deem, R. and L. Morley (2006) 'Diversity in the academy? Staff perceptions of equality policies in six contemporary higher education institutions', *Policy Futures in Education*, 4 (2): 185–201.

De Genova, N. (2010) 'The queer politics of migration', *Studies in Social Justice*, 4 (2): 101–126.

De Genova, N. (2017) *The Borders of Europe, Autonomy of Migration, Tactics of Bordering*, Durham: Duke University Press.

De Genova, N., G. Garelli and M. Tazioli (2018) 'Autonomy of asylum: The autonomy of migration: Undoing the refugee crisis script', *South Atlantic Quarterly*, 7 (2): 239–265.

Denis, A. (2008) 'Review essay: Intersectional analysis. A contribution of feminism to sociology', *International Sociology*, 23 (5): 677–694.

Derrida, J. (1982) 'Différance', in A. Bass (trans.), *Margins of Philosophy*, Chicago: University of Chicago Press, pp. 3–27.

Deveaux, M. (1994) 'Feminism and empowerment: A critical reading of Foucault', *Feminist Studies*, 20 (2): 223–247.

Dhamoon, R.K. (2011) 'Considerations on mainstreaming intersectionality', *Political Research Quarterly*, 64: 230–243.

Dhawan, N. and M.C. Varela (2016) 'What difference does difference make? Diversity Intersectionality and transnational feminist politics', *Wagadu: A Journal of Transnational Women's and Gender Studies*, 16: 9–43.

Diamond, L.M. and M. Butterworth (2008) 'Questioning gender and sexual identity: Dynamic links over time', *Sex Roles*, 59 (5–6): 365–376.

Dietze, G., E.H. Yekani and B. Michaelis (2018) 'Modes of being versus categories: Queering the tools of intersectionality', in G. Olson, D. Harrley, M. Horn-Schott and L. Schmidt (eds.), *Beyond Gender: An Advanced Introduction to Futures of Feminist and Sexuality Studies*, Oxford: Routledge, pp. 117–137.

Dines, N., N. Montagna and V. Ruggiero (2015) 'Thinking Lampedusa: Border construction the spectacle of bare life and the productivity of migrants', *Ethnic and Racial Studies*, 38 (3): 430–445.

Donnelly, E.R. and V. Muthiah (2019) 'Protecting women and girls in refugee camps', *LSE Centre for Women Peace and Security*.

Dorling, D. (2014) *Inequality and the 1%*, London: Verso.

Dunn, J.L. (2004) 'The Politics of Empathy: Social Movements and Victim Repertoires', *Sociological Focus*, 37 (3), 235–250.

Durkheim, E. (1893/1984/2014) *The Division of Labour in Society*, New York: Free Press.

Durkheim, E. (1895/1970) *The Rules of Sociological Method*, London: Routledge and Kegan.

Durkheim, E. and M. Mauss (1967) *Primitive Classification*, Chicago: University of Chicago Press.

Edmunds, J. (2012) 'The "new" barbarians: Governmentality, securitization and Islam in Western Europe', *Contemporary Islam*, 6: 67–84.

Efthymiou, S. (2019) *Nationalism, Militarism and Masculinity in Post War Cyprus*, Basingstoke: Palgrave Macmillan.

Ehrenreich, B. and A.R. Hochschild (eds.) (2002) *Global Women: Nannies, Maids and Sex Workers in the New Economy*, New York: Metropolitan Books.

Elson, D. (2002) 'Gender justice, human rights and neo-liberal economic policies' in M. Molyneux and S. Razavi (eds.) *Gender Justice, Development and Rights*, Oxford: Oxford University Press.

Elson, D. and R. Pearson (1981) '"Nimble fingers make cheap workers": An analysis of women's employment in third world export manufacturing', *Feminist Review*, 7 (1): 87–107.

Engels, F. (1884/2004) *The Origin of the Family, Private Property and the State*, London: Resistance Books.

Enloe, C. (1998) 'All the men are in the militias, all the women are victims: The politics of masculinity and femininity in nationalist wars', in L.A. Lorentzen and J. Turpin (eds.), *The Women and War Reader*, New York: New York University Press, pp. 50–62.

Equality and Human Rights Commission (2010) *The Equality Act*. www.equalityhumanrights.com

Erasmus, Z. (2017) *Race Otherwise: Forging a New Humanism for S. Africa*, Johannesburg: Wits University Press.

198 References

Erel, U. (2010) 'Migrating cultural capital: Bourdieu in migration studies', *Sociology*, 44 (4): 642–660.

Erel, U., J. Haritaworn and E.G. Rodrıguez (2011) 'On the depoliticisation of intersectionality-talk. Conceptualising multiple oppressions in critical sexuality studies', in Y.S. Taylor, S. Hines and M. Casey (eds.), *Theorizing Intersectionality and Sexuality*, Basingstoke: Palgrave Macmillan, pp. 56–77.

Erikson, R. and J. Goldthorpe (1992) *The Constant Flux: A Study of Class Mobility in Industrial Societies*, Oxford: Clarendon Press.

Esping-Andersen, G. (1990) *The Three Worlds of Welfare Capitalism*, Cambridge and Princeton, NJ: Polity Press and Princeton University Press.

Eurostat (2017) 'Migrant integration statistics', *EU Commission*, May 2017.

Eurostat (2018) 'EU citizens in other EU member states', *Eurostat News Release*, https://ec.europa.eu/eurostat/documents/2995521/8926076/3-28052018-APEN.pdf/48c473e8-c2c1-4942-b2a4-5761edacda37

Fanon, F. (1967) *Black Skin, White Masks*, New York: Grove Press.

Farahani, F. (2017) *Gender Sexuality and Diaspora*, Basingstoke: Palgrave Macmillan.

Farris, S. (2012a) 'Femonationalism and the regular army of labour called migrant women', *History of the Present: A Journal of Critical History*, 2 (2): 184–199.

Farris, S. (2012b) 'Migrants regular army of labour: Gender dimensions of the impact of the global economic crisis on migrant labour in Western Europe', *Sociological Review*, 63: 121–143.

Fathi, M. (2017) *Intersectionality, Class and Migration: Narratives of Iranian Women Migrants in the UK*, Basingstoke: Palgrave Macmillan.

Federici, S. (2006) 'The reproduction of labor-power in the global economy, Marxist theory and the unfinished feminist revolution', *Globalizations*, 3: 13.

Federici, S. (2012) *Revolution at Point Zero: Housework, Reproduction, and Feminist Struggle*, Oakland: Commons Notions/PM Press.

Fekete, L. (2009) *A Suitable Enemy, Racism, Migration and Islamophobia in Europe*, London: Pluto Press.

Fekete, L. (2018) *Europe's Fault-Lines, Racism and the Rise of the Far Right*, London: Verso.

Ferguson, S. (2016) 'Intersectionality and social reproduction, toward an integrative ontology', *Historical Materialism*, 24 (2): 38–60.

Ferree, M.M. (2009) 'Inequality, intersectionality and the politics of discourse: Framing feminist alliances', in E. Lombardo, P. Meier and M. Verloo (eds.), *The Discursive Politics of Gender Equality: Stretching, Bending and Policy Making*, London: Routledge, pp. 84–101.

Ferrett, M., M. Herbert and G. Brodeu (2019) '"When you're in a relationship you say no, but your partner insists". Sexual dating, violence and ambiguity among girls and young women', *Journal of Interpersonal Violence*. https://doi.org/10.1177/0886260519867149

Flemmen, M.P., V. Jarness and L. Roselund (2019) 'Class and status: On the misconstrual of the conceptual distinction and a neo-Bourdieusian alternative', *British Journal of Sociology*, 70 (3): 816–866.

Foucault, M. (1972) *The Archaeology of Knowledge*, London: Tavistock.

Foucault, M. (1975) *Discipline and Punish: The Birth of the Prison*, New York: Random House.

Foucault, M. (1982) 'The subject and power', *Critical Inquiry*, 1 (4): 777–795.

Foucault, M. (1985) *The History of Sexuality*, New York: Vintage Books.

Foucault, M. (1997) 'The birth of biopolitics', in P. Rabinow and J.D. Faubion (eds.), *Ethics, Subjectivity, and Truth*, New York: New Press.

Foucault, M. (2003) *Abnormal: Lectures at the College de France 1974–1975*, New York: Picador.

References **199**

Foucault, M. (2004) *Society Must Be Defended: Lectures at the college de France 1975–76*, London: Penguin Books.

Fraser, N. (1989) 'Foucault on power: Empirical Insights and normative confusions', in N. Fraser (ed.), *Unruly Practices*, Minneapolis: University of Minnesota Press, pp. 17–34.

Fraser, N. (1997) *Justice Interruptus: Critical Reflections on the 'Postsocialist' Condition*, London: Routledge.

Fraser, N. (2000) 'Rethinking recognition', *New Left Review*, May–June: 107–120.

Fraser, N. and L. Gordon (1994) 'A genealogy of dependency: Framing a keyword in the American welfare state', *Signs: Journal of Women in Culture and Society*, 19 (2): 309–336.

Freud, S. (1912/2005) *The Unconscious*, London: Penguin Classics.

Friedman, S. (2016) 'Habitus clivé and the emotional imprint of social mobility', *The Sociological Review*, 64: 129–147.

Friedman, S. (2019) *The Class Ceiling: Why It Pays to Be Privileged*, Bristol: Policy Press.

Fundamental Rights Agency (2013) 'Jewish Peoples' experience of discrimination and hate crime in European Union Member States', Luxembourg Publications, Office of the EU. https//: fra.europa.eu

Fundamental Rights Agency (2018) 'Experiences and perceptions of antisemitism', Second Survey on Discrimination and Hate Crime against Jews in the EU, Luxembourg Publications, Office of the EU. https//: fra.europa.eu

Gamble, A. (1988) *The Free Economy and the Strong State*, London: Palgrave Macmillan.

Gardiner, J. (1975) 'Women's domestic labour', *New Left Review*, 89: 47–58.

Garner, S. (2007) *Whiteness: An Introduction*, London: Routledge.

Genovese, E.D. (1971) *In Red and Black*, New York: Pantheon Books.

Georgiou, M. (2018) 'Does the subaltern speak? Migrant voices in digital Europe', *Popular Communication*, 16 (1): 45–57.

Gerth, H.H. and C.W. Mills (eds.) (1991) *From Max Weber: Essays in Sociology*, London: Routledge.

Giddens, A. (1973) *The Class Structure of the Advanced Societies*, London: Hutchinson.

Gidley, B. (2018) 'Spaces of informal learning and cultures of translation and marginality in London's Jewish East End', in S. Nichols and S.A. Dobson (eds.), *Learning Cities, Multimodal Explorations and Placed Pedagogies*, Singapore: Springer, pp. 169–182.

Gill, A. (2010) 'Reconfiguring "Honour" – Based Violence as a Form of Gendered Violence', in M. Idriss and T. Abbas (eds.), *Honour, Violence, Women and Islam*, London and New York: Routledge-Cavendish.

Gill, A., N. Begikhani and G. Hague (2012) 'Honour based violence in Kurdish communities', *Women's Studies International Forum*, 35: 75–85.

Gilroy, P. (1987) *There Ain't No Black in the Union Jack*, London: Hutchinson.

Gilroy, P. (1993) *The Black Atlantic: Modernity and Double Consciousness*, London: Verso.

Gilroy, P. (2004) *After Empire: Melancholia or Convivial Culture?: Multiculture or Postcolonial Melancholia*, Abington: Routledge.

Gimenez, M. (2001) 'Marxism and class, gender and race: Rethinking the trilogy', *Race, Class and Gender*, 8 (2): 23–33.

Gimenez, M. (2018) *Marx, Women and Capitalist Social Reproduction*, New York: Brill.

Goffman, E. (1956) *The Presentation of Self in Everyday Life*, Chicago: University of Chicago Press.

Goldberg, D.T. (1993) *Racist Culture, Philosophy and Politics of Meaning*, Oxford: Blackwell Publishers.

Goldthorpe, J. (1980/87) *Social Mobility and Class Structure in Modern Britain*, Oxford: Clarendon Press.

Goldthorpe, J. (1996) 'Class analysis and the re-orientation of class theory', *The British Journal of Sociology*, 47 (3): 481–505.

200 References

Goldthorpe, J. and A. Heath (1992) 'Revised class schema', Joint Unit for the Study of Social Trends, Working Paper No. 13.

Gramsci, A. (1971) *Selections from Prison Notebooks*, London: Lawrence and Wishart.

Grillo, R. (2008) *The Family in Question; Immigrant and Ethnic Minorities in Multicultural Europe*, Amsterdam: Amsterdam University Press.

Groenendijk, K. (2004) 'Legal concepts of integration in EU Migration Law', *European Journal of Migration and Law*, 6: 111–126.

Groenendijk, K. (2012) 'Integration of immigrants in the EU: The old or the new way?' in Pascouau, Y., Strik, MHA (eds), *Which Integratin Policies for Migrants? Interaction between the EU and its member states*, Nijmegen: Wolf Legal Publishers, pp. 3–14.

Grossman, N., H. Golden and T. Thurnell (2009) *Grist in Depth: Hiring Noncitizens: An Immigration Law Primer for US Employers*, Macon: Mercer University Press.

Guattari, F. (2015) 'Transdisciplinarity must become transversality', *Theory Culture and Society*, 32 (5–6): 131–139.

Guillaumin, C. (1995) 'I know it's not nice but . . . "The changing face of race"', in *Racism, Sexism, Power and ideology*, London: Routledge, pp. 99–107.

Habermas, J. (1984) *Theory of Communicative Action* (vol. 1), Boston: Beacon Press.

Hadjipavlou, M. (2010) *Women and Change in Cyprus: Feminisms and Gender in Conflict*, London: IB Tauris.

Hall, S. (1978) 'Marxism and culture', *Radical History Review*, 18: 5–14.

Hall, S. (1989/1996) 'New ethnicities', in D. Morley and C. Kuan-Hsing (eds.), *Critical Dialogues in Cultural Studies*, London: Routledge.

Hall, S. (1992) 'The West and the rest discourse and power', in S. Hall and B. Gieben (eds.), *Formations of Modernity*, Cambridge, MA: Open University and Blackwell, pp. 275–295.

Hall, S. (1996a) 'Race, articulation and societies structured in dominance', in H. Baker Jr, M. Diawara and R. Lindeborg (eds.), *Black British Cultural Studies: A Reader*, Chicago: University of Chicago Press.

Hall, S. (1996b) 'Who needs "identity"?', in S. Hall and P. de Gay (eds.), *Questions of Cultural Identity*, London: Sage, pp. 1–18.

Hall, S. (2000) 'The multi-cultural question', in B. Hesse (ed.), *Un/Settled Multiculturalisms*, London: Zed Books, pp. 209–241.

Hall, S. and M. Lamont (2013) *Social Resilience in the New Liberal Era*, Cambridge: Cambridge University Press.

Halsey, A.H., A. Heath and J.M. Ridge (1980) *Origins and Destinations: Family, Class and Education in Modern Britain*, London: Clarendon Press.

Hancock, A. (2007) 'When multiplication doesn't equal quick addition: Examining intersectionality as a research paradigm', *Perspectives on Politics*, 5 (1): 63–79.

Hankivsky, O. (2012) 'Women's health, men's health and gender and health', *Social Science and Medicine*, 74 (11): 1712–1720.

Harding, S. (ed.) (2004) *The Feminist Standpoint Theory Reader: Intellectual and Political Controversies*, New York: Routledge.

Hartman, H. (1979) 'The unhappy marriage of Marxism and Feminism', *Capital and Class*, 3 (2): 1–33.

Hay, C. (1999) *The Political Economy of New Labour*, Manchester: Manchester University Press.

Hekman, S. (1997) 'Truth and method: Feminist standpoint theory revisited', *Signs*, 22 (2): 341–365.

Heller, A. (1975) 'Towards a sociology of knowledge of everyday life', *Cultural Hermeneutics*, 3 (1): 7–18.

References 201

Herskovitz, M.J. (1938) *Acculturation: The Study of Culture Contact*, New York: J.J. Augustin.

Hertz, R. (1978) 'The pre-eminence of the right hand', in R. Needham (ed.), *Right and Left: Essays on Dual System Classification*, Chicago: University of Chicago Press, pp. 3–32.

Hickman, M. (2002) 'Locating the Irish diaspora', *Irish Journal of Sociology*, 11 (2): 8–26.

Hickman, M., H. Crowley and N. Mai (2008) *Immigration and Social Cohesion in the UK*, York: Joseph Rowntree Foundation.

Hochschild, A.R. (2000) 'Global care chains and emotional surplus value', in W. Hutton and A. Giddens (eds.), *Living with Global Capitalism: On the Edge*, London: Jonathan Cape, pp. 130–146.

Hochschild, A.R. (2012) *The Second Shift: Working Families and the Revolution at Home*, London: Penguin Random House.

Holland, J., C. Ramazanoglou and S. Sharpe (1998) *The Male in the Head: Young People*, London: The Tufnell Press.

Hood-Williams, J. and W. Cealey Harrison (1998) 'More varieties than Heinz: Social categories and sociality in Humphries, Hammersley and beyond', *Socresonline*, 3 (1): 1–9.

Hooks, B. (1981) *Ain't I a Woman? Black Women and Feminism*, London: Pluto Press.

Houtum Van, H. and J. Naerssen (2002) 'Bordering ordering and othering', *Tijdschrift voor Economische en Sociale Geografie*, 93 (2): 125–136.

Hussain, Y. and P. Baggaley (2012) 'Securitised citizens: Islamophobia, racism and the 7/7 London bombings', *The Sociological Review*, 60.

ILO (2017) 'Global estimates of modern slavery: Forced labour and forced marriage', *ILO*, Geneva, September.

Indra, D.M. (1999) *Engendering Forced Migration: Theory and Practice*, Oxford: Berghahn Books.

International Holocaust Remembrance Alliance (2016) https://www.holocaustremem brance.com/stories-working definition-antisemitism

IOM (2018) *Swing, W.L. Speech at International Organisation of Migration Speech on 16.7.2018.* gpaj.org, retrieved October 13, 2019.

Jeffries, V. and H.E. Ransford (1980) *Social Stratification: A Multiple Hierarchy Approach*, Boston: Allyn and Bacon.

Jenkins, R. (1997) *Rethinking Ethnicity*, London: Sage.

Jenkins, R. (2002) *Pierre Bourdieu*, London: Routledge.

Jensen, J., F. Polletta and P. Raibman (2019) 'The difficulties of combatting inequality in time', *Daedalus: Journal of the American Academy of Arts and Sciences*, Summer: 136–160.

Jessop, B. (2009) 'Cultural political economy and critical policy studies', *Critical Policy Studies*, 3 (3–4): 336–356.

Jewish Journal (2019) 'Reut report: How intersectionality poses a threat to the organized American Jewish Community'. https://jewish journal/analysis/301251/reut-report-intersectionality-poses-a-threat-to-to-the-orgnised-american-jewish-community/

Jibrin, R. and S. Salem (2015) 'Revisiting intersectionality: Reflections on theory and praxis', *Transcripts: An Interdisciplinary Journal in the Humanities and Sciences*, 5: 7–24.

Kalayji, L. (2018) 'Understanding transgender feminism and transphobic attacks', *Viewpoint*, https://discoversociety.org/2018/04/03viewpoint-understanding-anti-transgender-feminism/

Kandiyoti, D. (1989) 'The patriarchal bargain', in N. Yuval-Davis and F. Anthias (eds.), *Woman, Nation, State*, Basingstoke: Macmillan.

Knapp, G.-A. (2005) 'Race, class, gender, reclaiming baggage in fast travelling theories', *European Journal of Women's Studies*, 12 (3): 249–265.

202 References

Kofman, E. (1999) 'Female birds of passage a decade later', *International Migration review*, 33 (2): 269–299.

Kofman, E. (2005) 'Citizenship, migration and the reassertion of national identity', *Citizenship Studies*, 9 (5): 453–467.

Kofman, E., A. Phizacklea, P. Raghuram and R. Sales (2000) *Gender and International Migration in Europe*, London: Routledge.

Kofman, E. and P. Raghuram (2006) 'Gender and global labour migrations: Incorporating skilled workers', *Antipode* 38 (2): 282–303.

Kontos, M. (ed.) (2009) *Integration of Female Migrants in Labour Market and Society: A Comparative Analysis*, Frankfurt am Main: FemiPol, Institute of Social Research at the Goethe University.

Kontos, M. (2013) 'Negotiating the citizenship rights of migrant domestic workers: The right to family reunification and a family life: Policies and debates', *Journal of Ethnic and Migration Studies*, 39 (3): 409–424.

Koser, K. (1997) 'Social networks and the asylum cycle: The case of Iranians in the Netherlands International Migration', *The International Migration Review*, 31 (3): 591–611.

Krais, B. and J.M. William (2000) 'The gender relationship in Bourdieu's sociology', *SubStance*, 29 (3): 53–67.

Labour Party National Executive Council (2018) *NEC Statement on All Women Shortlists, Women's Officers and Minimum Quotas for Women*. https://labour.org.uk, retrieved October 13, 2019.

Laczko, F., A. Singleton and J. Black (eds.) (2017) 'Chapter 1', in *Fatal Journeys, Volume 3, Part 1: Improving Data on Missing Migrants*, Geneva: IOM, Global Migration Data Analysis Centre.

Lamont, M. (1992) *Money Morals and Manners: The Culture of the French and American Upper-Middle Class*, Chicago: Chicago University Press.

Lamont, M. (2000) *The Dignity of Working Men: Morality and the Boundaries of Race Class and Immigration*, Cambridge, MA: Harvard University Press.

Lamont, M. (2012) 'How has Bourdieu been good to think with? The case of the United States', *The Sociological Forum*, 27 (1): 228–237.

Lamont, M. (2019) 'From having to being: Self-worth and the current crisis of American society', *British Journal of Sociology*, 70 (3): 660–707.

Lamont, M., A. Morning and M. Mooney (2002) 'Particular universalisms; North African immigrants respond to French racism', *Ethnic and Racial Studies*, 25 (3): 390–414.

Lamont, M. and P. Pierson (2019) 'Inequality generation and persistence: Multidimensional processes: An interdisciplinary agenda', *Daedalus: Journal of the American Academy of Arts and Sciences*, Summer: 1–27.

Lawler, S. (2005) 'Disgusted subjects: The making of middle-class identities', *The Sociological Review*, 53: 429–446.

Layder, D. (2006) *Understanding Social Theory*, London: Sage.

Lenski, G.E. (1966) *Power and Privilege*, Chapel Hill: University of North Carolina Press.

Lentin, A. (2016) 'Racism in public or public racism: Doing anti-racism in post racial times', *Ethnic and Racial Studies*, 39: 33–45.

Lentin, A. (2019) 'Looking as white: Anti-racism apps, appearance and racialised embodiment', *Identities: Global Studies in Culture and Power*, 26 (5): 614–630.

Lentin, A. and G. Titley (2008) 'More Benetton than barricades? The politics of diversity in Europe', in G. Titley and A. Lentin (eds.), *The Politics of Diversity in Europe*, Strasbourg: Council of Europe Publishing.

References   **203**

Lerner, G. (ed.) (1973) *Black Women in White America: A Documentary History*, New York: Vintage.

Levine-Rasky, C. (2011) 'Intersectionality theory applied to whiteness and middle-classness', *Social Identities*, 17 (2): 239–253.

Levi-Strauss, C. (1949/1969) *The Elementary Structures of Kinship*, Oxford: Eyre and Spottiswoode.

Lewis, G. (2009) 'Celebrating intersectionality? Debates on a multi-faceted concept in gender studies: Themes from a conference', *European Journal of Women's Studies*, 16 (3): 203–210.

Lewis, G. and C. Hemmings (2019) '"Where might we go if we dare": Moving beyond the "thick, suffocating fog of whiteness" in feminism', *Feminist Studies*, online first. https://doi.org/10.1177/14647001 19871220

Li, Y. and A. Heath (2018) 'Persisting disadvantages: A study of labour market dynamics of ethnic unemployment and earnings in the UK (2009–2015)', *Journal of Ethnic and Migration Studies*, online first 1–22. https://doi.org/10.1080/1369183X.2018.1539241

Lovell, T. (2000) 'Thinking feminism with and against Bourdieu', *Feminist Theory*, 1 (1): 11–32.

Lukacs, G. (1967) *History and Class Consciousness*, London: Merlin Press.

Lutz, H. (2014) 'Intersectionality's (brilliant) career: How to understand the attraction of the concept', Working Paper Series: Gender, Diversity and Migration, No. 1, Goethe University, Frankfurt.

Lutz, H. (2017) 'Care as fictitious commodity; Reflections on the intersections of migration, gender and care regimes', *Migration Studies*, 15 (3): 356–368.

MacKinnon, C.A. (1982) 'Feminism, Marxism, method and the state: An agenda for theory', *Signs: Journal of Women in Culture and Society*, 7 (3): 515–544.

MacKinnon, C.A. (1997) 'Rape: On coercion and consent', in K. Conboy, N. Medina and S. Stanbury (eds.), *Writing on the Body: Female Embodiment and Feminist Theory*, New York: Columbia University Press.

Mackintosh, M. and M. Barrett (1985) 'Ethnocentrism and socialist feminism', *Feminist Review*, 20 (1): 23–47.

Macpherson, W. (1999) *The Stephen Lawrence Inquiry*, CM4262–1. www.gov.uk

Mannheim, K. (1929/1936) *Ideology and Utopia* (trans. L. Wirth and E. Shils), London: Routledge.

Margolis, J. (1999) 'Pierre Bourdieu: Habitus and the logic of practice', in R. Shusterman (ed.), *Bourdieu: A Critical Reader*, Oxford: Blackwell, pp. 64–83.

Marx, K. (1859/1977) *A Contribution to the Critique of Political Economy*, Moscow: Progress Publishers.

Marx, K. (1976) *Capital*, Vol. I, London: Penguin.

Marx, K. and F. Engels (1932) *The German Ideology*, Moscow: Marx and Engels Institute.

Mason, D. (1994) 'On the dangers of disconnecting race and racism', *Sociology*, 28 (4): 845–859.

Massey, D. (2013) *Space, Place and Gender*, Cambridge: Wiley.

Mbembe, A. (2003) 'Necropolitics', *Public Culture*, 15 (1): 11–40.

McCall, L. (1992) 'Does gender fit? Bourdieu, feminism, and conceptions of social order', *Theory and Society*, 21: 837–867.

McCall, L. (2001) *Complex Inequality: Gender, Class and Race in the New Economy*, New York: Routledge.

McCall, L. (2005) 'The complexity of intersectionality', *Signs: Journal of Women in Culture and Society*, 30 (3): 1771–1800.

204 References

McDowell, L. (2014) 'The lives of others: Body work, the production of difference and labor geographies', *Economic Geography*, 91 (1): 1–23.

McDowell, L., K. Ward, D. Perrons, K. Ray and C. Fagan (2006) 'Place, class and local circuits of reproduction: Exploring the social geography of middle-class childcare in London', *Urban Studies*, 43 (12): 2163–2182.

McNay, L. (1999) 'Gender, habitus and field: Pierre Bourdieu and the limits of reflexivity', *Theory, Culture and Society*, 16 (1): 95–117.

McWhorter, L. (2004) 'Sex, race and biopower: A Foucauldian genealogy', *Hypatia*, 19 (3): 38–62.

Mead, G.H. (1934) *Mind, Self and Society,* Chicago: Chicago University Press.

Meekosha, H. and R. Shuttleworth (2009) 'What's so critical about Critical Disability Studies?', *Australian Journal of Human Rights*, 15 (1): 47–76.

Meer, N. (2013) 'Semantics, scales and solidarities in the study of antisemitism and Islamophobia', *Ethnic and Racial Studies*, 36 (3): 500–515.

Meer, N., C. Dwyer and T. Modood (2010) 'Embodying nationhood? Conceptions of British national identity, citizenship, and gender in the "veil affair"', *The Sociological Review*, 58 (1): 84–111.

Meissner, F. and S. Vertovec (2015) 'Comparing superdiversity', *Ethnic and Racial Studies*, 38 (4): 541–555.

Mezzadra, S. (2011) 'The gaze of autonomy. Capitalism, migration and social struggles', in V. Squire (ed.), *The Contested Politics of Mobility. Borderzones and Irregularity*, New York: Routledge, pp. 121–142.

Mezzadra, S. and B. Neilson (2011) 'Borderscapes of differential inclusion: Subjectivity and struggles on the threshold of justice's excess', in E. Balibar, S. Mezzadra and R. Samaddar (eds.), *The Borders of Justice*, Philadelphia: Temple University Press, pp. 181–203.

Mezzadra, S. and B. Neilson (2013) *Border as Method, or the Multiplication of Labour*, Durham and London: Duke University Press.

Miles, R. (1989) *Racism*, London: Routledge.

Miles, R. (1993) *Racism after Race Relations*, London: Routledge.

Miles, R. and M. Brown (2003) *Racism*, New York: Routledge.

Miles, R. and N. Rathzel (1991) 'Migration and the articulation of racism', in S. Bolaria (ed.), *World Capitalism and the International Migration of Labour*, Toronto: Garmund Press.

Miller, T. (2010) *Making Sense of Fatherhood*, Cambridge: Cambridge University Press.

Modood, T., T. Berthoud, J. Lakey, J. Nazroo, P. Smith, S. Virdee and S. Beishon (1997) *Ethnic Minorities in Britain: Diversity and Disadvantage*, London: Policy Studies Institute.

Molyneaux, M. (1979) 'Beyond the domestic labour debate', *New Left Review*, 1 (116, July–August).

Morley, D., S. Hall, C. Critcher, T. Jefferson, J. Clarke and B. Roberts (1978) *Policing the Crisis, Mugging, the State and Law and Order*, London: Macmillan.

Morokvasic, M. (1984) 'Birds of passage are also women', *International Labour Review*, 18 (6): 886–907.

Morokvasic, M. (2004) 'Settled in mobility: Engendering post-wall migration in Europe', *Feminist Review*, 77 (1): 7–25.

Morokvasic, M. and C. Catarino (2010) 'Women, gender, transnational migration and mobility in France', in K. Slaney, M. Kontos and M. Liapi (eds.), *Women in New Migrations, Current Debates in European Societies*, Cracow: Jagiellonian University Press.

Mulholland, J., N. Montagna and E. Sanders-McDonagh (2018) *Gendering Nationalism: Intersections of Nation, Gender and Sexuality*, London: Palgrave Macmillan.

Murji, K. and J. Solomos (eds.) (2014) *Theories of Race and Ethnicity: Contemporary Debates and Perspectives*, Cambridge: Cambridge University Press.

Myrdal, G. (1944) *An American Dilemma*, New York: McGraw-Hill.

Narayan, Y. (2019) 'Intersectionality, nationalisms biocoloniality', *Ethnic and Racial Studies*, 42 (8): 1225–1244.

Nare, L. (2013) 'Migrancy, gender and social class in domestic labour and social care in Italy: An intersectional analysis of demand', *Journal of Ethnic and Migration Studies*, 39 (4): 601–623.

Nash, J. (2008) 'Rethinking intersectionality', *Feminist Review*, 89: 1–15.

Nash, J. (2011) 'Home truths on intersectionality', *Yale Journal of Law and Feminism*, 23: 445.

Nash, J. (2016) 'Feminist originalism: Intersectionality and the politics of reading', *Feminist Theory*, 17 (1): 3–20.

Nayak, A. (2006) 'After race: Ethnography, race and post-race theory', *Ethnic and Racial Studies*, 29 (3): 411–430.

Ndhlovu, F. (2016) 'A decolonial critique of diaspora identity theories and the notion of superdiversity', *Diaspora Studies*, 9 (11): 28–40.

Nentwich, J.C., M.F. Özbilgin and A. Tatli (2014) 'Change agency as performance and embeddedness: Exploring the possibilities and limits of Butler and Bourdieu', *Culture and Organization*, 21 (3): 235–250.

Newman, K. (2019) 'New angles on inequality', *Daedalus*, pp. 173–180.

Nicholson, L. (1994) 'Interpreting gender', *Signs: Journal of Women in Culture and Society*, 20 (1): 79–105.

Nieswand, B. (2017) 'Towards a theorisation of diversity. Configurations of person-related differences in the context of youth welfare practices', *Journal of Ethnic and Migration Studies*, 43 (10): 1714–1730.

Nussbaum, M. (2011) *Creating Capabilities*, Cambridge, MA: Harvard University Press.

Nussbaum, M. (2016) 'Women's progress and women's human rights', *Human Rights Quarterly*, 38: 589.

Oakley, A. (1972/1985) *Sex, Gender and Society*, Temple Smith (revised edition), Aldershot: Gower (1985).

Oliver, M. (1995) *The Politics of Disability*, Basingstoke: Macmillan.

Ong, A. (2006a) 'Neoliberalism as a mobile technology', *Transactions, The Institute of British Geographers*, 32 (1): 3–8.

Ong, A. (2006b) *Neoliberalism as Exception: Mutations in Citizenship and Sovereignty*, Durham and London: Duke University Press.

Pajnik, M. and G. Campani (eds.) (2009) *Precarious Migrant Labour across Europe*, Ljubljana: Politike Symposion Series, Peace Institute.

Pakulski, J. and M.J. Waters (1995) *The Death of Class*, London: Sage.

Pakulski, J. and M.J. Waters (1996) 'The reshaping and dissolution of social class in advanced society', *Theory and Society*, 25: 667–691.

Papadopoulos, D. and V. Tsianos (2013) 'After citizenship: Autonomy of migration and the mobile commons', *Citizenship Studies*, 17 (2): 42–73.

Papastergiades, S. (2000) *The Turbulence of Migration, Globalization, Deterritorialization and Hybridity*, Cambridge: Cambridge University Press.

Parekh, B. (ed.) (2000) *Multi-Ethnic Britain*, London: The Runnymede Trust.

Parennas, R.S. (2001) 'Mothering from a distance: Emotions, gender and intergenerational relations' in Filipino transnational families', *Feminist Studies*, 27 (2): 361–390.

Park, R.E. (1928) 'Human migration and the marginal man', *American Journal of Sociology*, 33 (6): 881–893.

206 References

Parkin, F. (1979) *Marxism and Class Theory: A Bourgeois Critique*, London: Tavistock.

Parsanoglou, D. and V. Tsianos (2019) 'Chronotopes of containment: Hotspots and the new European border architecture', paper given at the University of Kent on 6th June 2019, https:// www.kent.ac.uk.

Pateman, C. (1988) *The Sexual Contract*, Cambridge: Polity.

Patterson, S. 1963) *Dark Strangers*, London: Tavistock.

Pemberton, S. (2017) 'The importance of super-diverse places in shaping residential mobility patterns', A Report to the Leverhulme Trust, Keele: Keele University.

Però, D. and J. Solomos (2010) 'Introduction: Migrant politics and mobilization: Exclusion, engagements, incorporation', *Ethnic and Racial Studies*, 33 (1): 1–18.

Phipps, A. (2009) 'Rape and respectability: Ideas about sexual violence and social class', *Sociology*, 43 (4): 667–683.

Phillips, A. and B. Taylor (1980) 'Sex and skill: Moves towards a feminist economics', *Feminist Review*, 6: 79–88.

Phizacklea, A. (eds.) (1983) *One-Way Ticket*, London: Routledge Kegan Paul.

Phizacklea, A. and R. Miles (1980) *Labour and Racism*, London: Routledge Kegan Paul.

Piekut, A. and G. Valentine (2017) 'Spaces of encounter and attitudes towards difference: A comparative study of two European cities', *Social Science Research*, 62: 175–188.

Piketty, T. (2014) '"Inequality and what to do about it: Thomas Piketty", interview by M. O'Neill and N. Pearce', *Renewal: A Journal of Social Democracy*, 22 (3/4): 101–115.

Pilkington, H. and N. Acik (2019) 'Not entitled to talk: (Mis)recognition, inequality and social activism of young Muslims', *Sociology*, 1–18, online first.

Poulantzas, N. (1974) *Classes in Contemporary Capitalism*, London: New Left Books.

Poulantzas, N. (1980) *State, Power, Socialism*, London: Verso.

Powell, E. (1968) 'Rivers of blood', *Speech*. www.telegraph.co.uk/comment/3643823/ Enoch-Powells-Rivers-of-Blood-speech.html

Puar, J. (2007) *Assemblages: Homonationalism in Queer Times*, Durham and London: Duke University Press.

Raaper, R. and M. Olssen (2017) 'In conversation with Mark Olssen: On Foucault with Marx and Hegel', *Open Review of Educational Research*, 4 (1): 96–117.

Rancière, J. (2004) *Disagreement: Politics and Philosophy*, Minneapolis: University of Minnesota Press.

Rancière, J. (2010) *Dissensus on Politics and Aesthetics*, New York: Continuum.

Rattansi, A. (2004) 'New labour, new assimilationalism', *Open Democracy*, 6 October 2004. www.opendemocracy.net/arts-multiculturalism/article_2141.jsp.

Razack, S. (1998) *Looking White People in the Eye: Gender, Race and Cuture in the Courtrooms and Classrooms*, Toronto: University of Toronto Press.

Reay, D. (1998) 'Rethinking social class: Qualitative perspectives on class and gender', *Sociology*, 32 (2): 259–279.

Reilly, N. (2007) 'Cosmopolitan feminism and human rights', *Hypatia*, 22 (4): 180–198.

Richardson, D. (2007) 'Patterned fluidities: (Re)imagining the relationship between gender and sexuality', *Sociology*, 41 (3): 457–474.

Richardson, D. (2017) *Sexuality and Citizenship*, Cambridge: Polity.

Rippon, G. (2019) *The Gendered Brain: The New Neuroscience that Shatters the Myth of the Female Brain*, Oxford: The Bodley Head.

Robertson, S. (2019) 'Status-making: Rethinking migrant categorisation', *Journal of Sociology*, 55 (2): 219–233.

Robinson, C. (2000) *Black Marxism*, Chapel Hill: University of North Carolina Press.

Rogaly, B. and B. Taylor (2007) 'Welcome to "Monkey Island": Identity and community in three Norwich estates', in M. Wetherell, M. Lafleche and R. Berkeley (eds.), *Identity, Ethnic Diversity and Community Cohesion*, London: Sage.

References 207

Roggeband, C. and M. Verloo (2007) 'Dutch women are liberated, migrant women are a problem: The evolution of policy frames on gender and migration in the Netherlands, 1995–2005', *Social Policy and Administration*, 41 (3): 271–288.

Romero, M. and Z. Valdez (2016) 'Introduction to special issue: Intersectionality and Entrepreneurship', *Ethnic and Racial Studies*, 39 (9): 1553–1565.

Rubery, J. (2015) 'Change at work: Feminisation, fragmentation and financialisation', *Employee Relations*, 37 (6): 633–644.

Rudolph, H. and F. Hillman (1997) 'The invisible hands need visible heads: Managers, experts and professionals from Western countries in Poland', in K. Koser and H. Lutz (eds.), *The New Migration in Europe*, London: Macmillan.

Runfors, A. (2016) 'What an ethnic lens can conceal: The emergence of a shared racialised identity position among young descendants of migrants in Sweden', *Journal of Ethnic and Migration Studies*, 42 (11): 1846–1863.

Runnymede Trust (1997) *Islamophobia: A Challenge for Us All*. Runnymedetrust.org

Ryan, L. (2007) 'Who do you think you are? Irish nurses encountering ethnicity and constructing identity in Britain', *Ethnic and Racial Studies*, 30 (3): 416–438.

Ryan, L., U. Erel and A. D'Angelo (2016) *Migrant Capital*, London: Palgrave.

Sa'ar, A. (2005) 'Postcolonial feminism, the politics of identification and the liberal bargain', *Gender and Society*, 19 (5): 680–700.

Sager, M. and D. Mulinari (2018) 'Safety for whom? Exploring femonationalism and care-racism in Sweden', *Women's Studies International Forum*, 68: 149–156.

Sahlins, P. (1989) *Boundaries: The Making of France and Spain in the Pyrenees*, Berkeley: University of California.

Salazar, N., A. Elliot and R. Norum (2017) 'Studying mobilities: Theoretical notes and methodological queries', in *Methodologies of Mobility, Ethnography and Experiment*, Oxford: Berghahn, pp. 1–24.

Sassen, S. (1996) *Losing Control? Sovereignty in an Age of Globalisation*, New York: Columbia University Press.

Sassen, S. (2000) *Cities in a World Economy*, London and Thousand Oak: Pine Forge Press.

Sassen, S. (2014) *Expulsions: Brutality and Complexity in the Global Economy*, Cambridge, MA: Harvard University Press.

Savage, M. (2000) *Class Analysis and Social Transformation*, Buckingham: Open University Press.

Savage, M. (2010) 'The politics of elective belonging', *Housing, Theory and Society*, 26 (1): 115–161.

Savage, M. (2015) 'Introduction to elites. From the problematic of the proletariat to a class analysis of "wealth elites"', *The Sociological Review*, 63: 223–239.

Savage, M., F. Devine, N. Cunningham, M. Taylor, Y. Li, J. Hiellbrekke and B. Le Roux (2013) 'A new model of social class? Findings from the BBCs Great British Class Experiment', *Sociology*, 42 (2): 219–250.

Sayer, A. (2005) 'Class, moral worth and recognition', *Sociology*, 39 (5): 947–963.

Schierup, K. and A. Alund (2018) 'Re-imagineering the commons in precarious times', *Journal of Intercultural Studies*, 39 (2): 207–223.

Schraub, D. (2019) 'White Jews: An intersectional approach', *American Jewish Studies*, 43 (2).

Schutz, A. (1944) 'The stranger, an essay in social psychology', *American Journal of Sociology*, 149 (6): 499–507.

Scott, J. (1994) 'Class analysis: Back to the future', *Sociology*, 28 (4): 933–942.

Segal, P. and M. Savage (2019) 'Inequality Interactions', International Inequalities Institute, LSE Working Paper, 27 January 2019.

Sen, A. (2004) 'Capabilities, lists and public reason: Continuing the conversation', *Feminist Economics*, 10 (3): 77–80.

Shilliam, R. (2018) *Race and the Undeserving Poor: From Abolition to Brexit*, Newcastle upon Tyne: Agenda Publishing.

Simmel, G. (1908/1950) 'The stranger', in A.K. Wolff (ed.), *The Sociology of Georg Simmel*, New York: Free Press, pp. 402–409.

Simmel, G. (1994) 'Bridge and door', *Theory, Culture & Society*, 11 (1): 5–10.

Sivanandan, A. (1976) 'Race, class and the state', *Race and Class*, 17 (4): 347–368.

Skeggs, B. (1997) *Formations of Class and Gender*, Cambridge: Polity Press.

Skeggs, B. (2004) *Culture, Class, Self*, London: Routledge.

Skeggs, B. (2005) 'The making of class and gender through visualising moral subject formation', *Sociology*, 39 (5): 965–982.

Skeggs, B. (2019) 'The forces that shape us: The entangled vine of gender, race and class', *Sociological Review*, 67: 28–35.

Smith, D. (2005) *Institutional Ethnography: A Sociology for People*, Oxford: Altmira Press, Rowman and Littlefield.

Smith, D. (2010) 'You are here, interview with Dorothy Smith (by W.K. Carroll)', *Socialist Studies/etudes socialistes*, 6 (2): 9–37.

Sociological Research Online (1999) 'Rapid response/sociology online: The Stephen Lawrence murder and the Macpherson inquiry', *Socresonline*, 4 (1): 92.

Sokoloff, N.J. and I. Dupont (2005) 'Domestic violence at the intersections of race, class and gender: Challenges and contributions to understanding violence against marginalised women in diverse communities', *Violence Against Women*, 11 (1): 38–64.

Song, M. (1999) *Helping Out*, Philadelphia: Temple University Press.

Spelman, E.V. (1988) *Inessential Woman*, Boston: Beacon Press.

Spivak, G.C. (1994) 'Can the subaltern speak?', in P. Williams and L. Chrisman (eds.), *Colonial Discourse and Post-Colonial Theory: A Reader*, Hemel Hempstead: Harvester.

Squire, V. (2011) 'The contested politics of mobility. Politicizing mobility, mobilizing politics', in V. Squire (ed.), *The Contested Politics of Mobility*, London: Routledge, pp. 1–25.

Standing, G. (2011) *The Precariat, The New Dangerous Class*, New York: Bloomsbury.

Standing, G. (2014) *The Precariat Charter, From Denizens to Citizens*, New York: Bloomsbury.

Staunes, D. (2003) 'Where have all the subjects gone/bringing together the concepts of intersectionality and subjectification', *Nordic Journal of Feminist and Gender Research*, 11: 101–110.

Stiglitz, J. (2012) *The Price of Inequality*, London and New York: W. W. Norton & Company.

St. Lewis, B. (2014) 'Can race be eradicated?: The post racial problematic', in K. Murji and J. Solomos (eds.), *Theories of Race and Ethnicity: Contemporary Debates and Perspectives*, Cambridge: Cambridge University Press, pp. 114–137.

Stoler, A.L. (2013) *Imperial Debris*, Durham: Duke University Press.

Sullivan, N. (2003) *A Critical Introduction to Queer Theory*, Edinburgh: Edinburgh University Press and Melbourne: Circa Books.

Taylor, C. (1984) 'Foucault on freedom and truth', *Political Theory*, 12 (2): 152–183.

Taylor, C. (2011) 'Race and racism in Foucault's College de France Lectures', *Philosophy Compass*, 6 (11): 746–756.

Taylor, Y., S. Hines and M. Casey (eds.) (2011) *Theorizing Intersectionality and Sexuality*, Basingstoke: Palgrave Macmillan.

Tazzioli, M. and G. Garelli (2018) 'Containment beyond detention: The hotspot system and disrupted migration movements across Europe', *Environment and Planning D: Society and Space*. https://doi.org/10.1177/0263775818759335

Thomas, W.I. and F. Znaniecki (1918–22), *The Polish Peasant in Europe and America*, Boston: Badger.

References 209

T.I.P. (2019) 'Trafficking in persons report Trafficking in Persons (2019)', U.S. State Gov Report, June 2019. https://www.state.gov/wp-content/uploads/2019/061/2019, retrieved October 2, 2019.

Tilly, C. (1998) *Durable Inequality*, Berkeley: University of California Press.

Titley, G. and A. Lentin (eds.) (2008) *The Politics of Diversity in Europe*. Strasbourg: Council of Europe Publishing.

Tomlinson, B. (2013) 'Colonising Intersectionality? Replicating racial hierarchy in feminist academic arguments', *Social Identities*, 19 (2): 254–272.

Trimikliniotis, N. (2020) *The Migration Dissensus*, London: Routledge.

Trimikliniotis, N. and U. Bozkurt (2012) *Beyond a Divided Cyprus: A State and Society in Transformation*, London: Springer.

Trimikliniotis, N., D. Parsanoglou and S.V. Tsianos (2015) *Mobile Commons, Migrant Digitalities and the Right to the City*, Pivot Series, London and New York: Palgrave.

Trimikliniotis, N., D. Parsanoglou and S.V. Tsianos (2016) 'Mobile commons and/in precarious spaces: Mapping migrant struggles and social resistance', *Critical Sociology*, 42 (7–8): 943–946.

Tronto, T. (2005) 'Care as the work of citizens: A modest proposal', in M. Friedman (ed.), *Women and Citizenship*, Oxford: Oxford University Press, pp. 130–145.

Tyler, I. (2015) 'Classificatory struggles: Class, culture and inequality in neo-liberal times', *Sociological Review*, 63: 493–511.

UK investment visa Tier 1. www.gov.uk-tier-1-investor, retrieved September 3, 2019.

UNCHR (2018a) *Global Trends*, unchr.org, retrieved September 2, 2019.

UNCHR (2018b) *Figures at a Glance*. Geneva: UNHCR. www.unchr.org/figures-at-aglance.html

United Nations – General Assembly (2000) 'UN Convention against Transnational Organised Crime, A/RES/ 87455/25', Palermo, Italy.

Urry, J. (2003) *Global Complexity*, Cambridge: Polity Press.

Urry, J. (2007) *Mobilities*, Cambridge: Polity Press.

Valentine, G. (2008) 'Living with difference: Reflections on geographies of encounter', *Progress in Human Geography*, 32 (3): 323–337.

Valluvan, S. (2016) 'What is post race and what does it reveal about contemporary racism', *Ethnic and Racial Studies*, 39 (13): 2241–2251.

Valluvan, S. (2019) 'The uses and abuses of class: Left nationalism and the denial of working class culture', *The Sociological Review*, 67 (1): 36–46.

Vertovec, S. (2007) 'Super-diversity and its implications', *Ethnic and Racial Studies*, 30 (6): 1024–1054.

Vertovec, S. (2019) 'Talking about superdiversity', *Ethnic and Racial Studies*, 42 (1): 125–139.

Vertovec, S. and S. Wessendorf (2006) 'Cultural, religious and linguistic diversity in Europe: overview of issues and trends', in R. Penninx, M. Berger and K. Kraal (eds.), *The Dynamics of International Migration and Settlement in Europe: A State of the Art*, Imiscoe: Amsterdam University Press, pp. 171–201.

Vickers, T., J. Clayton, H. Davison, L. Hudson, M.A. Canadas and P. Biddle (2019) 'Dynamics of precarity among "new migrants": Exploring the worker-capital relation through mobilities and mobility power', *Mobilities*, 14 (5): 696–714.

Virdee, S. (2014) *Racism, Class and the Racialised Outsider*, London: Palgrave Macmillan.

Walby, S. (2007) 'Complexity theory, systems theory and multiple intersecting inequalities', *Philosophy of Social Science*, 37: 449.

Wallerstein, I. (2014) 'Conclusion', in I. Wallerstein (ed.), *The World Is Out of Joint, World historical Interpretations of Continuing Polarizations*, New York: Routledge, pp. 163–170.

210 References

Webb, J., T. Schirato and G. Danaher (2002) *Understanding Bourdieu*, London: Sage.

Weber, L. (2001) *Understanding Race, Class, Gender and Sexuality: A Conceptual Framework*, Boston: MacGraw-Hill.

Weber, M. (1946) *From Max Weber: Essays in Sociology* (eds., Gerth and Mills), New York: Oxford University Press.

Weber, M. (1947/1964) *Theory of Social and Economic Organisation*, London: Macmillan.

weforum.org (2019) '5000 women a year are still being killed in the name of "honour", Stephanie Thomson of *The Guardian*, retrieved September 5, 2019.

Wessendorf, S. (2014) *Commonplace Diversity. Social Relations in a Super-Diverse Context*, Basingstoke: Palgrave Macmillan.

West, C. and S. Fenstermaker (1995) 'Doing difference', *Gender and Society*, 9: 8–37.

Wetherell, M. and J. Potter (1992) *Mapping the Language of Racism*, Hampstead: Harvester Wheatsheaf.

Wilford, R. and R. Miller (eds) (1998) *Women, Ethnicity and Nationalism*, London: Routledge.

Williams, F. (1989) *Social Policy: A Critical Introduction*, Cambridge: Wiley and Son.

Wimmer, A. and N. Glick Schiller (2002) 'Methodological nationalism and beyond: Nation state building, migration and the social sciences', *Global Network*, 2 (4): 301–334.

Winker, G. and N. Degele (2011) 'Intersectionality as multi-level analysis: Dealing with social inequality', *European Journal of Women's Studies*, 18 (1): 51–66.

Wise, A. and S. Velayutham (eds.) (2009) *Everyday Multiculturalism*, London: Springer.

Wodak, R. (2010) *The Politics of Fear: What Right-Wing Populist Discourses Mean*, London: Sage.

Wodak, R., M. KhosraviNik and B. Mral (2013) *Right Wing Populism in Europe: Politics and Discourse*, London: Bloomsbury Academic.

Woodhams, C., B. Lupton and M. Cowling (2015) 'The snowballing penalty effect: Multiple disadvantage and pay', *British Journal of Management*, 26 (1): 63–77.

Wright, E.O. (1982) 'Class boundaries and contradictory class locations', in A. Giddens (ed.), *Class, Power and Conflict*, Berkeley: University of California Press, pp. 112–129.

Wright, E.O. (1985) *Classes*, London: Verso.

Yiftachel, O. (2009) 'Critical theory and "gray space": Mobilisation of the colonised', *City*, 13 (2–3): 240–256.

Yuval-Davis, N. (1994) 'Women, ethnicity and empowerment', *Feminism and Psychology*, 4 (1): 179–197.

Yuval-Davis, N. (1997) *Gender and Nation*, London: Sage.

Yuval-Davis, N. (2011) *The Politics of Belonging: Intersectional Contestations*, London: Sage.

Yuval-Davis, N. (2019) 'Perceptions of Jews or perceptions of antisemitism?', *Open Democracy*, 22 May 2019.

Yuval-Davis, N., F. Anthias and E. Kofman (2005) 'Secure borders and safe haven and the gendered politics of belonging: Beyond social cohesion', *Ethnic and Racial Studies*, 28 (3): 513–535.

Yuval-Davis, N., G. Wemyss and K. Cassidy (2019) *Bordering*, Cambridge: Polity.

INDEX

Agamben, Giorgio 14, 15, 33–34
Althusser, Louis 18, 24, 74
anti-Jewish racism 17, 155, 157, 159–160, 162–164, 166
anti-Muslim racism 17, 154–155, 157, 159–162, 166
anti-racism 17, 129
anti-Roma racism 17, 155
Antonsich, Marco 193
Arendt, Hannah 15, 34
Atkinson, Tony 92

Barrett, Michelle 66
Bassel, Leah 85
Begum, Shamima 25, 150
belonging 11, 13, 24–26, 46, 141, 186
Bilge, Sirma 62, 66, 67
binarisation 51–52, 116–118
biocoloniality 50
biopolitics 15, 36, 39, 50, 58–59
'blackening' 157
Black Skin, White Masks (Fanon) 53
Blair, Tony 173
Blunkett, David 157–158
border making 22–26, 37, 45, 53, 141–150, 168–172, 181
borders: belonging and 24–26, 166; crossing 21, 183; of ethnic groups 53, 59; mapping out 30; multiform and locations of 9; national 15, 24, 27, 80, 122, 141–155, 174, 181; personal borderscapes 3–8; policing 21, 24, 122, 158, 167, 168, 173; practices 168–172; unfixing 23

boundaries: of belonging 24–26, 60, 106, 125, 133; of categorisations 15, 39, 51; class 80, 97, 99, 113; crossing 122, 183; cultural 92, 155, 171, 183; diversity and 40; four Ds and 23; gender 78, 79; mapping out 30; multiform and locations of 9; national 13, 24, 49, 59, 80, 121, 142–144, 146, 149–150, 158, 174, 181; naturalisation and 52–53; policing 24, 144, 150; practices 179; racist 153, 156; social location and 27, 42; symbolic 92, 94, 99; as translocationally constituted 9–11, 180; work of and intersections 89
boundary making 12, 17, 22, 23, 31–32, 40–44, 82, 120, 169, 181
Bourdieu, Pierre 11, 33–36, 38, 39, 42, 46, 52, 56–58, 60, 70, 78, 84, 85, 91–92, 97–98, 100, 102, 111, 119, 178, 180
Bradley, Harriet 95
Brah, Avtar 67
Brexit 17, 22, 92–93, 98, 137, 145, 153–155, 159, 167, 168, 187
Brown, Gordon 172
Butler, Judith 10, 31, 33, 35, 38, 119, 139

Cameron, David 157, 172, 173
capitalism: class categorisation in 28, 50–51, 57, 59–60, 79, 96, 179–180, 187; class inequalities and 92; gender categories 117; gendered 10; ideological imprint of 17, 36; industrial 33; intersectionality and 68; Jews as embodiment of 163; logic of 46, 48, 106–109, 113–115; migrants and 21, 153; nationalism and

212 Index

143; race and 40; third wave feminist analysis of 120; violence and 139
Carastathis, Anna 65, 67
Carchedi, Guglielmo 20
care work 134–137
categories: attributions 53–54; of belonging 24–26, 46; binarisation and 51–52; as building block for inequality 58–60; of collective 'other' 13, 141, 142–143; commonalities 50–51; of difference 9–12, 25, 33, 40–44, 48–58, 67–70; differential saliency and 46–48, 59; dismantling and retrenchment 15–21; as family of concepts 142–143; forms of 46–48; heuristic of diversity and 40–44; hierarchisation and 54; homogenisation and 53–54; inferiorisation and 55; as knowledge and power, 36–38; 'mutual constitution' and 49, 74–76, 179; naturalisation and 52–53; problematic of 'groups' 44–46; resource allocation and 51, 54–55; social 79–83; social categories 79–83; social relations around 30–32; theorising 10, 32–40, 48–58; work of and intersections 55–58; *see also* categorisation; class; ethnicity/race; gender
categorisation: in everyday life 43; forms of 47; racial 156; relationality of 61–66; social relations around 31, 33, 46, 86, 179, 187
Cealey Harrison, Wendy 46
Choo, Hae Yeon 67
Cities of Sanctuary movement 185
citizenship 59, 104, 120, 186
class: attributions 53–54, 100–103; binarisation and 51–52; characteristics of 100, 180; cultural/symbolic aspects 109–111; *definitional* approach 49; delimiting 112; differential saliency and 47; equating the economic with 103–107; fixities of 16, 19–20; hierarchisation and 54; homogenisation of 53–54; inferiorisation and 55; intersectionality and 113–115; judgements of 100–103; material/economic aspects 109–111; naturalisation of 53; as object of analysis 77–85; operation of 102–103; as production role and relation 111–113; resource allocation and 54–58, 107; social location and 27, 74–75, 96; social ontology 79; social stratification and 12, 93–94, 113–114; stigma and 55, 101; theorising 32–40, 48–56, 62–63, 66–67, 96–100, 113–115; thinking with and beyond 94–96
collective attributions 53–54, 103
collective 'other' 142–143

collectivity 13, 30, 115, 142–144, 147, 163
Collins, Pat Hill 11, 31–32, 53, 62–64, 66, 69–72, 82, 85, 123, 184
coloniality 18, 20, 50, 71–73, 100, 141
Combahee River Collective 53
commonalities 50–51
concrete social relations 11, 83–85, 100
contradictory locations 19
conviviality 42, 167–168
Corbyn, Jeremy 155
Cox, Oliver 40, 50
Crenshaw, Kimberle 62, 66, 72
cultural capital 92, 98, 103, 111, 131
cultural racism 155
cultural rights 48

danger 23, 166
Davis, Kathy 67
deficiency 23, 166
De Genova, Nicholas 59
Denis, Ann 67
Derrida, Jacques 52
deviance 23, 166
Dhamoon, Rita Kaur 67
dialogue 181–184
difference: attributions 53–54; binarisation and 51–52; as building block for inequality 58–60; categorisation and 48–58, 67–70; commonalities and 50–51; differential inclusion 11, 23, 136, 177; differential saliency and 46–48, 69, 74; at *experiential* levels 59; heuristic of diversity and 40–44; hierarchisation and 54; homogenisation and 53–54; at *intersubjective* levels 59; management of 141–142; naturalisation and 52–53; at *organisational* level 59; relationality of 61–66; at *representational* level 60; resource allocation and 51, 54–55; social locations of 32; social ontologies of 78–79; stigma and 55
disgust 23, 166
Distinction (Bourdieu) 99
diversity 13, 37, 40–44, 69, 142, 147, 151, 167–172, 186
domestic violence 75, 125–126
Dorling, Danny 92
doxa 78–79
Dupont, Ida 126
Durkheim, Émile 33, 61, 172

Elson, Diane 103
Engels, Friedrich 108
equality 17, 19, 29, 40, 42, 55, 56–57, 92, 103, 115, 117, 121, 123, 127, 129, 140, 148, 153, 185–187, 189

Index 213

ethnicity/race: attributions 53–54, 100–103; binarisation and 51–52; border making and 13, 141–150; boundary making and 23, 183; *definitional* approach 49; dismantling of categories 15–16; fixities of 16, 19–20; fluidities of 28; group-making and 44–46; heuristic of diversity and 40; hierarchisation and 54; homogenisation of 53–54; inferiorisation and 55; naturalisation of 52–53; as object of analysis 77–85; practices and outcomes 165–166; race making 155–159; resource allocation and 54–58, 107; social location and 27, 74–75, 91, 179; social stratification and 12; solidarity-making 99; stigma and 55; theorising 32–40, 48–56, 62–63, 66–67, 70; *see also* racism
ethnos 79, 81, 141
experiential societal arena 86

Fanon, Frantz 35, 53
Federici, Silvia 40, 134
feminism 12, 17, 19, 34, 40, 55, 63–64, 67, 68, 71, 109, 113, 119–120, 124, 129, 132, 139, 183–184
femonationalism 17, 120, 123
Ferguson, Sarah 40
Ferree, Myra M 67
fixities: belonging and 25; categorisation and 57, 79–80; dismantling 11, 15–20; everyday assumptions of 43; gender 118, 138, 183; multiplicity of forms and 151–153; as process relating to agonistic nature of social life 27, 181; retrenchment of 28, 187; in trans/national space 141–143
fluidities: belonging and 25; border making and 19–20; categorisation and 49, 57, 114; gender 118, 138; as process relating to agonistic nature of social life 27, 181; in trans/national space 141–143
forced marriage 128
Foucault, Michel 11, 18, 33–34, 36–38, 46, 48, 50, 58–59, 98, 119, 177, 179
four Ds 23, 166
Frankfurt School 176
Fraser, Nancy 18, 40
Freud, Sigmund 36
Friedman, Sam 20

gender: attributions 53–54, 100–103; binarisation and 51–52, 116–118; care work 134–137; consumption/ lifestyles of 110–111; *definitional* approach 49; dismantling of categories 16; domestic violence 125–126; fixities of 16, 19–20; fluidities 19–20, 118, 138; fluidities of 28; forced marriage 128; forms of domination 116–117; global gendered economy 133–137; hierarchisation and 54; homogenisation of 53–54; honour-based violence 127–129; inferiorisation and 55; judgements of 100–103; migration 151; nationhood and 121–123; naturalisation of 52–53; as object of analysis 77–85; rape 124–125; relationality of 116–118; resource allocation and 54–58, 107; service sector jobs 137; sexuality and 118–121; social location and 27, 74–75, 91, 96; social ontology 79, 80; social stratification and 12; stigma and 55; theorising 32–40, 48–56, 66–67; trafficking 76, 129–132; transgendering/undoing 17, 138–139, 188; violence 75, 76, 116–117, 123–132
Global Alliance Against Trafficking in Women (GAATW) 130
Goldthorpe, John 97–98, 101
governmentality 10, 16, 18, 30, 36–37, 51, 58–60, 71, 74, 77–78, 87–88, 119, 147, 155, 168, 170, 172, 179, 187
Gramsci, Antonio 36
Grenfell Tower disaster 150, 151, 159
'groups' 44–46, 79–83, 101–102, 112, 180

habitus 33, 34–36, 52, 57–58, 84, 92, 98, 119–120
Hall, Stuart 14, 40, 42, 77, 181
Hancock, Ange-Marie 67
Harding, Sandra 71, 177
Hartman, Heidi 109
hate crimes 84
Heath, Anthony 97
Hekman, Susan 177
Hertz, Robert 51
hierarchy: categories and 54; class processes and 94, 99, 180; difference and 52; economic hierarchy 51, 102, 106; globalisation and 127; links between identity and 61–62; in social field 35; social hierarchy 48, 51–52, 76, 84–85; societal arenas and 69; symbolic violence and 34; translocational intersectionality of 26
hierarchy making, 9, 30, 82, 143, 189
homogenisation 53–54
homonationalism 17
honour-based violence 122, 127–129
Hood-Williams, John 46

identity politics 13, 21, 26, 39, 46, 53, 59, 178, 182, 184–185
ideological state apparatuses 18

214 Index

in-betweenness 20, 22
'inequality regimes' 58–60, 91
inferiorisation 55
institutional racism 148
integration 13, 37, 41, 56, 142, 146–147,
  157, 168–169, 171–173, 186
intersectionality: applicability 70;
  characteristics of 64–65; class and
  113–115; critiques 13, 28, 49; as heuristic
  device 70–71; lack of theoretical framing
  68; limitations 68; listing of a priori and
  taken for granted differences 69–70;
  mutual constitution and 74–76; object
  of analysis in 68, 77–85; politics of
  178–181; positions of 66–67; problem of
  equivalence or flattening 69; proliferating
  and individualising oppression: 68;
  quandaries and difficulties involved
  67–70, 74; relationality of 19, 61–66;
  societal arenas of investigation in 85–88;
  translocational lens for 10, 73–74, 88–90;
  whitening of coloniality and 71–73
intersubjective societal arena 86

Johnson, Boris 145

Lamont, Michelle 92
Lenski, Gerhard E. 62
Lerner, Gerda 62
Levine-Rasky, Levine-Rasky, C. (2011)
  'Intersectionality theory 67
Lukacs, György 36

MacKinnon, Catharine 124
Mannheim, Karl 71, 176
Marx, Karl 13–14, 16, 33, 36, 46, 61,
  70, 71, 98, 104, 106, 108, 113,
  179–181, 187
Massey, Doreen 26
May, Theresa 145–146
Mbembe, Achille 22
McCall, Leslie 67
Mcintosh, Mary 66
migrant commons 16, 185, 188
migrants: belonging 25; border making
  and 141–150; boundary making and
  23; categorisation of 147–148; in global
  gendered economy 133–137; markings
  of 44; trafficking 76
migration: age of 13, 144–147; crisis
  21–24; management of 174; specificity
  of 148–151
Miles, Robert 113
'mutual constitution' 12, 49, 74–76, 179

Nash, Jennifer C. 67, 76
nationalism 22, 32, 125, 143–144, 146,
  153–154
nativism 17, 21–22, 37, 38, 143, 145, 153,
  155–156, 158, 188
naturalisation 52–53
Nayak, Anoop 38
necropolitics 22
neo-liberalism 10, 13, 15, 17, 22, 39, 48,
  65, 72, 88, 103, 121, 137, 139, 170, 174,
  178, 187, 189

organisational societal arena 86

Pakulski, Jan 99
panopticon 18
Papastergiades, Nikos 142
Parkin, Frank 24
Pearson, Ruth 103
personal borderscapes 3–8
Phizacklea, Annie 113
Phoenix, Ann 67
Piketty, Thomas 92
politics of translocation 13, 89, 178–181,
  183, 184–186
populisms 15, 17, 141, 153–155, 187
post-structuralism 33
Poulantzas, Nicos 20
power: categories around difference as
  modes of 11; societal arenas of investigation
  with different technologies of 85–88;
  theorising 18, 33–40; translocational lens
  for addressing modalities of 10, 88–90;
  translocational nature 64
Prevent programme 21, 154, 168

racism: anti-Jewish 17, 23, 157, 159–160,
  162–164, 166; anti-Muslim 17, 23,
  154–155, 157, 159–162, 166; anti-
  Roma 17, 23, 155; cultural 155–156,
  170; differential saliency and 47; hate
  crimes 84; institutional 148; new forms
  of 145–146, 153–154, 188; practices
  and outcomes 55, 140, 165–167; race
  making and multiple targets of 155–159;
  re-energisation of 16; resource allocation
  and 55; state 37; vernacular 18
rape 124–125
refugees: belonging and 24; camps 14–16;
  categorisation of 47–49, 56, 142, 188;
  hostility to 23; markings of 44; migration
  crisis and 21, 144, 146–151, 155–156;
  rights 159; social locations of 32;
  theorising 34; trafficking 76

relationality 19
representational societal arena 86
reserve army of labour (RAL) 107, 108, 113, 117, 181
resource allocation: border making and 11, 21, 30, 45; building blocks for 75; categorisations for 89; differential forms of 44, 51, 110, 112, 177–178, 187–188; social location and 27; unequal 54–58, 84, 92, 94, 106–107, 114
Richardson, Diane 59, 121
Robinson, Cedric 107

Sahlins, Peter 141
Savage, Michael 91, 92, 98–99, 101, 113
Schutz, Alfred 36
service sector 137
sexual citizenship 59
sexuality 12, 16, 17, 48–55, 74–75, 77–85, 118–121
'situated knowledge' 176–178
'situational' 27, 176
Smith, Dorothy 70–71, 88, 177
social capital 98–99, 114, 131, 132
social categories 79–83
social field 34, 35, 85
social hierarchy 48, 51–52, 76, 84–85
social justice 16, 54, 64–66, 178–179, 187
social location: belonging and 26; categorisation and 188; class and 95–96; *contradictory* 28; of difference 32; *different modes of oppression* in 74; disparities of 183–184; heterogeneity of 184; *hierarchical* 32, 83–84, 111; inequality and 91, 96, 100, 107–109; of migrants 127; of refugees 32; resource allocation and 27; rise of populisms and 17; social mobility and 89; as social spaces 27
social media 18
social ontologies 78–79
social regulation 15
social stratification: intersectional approach to 12, 93–95, 113–114, 179–180; status group and 62; symbolic violence and 124; theorising 179–180
societal arenas of investigation 12, 85–88
Society Must be Defended (Foucault) 37
Sokoloff, Natalie J. 126
solidarity politics 13, 20, 178, 182, 184–188
state racism 37
'status' 62, 93–94, 105
Stiglitz, Joseph 92
stigma 55, 101

stratification: contemporary forms of 149; intersectional approach to 12, 90, 93–95, 100, 109, 111–114; traditional approaches to 62, 89, 91; *see also* social stratification
super-diversity 43–44, 69, 151
Swing, William Lacy 151
symbolic violence 34, 119, 123, 124

Taylor, Charles 38
telos 186–189
Tilly, Charles 33–34, 38–39, 50, 88, 118
trafficking 76, 129–132
'trans' 27–28
transgender movement 17, 20–21, 138–139, 188
translocation: notion of 26–28; politics of 13, 178–181, 184–186
translocational intersectionality 26–28, 73–74, 179; *see also* intersectionality
translocational lens 10, 11, 26–28, 48, 60, 63, 70, 73–74, 88–90, 140, 174, 176, 177, 179
translocational positionality 10, 19, 26, 74, 186–187
'transversal politics' 183
Trimikliniotis, Nicos 152, 172–173
Trump, Donald 17, 42, 92, 98, 154, 187
Tyler, Imogen 91, 96, 97

United Nations: Convention against Organised Crime 130; Global Compact for Safe, Orderly and Regular Migration 146; Global Compact on Refugees 146; poverty rates 14; refugee camps 144
United Nations High Commissioner for Refugees (UNCHR) 14

Vertovec, Steven 43
violence 75, 76, 116–117, 123–132
Virdee, Satnam 107

Wacquant, Loic J. D. 35
Wallerstein, Immanuel 13
Waters, Malcolm 99
Weber, Max 18, 24, 40, 61–62, 93, 98, 105, 108
'whitening' 13, 72, 101, 157, 178
Windrush scandal 24, 47, 145, 146, 150, 151, 159
Wright, Erik Olin 20

Yiftachel, Oren 152
Yuval-Davis, Nira 65, 66